SOUTH BRANCH

D0679871

364.133 Am88t

Amster, Gerald.

Transit point Moscow

FEB   1985

FEB 5 1985

TRANSIT POINT MOSCOW

ALSO BY BERNARD ASBELL

*Mother and Daughter: The Letters of
Eleanor and Anna Roosevelt (Editor)*

White Coat, White Cane (With David Hartman, M.D.)

The Senate Nobody Knows

The F.D.R. Memoirs

*President McGovern's First Term (written under
the name Nicholas Max)*

What Lawyers Really Do

Careers in Urban Affairs

The New Improved American

When F.D.R. Died

TRANSIT POINT
MOSCOW

EVANSTON PUBLIC LIBRARY
1703 ORRINGTON AVENUE
EVANSTON, ILLINOIS 60201

GERALD AMSTER AND
BERNARD ASBELL

HOLT, RINEHART AND WINSTON
NEW YORK

Copyright © 1984 by Gerald Amster and Bernard Asbell
All rights reserved, including the right to reproduce this
book or portions thereof in any form.
First published in January 1985 by
Holt, Rinehart and Winston, 383 Madison Avenue,
New York, New York 10017.
Published simultaneously in Canada by Holt, Rinehart and
Winston of Canada, Limited.

Library of Congress Cataloging in Publication Data
Amster, Gerald.
Transit point Moscow.
1. Narcotics, Control of. 2. Smugglers—Soviet
Union—Biography. 3. Smuggling—Soviet Union.
4. Prisons—Russian S.F.S.R.—Mordovskaia A.S.S.R.
I. Asbell, Bernard. II. Title.
HV5805.A48A36 1984   364.1'33   84–10788
ISBN 0–03–064156–X

First Edition

Design by Kate Nichols
Printed in the United States of America
1 3 5 7 9 10 8 6 4 2

ISBN 0-03-064156-X

TRANSIT POINT MOSCOW

1

MORDOVIA

In a few moments they'll open the door of this railroad car and I'll be officially welcomed by the military reception party waiting below.

To my knowledge, no American has ever laid eyes on this place. In fact, the government hosting me, the Union of Soviet Socialist Republics, has never in all its days granted any casual sightseer from any corner of the world permission to visit this village, much less the official installation that lies just beyond it.

In that sense, I, Gerald Amster, a native of Paterson, New Jersey— adventurer, pioneer, a first among my countrymen—join ranks at age thirty-three with such explorers and first-timers as Christopher Columbus, Charles Lindbergh, and John Glenn.

At last, with a metallic lurch and squeal and groan, the sliding door of our private car clangs open. My five traveling companions— two other Americans assigned to come here with me, two English- men, and a Malaysian—and I step down to meet and review a detachment of twelve Soviet guardsmen. They salute us with raised *kalashnikavy*, Red Army–style light machine guns, each guard also wearing a *marenko*, a holstered pistol.

1

Impressed, we wordlessly signal our readiness to go anywhere they want us to go, do anything they say.

One ordeal had just ended; I felt as though three thousand pounds had slid off my back. Three months earlier the Russians had arrested my two American companions and me at six o'clock on a Sunday morning, June 27, 1976, at Sheremet'evo Airport, Moscow, when we waited for a change of flights on a journey from Kuala Lumpur to Amsterdam. For long days and nights in Moscow's notorious Lefortovo Prison, the KGB grilled us. Next, the psychiatric exams. Then the trial: a showpiece to entertain the international press, including reporters of my own country. Finally this episode today: arrival at a Soviet labor camp, in a grimy, stinking converted railroad boxcar.

So now, in October, one ordeal having ended, a new one, our long labor-camp penance, was about to begin. All I knew about Soviet labor camps came from headlines on the imprisonment and release of Alexander Solzhenitsyn, which hadn't seemed to have much to do with me—until this moment.

The other five prisoners and I leaped down from the boxcar, trying to slap from our clothes and hands the layer of greasy dirt from the wood planks that had served as our bunks. In the sharp chill of Russian October we shuffled in double file toward a clump of dwellings. Our guards muttered, *"Bystree, bystree, bystree,"* meaning "faster, faster, faster," a word we were to hear so often we'd grow deaf to it, while automatically obeying.

This clearing by the side of the railroad track was the stop for the village of Leplai, population about five hundred, and for Labor Camp Number 5-1 (Camp Number 5, of Section 1). We had traveled only about 250 miles east and slightly south of Moscow, to an "autonomous" Russian state called Mordovia. It might as well have been Siberia. Mordovia's main industry is a thirty-mile chain of labor camps, each a fenced island in a morose sea of woods. That's what led Solzhenitsyn to invent the metaphorical term "archipelago." The "islands" were linked only by the rickety rail line behind us.

We trudged into the village of Leplai and right down its main street, actually a broad path of gravel and frozen mud ruts, where chickens, a couple of sheep, and a goat freely pecked and meandered. To the side loafed an aged horse, harnessed to a wagon. This village had no cars, no trucks, no road leading to it or through it on which a motor vehicle could come from, say, Saransk, the capital of Mordovia. Just the railroad. One tiny building was a *magazin*, Leplai's only store. Chimneys of the tumbledown dwellings puffed out the perfume of burning logs, the sole local fuel. Behind each shack lay a wood pile, mostly white birch.

Also behind each shack tilted an outhouse. At roadside a woman, head wrapped in a babushka, worked a water pump, filling a pail. Down the way was another public pump. No indoor plumbing anywhere. (Over the coming years I was to ride prison trains many times from this place to Moscow and on one occasion a train and truck to the vicinity of Leningrad for a "psychiatric" examination. I was to see many villages, the ones tourists and journalists can't get permission to visit. They are all the same, all like the little prison-camp town of Leplai, no better, no worse.)

Children at play and women sweeping at their doorways and hanging laundry paused to watch us. We three Americans, still wearing tropical suits custom-tailored for us in Kuala Lumpur, but covered with worn-out army coats furnished us in Moscow, were obviously foreigners to these onlookers. Actually, that would not have surprised them. Camp 5–1 is reserved for foreigners, the only one so designated in the Soviet Union. The Soviets always segregate foreign convicts in a special camp away from their own (except for very special foreigners such as Francis Gary Powers, the U-2 pilot; he was locked not in a camp, but a fortresslike prison called Vladimir).

A child tagged alongside one of our guards, pleading something in Russian, something familial. Could this be the guard's own child?

3

Of course. This village, and others nearby like it, existed to house the people who worked at the camp. What other reason was there for these families to live here?

If our guards—the ruling class of this life we now approached— if *they*, upon leaving the camp at the end of a day's work, lived in this mud-encrusted squalor, what miseries awaited *us* as prisoners in Labor Camp 5–1?

The cottages thinned out, but the gravel road stretched on, perhaps a quarter-mile, to a long, somber wooden fence about eight feet high, each vertical wood slat rising to a point. Along the top of the fence, reaching several feet above the wood slats, stretched barbed wire, no doubt afire with an electric charge, thorny strand upon strand drawn tightly less than five inches apart, too close together for a man to squeeze between them.

The road met the fence at a pair of green solid metal doors that were high, awkwardly high, perhaps sixteen or eighteen feet. As we approached, one door of the iron pair dragged open grudgingly, long enough to admit us; then an armed man behind it dragged and clanged it shut.

We faced an inner fence, another broad spool of barbed wire, and another mammoth metal gateway. This one shielded the base of a high, glassed-in observation tower. Up there, impassively watching us, more guards, more *kalashnikovy*.

Admitted through the second gateway, we waited at a door to the base of the hulking watchtower building. A loud buzzer released its lock and we entered a dark, unheated, gloomy room. A guard sat at a desk, and behind him loitered several others. All had faces of an Oriental cast, although not as clearly Eastern as our Malaysian companion. Coldly, silently, they took our measure, as though we'd landed from another planet. For at least five minutes we just stood there, wordless, regarding each other, waiting for we didn't know what.

Finally, from behind yet another door, we heard keys jangle. The door opened. A man wearing chevrons and a red armband— the officer of the day—ambled in and looked us over. He asked in Russian whether we understood Russian. I understood the question, but didn't venture an answer. During our months in Moscow, I'd picked up a smattering of the language through dealing with KGB interrogators, prison guards, and, most particularly, a Russian cellmate. I have a facility with languages and once taught at Berlitz in New York, but I couldn't yet handle a conversation here.

In Russian I tried to make a language connection. "*Angliiskii?* English?"

"Ah, *vy anglichane.*"

Pointing to the two Englishmen, I said, "No, *ani Anglichan.*" Of the Malaysian I said, "*On panimaet angliiskii.* He understands English." Then, designating Peter Benack, Darrell Lean, and myself, I said, "*My amerikanets.*"

"*Amerikantsy!*" His face lit. He tilted his head with a kind of effeminate surprise and politeness.

After all the severe looks we'd seen among our captors, this guy was different. He seemed friendly and benign, his softness, in a baby-faced fellow of only twenty-six or so, coming off as fat, pink, and piggish.

"Ah, *amerikantsy,*" he repeated, mysteriously delighted.

I thought of trying to connect with him in French or Spanish, even Dutch, but first put forward my best foot: "*Deutsch?*"

The offer of German took. "*Ja, Deutsch, gut.*"

He led us through the door that had brought him, which he unlocked and relocked behind him, then down a dark corridor and into an airy, chilly room. Planting himself on a squeaking wooden chair, he motioned us to a couple of benches facing him. "*Dokument nety.* No documents," he said with a trace of apology. Then, switching back to atrocious but workable German: "We wait. Soon come papers from train. Soon come woman, he give clothes for you and—" A confused hand motion said "and so forth."

5

Apparently inmates arrive with no advance notice, except a sighting by the guards in the observation tower above, who spot a train and then a squad marching down the street.

Our host made it known, by pointing to himself and reciting it, that his name was Ramashin.

"*Amerikantsy,*" he repeated, again the tilt of his head possessed by the miracle of it. He looked at me. Then at Pete and Darrell. Then at me again.

"For what here?"

I said the word that is essentially the same in his language and ours. "Contraband."

He nodded like an impressed relative. "*Srok skol'ka?* How long sentence?" (From my first grasp of it through my Moscow cellmate, the Russian language had struck my ear strangely because of its lack of the articles *a* and *the* and any form of the verb *to be*. In fact, to this day, when I hear Russian or speak it, the translation in my head never breaks free of that structural difference. So I translate Russian here as I heard it.)

"*Vosem' let.* Eight years."

He pursed his fat lips and rounded his eyes appreciatively. His eyes put the same query to Darrell.

I answered for him. "Contraband. Seven years. He pleaded not guilty to one charge."

Ramashin's face bespoke a regretful "tut-tut." Under Soviet law, a defendant who pleads not guilty, even to only one charge of many, and is then found guilty has forfeited the hope of any reduction of sentence for good behavior. He looked at Pete.

"Contraband," I said. "Five years."

The others: contraband, contraband, contraband. No, our offenses were not committed together. The Englishmen were separate, and so was the Malaysian.

"*Amerikantsy,*" he said still again, with undiminished savor. He got up and strolled toward our benches, ran a finger along Pete's package of belongings, along Darrell's, then lingered at my duffel bag. It bulged to its mouth with all sorts of gifts brought me by an aunt who had flown to Moscow from New York during my trial. He half-lifted out a gleaming object, my Philips electric razor.

"*Pobrit'sia.* To shave," he said with covetous admiration. Then he sat down again and gazed at us.

"Don't worry, you not sit long time."

The words came as music. In the phraseology of Russian prisons, the verb "to sit" means "to do time." A prisoner will ask, "How long have you been sitting? How much longer do you sit?" Ramashin continued:

"This camp, all foreigners. Foreigners not sit long. October, one year from now, sixty years from October Revolution. Big, big amnesty come. Many, many foreigners go home. Soon, Olympics in Moscow. Many go home, you will see."

As Ramashin's sentences hobbled along, I translated for the others.

"You do your work, you make no trouble, you go home soon. Many amnesty. Last year, two Germans and four Dutch come, all together, all for same as you, all contraband. Germans get ten years, Dutch eight. All together, fifty-two years. Before one year, all out, go home. Amnesty. Your President Ford, he go to Vladivostok, see Brezhnev. Make detente." Ramashin flopped his hamlike hand in a not-to-worry gesture. "American, you work good, make no trouble, amnesty. You go home, buy all electric shaver you want. Maybe you leave that one here, I keep for you in case you come back, hah? Ha, ha, ha."

At Lefortovo Prison in Moscow, as we awaited trial, Russian inmates had fed us—Pete, Darrell, and me—the same absolute certainty of early release. So had the guards, even our KGB investigators. We ate up every delicious word, yet didn't know whether to believe it. And now this guy Ramashin, who sees them all come and go. Why would he con us?

From that moment my optimism took firm flight. We just weren't going to be here long.

If that was the high moment of the day, the low followed promptly.

A guard led in a stooped, miserable fellow with shaven head and worn blue-gray, Mao-style work clothes, clearly a prisoner, whose hand grasped a pair of barber's clippers.

Ramashin got up and strolled out.

"*Idi siuda.* Come here," commanded the guard of our Malaysian colleague.

The prisoner ran his instrument up the back of the Malaysian's head as if mowing a roadway through a wheatfield, chunks of hair plopping to the floor. As though expecting the treatment, our companion just sat there and took it. Then another fierce pass and another, then up the sides and around the ears, the barber turning that Oriental's head into a bald duplicate of his own.

"He bloody well won't do that to me," swore one of the Englishmen.

Until he said that, I hadn't imagined myself as victim of the clippers.

"*Idi siuda,*" said the guard, this time at me.

"No," I said. I blurted it without thinking, not as protest, simply declining the offer.

Paying no attention, the prisoner stood behind me, put his palm atop my head, and invaded the back of my skull as though it belonged to . . . to anyone, to no one. His instrument, without my consent, yanked and tore and sheared, and my hair, my own hair, the hair of *my* head, rained down over my shoulders. In a minute it was all done. I looked from wall to wall for the barbershop mirror. The walls returned nothing. I felt for my head. It was sore. It was sandpaper. It was all skin and skull. It was not me. Worse still, it *was* me.

My head burned. Then it didn't, because I couldn't feel the pain for the pounding in my belly, the insult of it.

What right do they have? *What right?*

And the pounding recited the unthinkable, over and over.

What right? What right?

They've got the rights, every one, and you've got none at all.

After an hour of waiting, just waiting and staring at our expressionless guard, we heard a voice through the door, a woman's voice, saying something quarrelsome. The guard motioned us to follow him. In a storeroom down the hall, a wrinkled sack of a woman hobbled between counter and bins. She measured each of us with a narrowed eye, plopped down sets of frayed cotton Mao suits, shorts, pairs of socks, two each, and commanded us to undress: *"Razdevaetes', razdevaetes'."* Any shyness we felt was quashed by her lack of interest. The clothes we removed and the belongings in our bags she ordered placed on the counter. The guard stood by silently, validating her authority. Licking a stubby pencil, for two hours she laboriously inscribed a slip of paper for each item, every single one separately, plunking it down before its owner like a payment of currency. Receipts. We wouldn't see these belongings, these identity cards of our individual lives, again until . . .

Then outside again, past still another locked gate, through which a gang of prisoners peered at us, shouting words I didn't understand. Questions? Taunts?

The guard led us into a storehouse. From stacks of bed parts, each of us took head frames, foot frames, springs, and carried them back to the gate. In the cold air our fingers stung, gripping the heavy iron. Don't they have people to do these things? (My internal voice responded promptly: Sure they do. Us.)

We lugged our bed parts into one of two huge barracks buildings, and into a room that was one of four in the building. In its air were suspended the odors of crowded men—their sweat, their breath, their stale smoke. Beds, single and some double-decker, jammed almost every square yard of the floor, except for a narrow aisle. We mounted our bed parts atop beds already there to form new double-deckers. In a space of about five hundred square feet I counted twenty-two bunks.

A dozen or more prisoners gathered around us, ominously eager. What did they want?

"Otsiuda? From where?" one asked.

"Amerikanets," I said, designating Pete, Darrell, and myself. *"Oni Anglichan."* Not knowing how to say "Malaysian," I let our sixth man fend for himself.

"Amerikantsy!" chorused a couple of voices, as struck as Ramashin.

Questions came in a babble. "What are you here for?" one asked in British-accented English. "How long?"

Our arrival, new faces turning up, was a stirring event. In a night of silence we were the excitement of a creak in the floor, for a motionless, bedridden patient a turned position.

Then came the familiar, comforting words: "Americans? English? You not sit long. Six months, a year. Out, go home."

I opened what was left of my belongings to pack them away in a flimsy table with drawers beside my bed, a *tumbochka.* The prisoners gathered around to gape. One reached excitedly for my Philips razor, palming it lovingly. His face was mean and sweet, with knife scars. In honeyed voice and inscrutable tongue, he implored me to do something or other, cradling and fondling the Philips like an infant.

"He wants you," said the British prisoner, "to give him the razor when you leave."

I didn't know what to say, and must have looked it.

"You better be prepared to keep the promise if you make it," the Englishman cautioned, with a faint leer toward Scarface.

These are my roommates, my world, my new life.

It won't be for long. It can't be long. They said so themselves.

I look back now over the strangeness, the surprises, the shocks of the next few hours, the next few days and nights, and it all grinds into a muddy stew. Too much to remember all at once. Too much to spill at one time. Each particle has its particular flavor; each needs to be separated out for telling. I'll get to all of it.

Out of that thick mush of recollections, however, one survives whole. One awareness dominates, defines, *is* for me what life in a Soviet labor camp was about. It goes by a short, simple word.

Work? Hard, driving, lousy drudgery filled all our days and deadened our senses. I'll get to telling about it. But the work wasn't the worst of it.

Torture? Prisoners were subjected to punishments that I would call cruel, but in the camp for foreigners, at least, I never saw an act of physical assault or torture committed by our keepers.

Greed? Corruption? They reached everywhere, entwining prisoners, guards, and higher officials, and arising from the same exploitation of the helpless that Soviets are so quick to condemn in capitalistic American life. Yet the chief victims, the prisoners, learned to take corruption for granted.

Bigotry and hatred? They are embedded in the official administration of the camps, in the very culture of the Soviets, as well as in the language and minds of guards and prisoners. But after a while, an outsider hardly notices.

Boredom, loneliness? Everywhere, without end. But in a prison camp, what else?

No, all of those were somehow bearable.

The awareness that never let go of my throat and my gut, that I could never make peace with, was simpler, more fundamental, than any of those. It was the awareness of *food*.

More correctly, the *absence* of food, my incessant craving for it.

Paradoxically, the absence of food energized my life. It ran me. It controlled my behavior with fellow prisoners. It made of me a panderer, a flatterer, an entertainer, and, yes, a sometime informer. It turned me into a seeker of favors from the KGB. It gave me ulcers, at times made me want to die. It sent me to the hospital camp for weeks on end. But that, in turn, brought the unexpected side benefit of intimate and extended association with Russian prisoners. I learned how life goes for the several million Soviet citizens said to be penned in labor camps, a life quite different from ours in foreigners' Camp 5–1.

For my first supper in camp, all the men in my barracks filed into a room of worn tables and benches, more than a hundred of us. We were one of three eating shifts, an unusual arrangement for

11

an unusual time. Camp facilities were strained by a population of almost five hundred foreign offenders. (Soon, several overdue amnesties brought the number down to a more normal one hundred or so.)

After the near starvation of two days in transit and the strains of bed-carrying and settling, I shuffled along the serving line with a certain eagerness. A server flung something dark and dry on my plate, and I looked beyond him for something more inviting. Nothing more. That was it: a wad of kasha, a gritty, groaty cereal that had been a staple in the Moscow prison during our trial.

From that night forward, every day, usually three times a day, we ate kasha. A couple of mornings a week, breakfast kasha was enhanced by a metal bowl of "fish soup." In all my time there, no matter how hungry I was, I never swallowed any. The fish soup was a thin layer of something greasy suspended over salty water, and floating in it either the head or ribs of a fish. For lunch, besides the kasha we'd get soup, usually of pickled tomato chunks and some potato. One festive meal a week, Sunday evenings, we got a spoonful of mashed potatoes with our kasha. Sometimes the potatoes came with a piece of fish about an inch square, so salted it was difficult to get down. I'd eat it. I was told this fish might have been preserved for as long as twenty years in a special marinade that would keep it practically forever.

At lunch and dinner we got one piece of black bread. Not pumpernickel—far from it. The bread was hard, sour, and bitter, especially the rocklike crust. Old-time prisoners said it contained sawdust. Greasing the bread with a dab of margarine helped. In the *magazin*, the camp store, one of the few items we could buy with our few monthly rubles of work wages was a kilo of margarine. A prisoner would store it in his *tumbochka*, the night table by his bed, then worry all his days and nights that someone might steal it. Also, we could buy a small tin of "fish preserve": ground fish bones and throwaway parts, mixed with barley, kasha or rice.

In the barracks after our first supper, a couple of fellow prisoners, following a custom of generosity toward new arrivals, offered us part of their tins of fish preserve. I couldn't believe its poisonous taste, thinking it a dirty trick. But after a while I developed a taste for it as a luxury.

Then another huddle of prisoners joined in a solemn and intense activity. Two men checked the doors, making sure they were free of guards. (For the first time I noticed that guards were scarcely seen in the barracks, or even around the camp. They kept watch at the gates and walls, but interfered little with the life of prisoners.) In the middle of the dimly lit concrete floor the men set a match to a wad of newspaper that was rolled to burn slowly and long, and stashed the wad beneath a small pot of water that perched on a makeshift wire stand. Soon the water bubbled into a boil.

Reverently, one of them tore open a small package and emptied its dark, dusty contents into the steaming water. A Swiss prisoner who spoke a cultured English, catching my curious look, explained, "Tea. Fifty grams. A few kopecks at the *magazin.*" More than an ounce and a half. It seemed a lot of tea for the tiny pot.

The tea slowly sank and eventually permeated the water. One of the alchemists put out the fire and covered the brew with the foil of the package, letting the leaves soak further. When the brewing was done, the teamaker observed a ritual, a lot like the sharing of marijuana. He poured the tea into a tin cup, sipped from it, then passed it around to others. It was a powerful, hot nectar, dense with caffeine and extremely bitter. Nobody sweetened it. The stuff was considered invigorating. Men explained to me in word and muscular gesture that it gave prisoners the energy to do their work, endure the struggle to meet their *norma,* their production quota.

Tea made in this concentrated form was illegal because, for one thing, a fire, which was forbidden, had to be lit inside the barracks, to keep it out of sight of the guards. (The ceilings of the prison buildings were black from smoke and sparks of years and years of illegal tea-brewing.) Second, this form of supercaffeinated tea was considered a drug. The tea, which I could take or leave, but to which Darrell became devoted, demonstrated to me how desperate a man in prison can become for kicks, any kicks at all.

13

In the middle of my first night in camp, I awoke. I didn't know whether it was the tea or my terror at this strange place, but my groin screamed for a piss. I pulled on my pants and coat and shoes and headed into the damp, wintry night. Icy crystals of snow descended and settled silently, as though trying to stay secret till morning. The long walk to the outhouse, a distance of three or four city blocks, snaked under dim lights, no doubt making it easier for guards to watch us from the tower; certainly it was not for our convenience.

Why didn't I just leave the path and do it against a tree? We'd been warned against that, under threat of time in the isolator, whatever that was. Why hadn't I just stayed in the barracks and pissed quietly into one of the sinks, in a separate room? Who'd know? Against that, too, we were warned. For this the punishment would be administered by our own comrades, beating the sneak into a meatball. I made it all the way and back, finally slipping beneath my threadbare blanket, wrapping myself against the chill. The barracks trembled with snores and wheezes. I thought I heard the whimpering sob of someone's nightmare. After the fresh, nippy outside air, the room stank with phlegmy breath and passed gases. I tried not to breathe, then had to.

What am I doing here? How did I get here?

What do these smelly men, this animal pen of a place, this strange, terrible new life, have to do with *my* life? How can I comprehend this as a consequence of the simple, hopeful, yes, I dare to say *innocent* moment of temptation—only what? ninety days ago?—sitting in the early-summer sun of Amsterdam with my friend, thinking of ways to make life a little better, a bit more economically secure?

There's been a mistake, God.

God, listen. You must undo this for me.

God, God, God, how can this have happened?

2

AMSTERDAM

Back in April I'd have let that stranger's leer, his half-smile, slide right past me. After all, that's what Orientals do, don't they? They smile a lot.

But this was June and I knew better. Since arriving in Amsterdam I'd been hanging out every afternoon, sometimes all afternoon, with my traveling companion, Darrell Lean, studying this city from the sidewalk cafés along the Damrak, the busy stretch between the Royal Palace and Central Station. In Amsterdam, when a Chinese stranger smiles at you from the next table of a café called the Hong Kong, he usually means business.

He entered lightly into one of our silences.

"English?"

"We're Americans," I said.

"Ah yes. On holiday?"

A spoonful at a time, I put out that I'd been floating around Europe for two years, setting foot briefly in North Africa. I'd been in Amsterdam two months, Darrell not as long.

"So you work here."

No, I replied. But looking for work, so I can stay longer.

He nodded slowly, almost invisibly, with the sympathetic invitation and understanding of a Viennese shrink. I almost expected him to purr, "Do you want to talk about it?" Instead he asked:

"A special kind of work?"

Let him fish if he wants.

For a while, to help pay my way, I went on, I bought and sold Krugerrands, trying to ride the surf of the gold market. But you can't build a business working at café tables, trading out of your shirt pocket. (Maybe this guy had seen me around, watched me. I know I had seen him.) I'd also tried selling for a forceful character who handled old Polish government bonds at low prices. I found them almost impossible to sell, because people didn't believe the present government would redeem pre-Communist bonds at their upcoming due date. So I had to quit. The hell of it was that the Poles *did* pay off those old bonds. I could have made a fortune buying the damn things instead of trying to peddle them. Anyhow, I confirmed for myself that selling was not for me, especially when I didn't have a lot of faith in the product.

Ordinarily, I don't go around dumping my job history on strangers at cafés. But this Chinese guy was clearly sending me a signal that he had a proposition. So I wanted to give him an equally clear signal that my pad of traveler's checks (originally eight thousand dollars that I'd inherited from my father) was getting thin. I had an open mind.

Next day he was there again, same table, same nosy small talk. On the third day he remarked, as though passing the time, that some young tourists picked up attractive money just agreeing to go somewhere, usually to an interesting country, expenses paid, to "bring something back."

"Yeah, I've heard."

His gaze drifted down the Damrak toward American Express, a few doors away. Its sidewalk was cluttered, as always, with knapsack-laden kids, mostly Germans and Americans, trying to sell or buy used vans and campers.

"Today," he speculated so quietly I had to strain to hear, "Caucasians should be able to pick up money quite easily. Especially with American passports. Now, you take the Chinese." He shrugged humbly. "The Chinese are not popular with customs these days. Too many times in trouble."

I said nothing, tried to show nothing of my rising alertness.

Suddenly he introduced himself as Mr. Lee. What else? I almost said I was Mr. Smith and my friend was Mr. Brown. He shed a layer of caution:

"If you are interested, I may know someone who would talk to you."

"A trip like that could be risky."

That bugged him. "Not very risky. But yes, some risk. Always some risk."

"What do you suppose it would be worth?"

"The people you would meet, I believe they are very generous."

"Well, talking to them won't hurt."

His eyes narrowed sternly. "If you are not seriously interested, I don't think—"

"We're interested."

"There is a place on Rembrandt Square called Short's of London. Can you meet someone there tomorrow at three?"

"How will I know him?"

"He will know you."

Mr. Lee rose to go, then sat down again. "It is possible you would need a third person. Do you have a reliable friend with an American passport who would, mmm, fit in?"

"Sure."

I didn't have the slightest idea who the third guy might be.

At Short's of London, a lone man waited in a dark booth: Mr. Lee himself. This time no headwaiter's politeness, all business. I would need a third person. We would leave in a couple of days for Kuala Lumpur. That's in Malaysia, he said, southeast of Vietnam, a short hop from Singapore. Suddenly the half-smile again. Malaysia is a wonderful place for a few days' vacation, he let on intimately, and we'd be furnished with spending money.

The romance of it rushed up my back. Singapore! Humphrey Bogart lurking in a smoky tropical bar. James Bond twirling ice in a neglected glass, waiting, watching. Can this be happening? Yes, this is me. This is true. He's offering it. And money, enough to keep me in Europe for who knows how long. It's mine for the taking, right now.

"What would we carry?"

Mr. Lee winced slightly, as if in distaste for unnecessary detail. "Nothing too serious," he shrugged, "don't worry."

No doubt a parcel of what Europeans call Buddha sticks, or what Americans call Thai sticks, the best grass in the world.

How would we carry it?

Don't worry, Mr. Lee assured us. In Kuala Lumpur we'd be given new luggage. We wouldn't even know we were carrying anything.

The pay, I reminded him. What are we offered for this trip?

Twenty thousand Dutch guilders, Mr. Lee said. Eight thousand American dollars. When we got back, he added, we could invest part of our pay to buy a small portion of our cargo. At Malaysian prices.

That means dirt cheap. In the streets of Amsterdam—or anywhere else—we could turn a profit of four, five hundred percent.

"The eight thousand dollars. That's for each of us," I prompted.

"Of course."

A single delivery, twenty-four thou. This is heavy industry.

Over and above the thrill of the money, a comfort settled on me like a satin quilt. Guys who work on this scale are professionals. We're in good hands.

Let me make two things perfectly clear, as Richard Nixon might say in doubletalk.

First, I did not consider myself a drug dealer.

18

Second, I want to emphasize how natural, practically unavoidable, it was for a decent, rosy-cheeked boy like me to meet, even associate with, street dealers in Amsterdam. Grass was sold almost as freely as tulips. The fine for selling it in Amsterdam in 1976 was smaller than for defying a parking meter in New York. In a downtown canal, moored opposite the police station, there floated a conspicuous houseboat surrounded by flower boxes of cannabis. (While possession of grass was technically illegal, growing it was not, and the law hadn't decided where growing ended and possession began.) Recently, five newly elected young members of the city council had made a public show of lighting up and turning on—at their first council meeting. Every Saturday, Hilversum Radio reported the latest quotations from the commodities market: current street prices for soft drugs, as well as listings and reviews of drug clinics.

The police were equally tolerant of other drugs, notably opium, when used by the city's many Chinese. Along the Zeedjik, the main street of the red-light district, the knowing person could take a visitor up any of a score of narrow staircases to smoky, sweet-smelling flats and find Chinese, a dozen or so to a room, mostly lounging on cots, puffing pipes, floating in another world. Occasionally a cop visited, snooped about, shook the hand of a well-dressed man in charge, accepted a cigar. "We leave them alone," a policeman once explained to me in a bar, "as long as they allow only Chinese in. It's better than driving them underground."

Decades ago, hundreds of Oriental sailors jumped ship in this hospitable port. They must have sent nice cards and letters home, because since World War II, immigrants from Hong Kong and Singapore have poured in, swelling the Chinese section of town. Among them trickled members of the "triads," secret crime "families" sometimes called "the Chinese Mafia." In the early 1970s, these triads, headed by a shrewd character named Yong Fatt Tong, made Amsterdam the drug smuggler's world capital, for importing, cutting, packaging, and distribution throughout Europe and the Western Hemisphere.

The triads, running into more success than they could stand, split into two rival gangs, Hong Kong Chinese versus Malaysian Chinese. In 1975, the year before I arrived in Amsterdam, Yong Fatt Tong's rivals shot him dead and murdered three successive replacements, floating corpses down the city's canals with almost the scheduled regularity of the sightseeing boats. (I should add that the Chinese have since lost their dominance to an influx of Turks, Indians, Pakistanis, and Arabs.)

But all of that was too remote to concern me at the time. My immediate business was to line up a third man—and those jet tickets to the other side of the world.

For the third guy we needed, I couldn't think of anybody I trusted enough in Amsterdam, or anywhere in Europe. But I remembered this American named Peter Benack, a quick-minded guy about my age, whom I'd met a few months earlier in Berlin. I'd lent him some money, and I was sure he would have paid me back if somebody hadn't robbed him. On my recent quick trip back to the States, he'd invited me to visit him in Las Vegas, where he owns apartments and makes real-estate deals. So I called him.

"Hey, Pete, this is Jerry. Remember, the guy you met in—"

"Yeah, yeah, yeah, Jerry, how you been?"

"I'm calling from Amsterdam, Pete. You remember when we were talking that if anything comes up in Europe where we could both make some quick cash, I—"

"Yeah, yeah, you got something?"

Pete had that pseudo-Mafia way: "Yeah, yeah, you got something?" He even looked the type: muscular, fattish, sweaty, thick hair, flashy shirts.

I said, "Yeah, I can't discuss it on the phone. We'd have to make a little trip. You'd have to get here and—"

"Got ya. Got ya."

"Could you get here right away?"

"Get where?"

"To Amsterdam."

"Christ, I'm in Las Vegas."

"I know, I know."

"That trip costs. How good is this thing?"

"I told you I can't talk about it till you get here. If you come right away, I'll pay half your ticket."

"That good, huh?"

"Yeah, no kidding."

"Okay. I'll be on a plane tomorrow."

That was a Friday. Sure enough, after another couple of calls for arrangements, he arrived in Amsterdam on Sunday. I met him at the airport with Darrell.

Even before we got into the city, I explained to Pete what our deal was. I think he'd already assumed the "little trip" involved carrying substances, but now he wanted to know more.

"What kind of stuff?"

"He didn't say."

"You didn't ask?"

"Ask what? You don't ask."

"Well, what do you think?"

"Must be Thai sticks."

"Twenty-four grand for Thai? Have to be an awful lot of stuff."

"Well, what do *you* think?"

"*You* talked to him. You know what it *could* be."

"How could it be? He's not going to lay something that heavy on us the first time. He doesn't even know us."

Pete's face looked nervous, not the way he'd sounded on the phone.

This was no time for nervous second thoughts. "Anyhow, why ask? Why do we have to know? We're not *doing* it. We're just getting it. Somebody's going to have that twenty-four thou next week."

Suddenly Pete said, nodding like a jack-in-the-box, "Okay, okay."

Later that Sunday he told me only one thing gave him a problem. Jabbing a thumb toward Darrell, he whispered, "What's with him?"

From the moment he'd seen us through the big customs window at the airport, even before we could meet and shake hands, Pete

21

had nailed Darrell as some kind of shaggy-haired punk. He never stopped worrying that Darrell was the weak link in our deal. I think what made him feel that way was that Darrell was missing a front tooth.

I'd known Darrell for a few years in New York as an off-and-on sort of kid brother. Actually, I was interested in his older sister, who was a champ at hard-to-get. He was twenty-six, skinny as a twig, and even taller than I am. I'm a beefy six-feet-one. On that trip I'd made back to the States, mainly to see the lawyer who pays out on my father's will, I ran into Darrell again as I was getting turned down by his sister. Maybe I had a feeling for Darrell because as a child he'd suffered by his parents' divorce. I'd gone through that too.

Darrell's missing tooth encouraged people not to take him too seriously. Actually, I hadn't always taken him seriously, mainly because I'd tell him what to do, and he'd just do it.

He lived in Queens with his aunt and grandmother, and always had trouble with them. When I ran into him he was itching to get away, and said he wished I'd let him go to Europe with me. He had a job installing burglar alarms, from which he'd saved enough to cover the fare and stay afloat for a few weeks. I said sure, he could come.

Darrell, who I don't think ever won anything in his life, always had to feel he was beating out somebody who had something. As our jet was lifting over Kennedy Airport for Amsterdam, the first takeoff in his life, he looked down at the houses of Queens, at all the nine-to-fivers, all the salesmen piloting their samples around in Oldsmobiles, and said, "So long, suckers." (That lingered in my mind during many long, wakeful nights in prison camp.)

"What the hell we need him for?" Pete demanded.

"They said they needed three guys. That's why I called you."

"He gets a *split?*"

"I've been thinking about that. Look, they're going to pay me, for all of us. You might say I'm the contractor. When they give me twenty thousand guilders for each of us—you can be there to see it if you want—I'll give Darrell ten thousand, and we'll split the other ten."

"Doesn't he know—?"

"No. I already told him it's ten."

"How much is ten?"

"Four thousand dollars."

"Two each."

"Right. Total, four for him. Ten grand for each of us."

Disarmed, Pete grimaced his agreement.

Early in the evening of June 21, 1976, at Amsterdam's Schiphol Airport, Mr. Lee gave the three of us our airline tickets (via Bahrein, Bangkok, and Singapore) and pocket money of one thousand Dutch guilders each (about four hundred dollars). He said not to worry, the people meeting us at Kuala Lumpur would recognize us. I felt important, looked after. I can't remember a lighter, springier, more melodious moment in all my life.

A jolt struck a few minutes later, at the check-in counter.

"Will you be returning to Amsterdam?" the blond clerk asked.

"Yes."

"You are ticketed only one way?"

"Yes."

"You'll have to register with the airport police, that window past the currency exchange."

"For what?"

"Rules."

"Does everyone have to do that?"

"On this flight, yes, if you're returning."

"We're not absolutely sure we're returning."

"Speak to them about it."

In front of the bustling currency exchange, where we melded into the crowd, Pete and I huddled. Darrell listened.

"What's so special about this flight?" huffed Pete.

"It's to Singapore."

"Sure it's to Singapore. Singapore Airlines."

23

"They know a lot of stuff comes in here from Singapore."

"You said this place was no hassle."

"I said it was less hassle than anywhere else. This must be new. I never heard of it."

"So we're supposed to walk right up to them and say, 'Here I am. Lock me up for the rest of my life.' "

"C'mon, Pete, I told you, nobody here gets that. At most a year, and it's like a country club. Everybody knows, Denmark, Sweden, Holland, real country clubs. With American passports, if the worst happened, the *worst*, they'd deport us, send us home. That's what they do."

"What do they want us to register about?"

"It's for the computer. It's just to make people nervous, to discourage them. They put us in the computer, then check us off on the way back. Those guys aren't customs. They don't look in your bags. It's all right."

We went to the window to register. Reason for trip to Singapore? Tourism. Returning to the Netherlands? Expect to. Why no return ticket? Not sure of travel plans.

Mark, mark, stamp, stamp. No hassle at all.

I felt good about convincing Pete; it made me feel I must be right. At those crisis moments something optimistic in me takes over. Actually, it's more complicated than that. Something funny rises up inside me, starting in my chest, reaching up through my neck, surging to my ears, something two-pronged, like the shape of a wishbone. One side of it is surprise, alertness, you might even say fear. I see—and fear—the possible consequences. You might say that for a flash of a moment I hear other people's voices, see their reality. But then the other side takes over. It says, If you listen to their reality, you won't want to take the risk. That part of me wants me to lie, even to myself. It wants me to belittle the risk, concentrate on the possible profit. That side wins just about always. And most times in my life, it's been right. The risk turns out not so bad. And the profit is there. But still, at moments of quick decision, that

24

conflict rises up inside me. It bothers me until the wishbone snaps in favor of going ahead and doing it, taking the risk.

So I felt good again after convincing Pete.

On Singapore Airlines, from which Europe and America ought to take lessons in how to run a classy flight, we took off into what had to become the adventure of my life.

3

KUALA LUMPUR

In about sixteen hours of the unreal time of jet travel, we flew eastward through two full nights and a day, stopping at Rome, at Bahrain (in the United Arab Emirates), and at Bangkok, Thailand. Finally we landed in early morning at Singapore's glossy air terminal, for a one-hour layover and a change of planes. The three of us, tired, and tired of each other, strolled separate ways.

Just as I stepped aboard an up escalator to look around, a man called softly from behind me:

"Mr. Amster."

The caller, an Oriental of about forty, stood at the bottom of the moving stairs, looking up at me as though he'd missed a train. Should I respond? We had nothing on us, why not? I had to ride to the top so I could descend to meet him.

Without extending his hand, in faintly British syllables he addressed me again, almost under his breath: "Mr. Amster. My name is David."

And mine is Chiang Kai-shek. "How did you know me?"

"I have been on the plane since Amsterdam. Your escort." A hint of a subservient bow, like a houseboy, which this guy surely wasn't. The open collar of his orange shirt, printed boldly with multihued flowers, gave rise to a thick neck and head with a boxer's broad, flat nose. Through his perfect courtesy peered eyes as merciless as an insurance adjuster's.

Our escort? A mixture of surprises swirled in me.

"On the flight to Kuala Lumpur," he said, "I will be aboard with you. It will be short, less than an hour. Do not speak to or otherwise pay attention to me. After you pass through customs, look for me outside, but make no direct contact with me. I will get a taxi and instruct the driver to take you to the Kuala Lumpur Hilton. Rooms are reserved in your name. Please wait in your room for my call."

I remained shaken that this man had traveled with us, watched us, since Amsterdam, without our knowing it. Had I behaved all right? Had I done anything foolish to damage the good impression I wanted to make on these people?

Had he seen what happened as we approached Bangkok? He must have. I was sitting at the right window, Pete on the aisle, Darrell between us. Annoyed with Darrell over something, maybe with me too, Pete made a big, noisy show of abandoning us and moving to an unoccupied window seat of his own. The hell with him, I figured. Moments later, as we descended, I saw rice paddies, acres and acres of glassy furrows, just like Vietnam on TV.

I said, "Look, Darrell, rice paddies." He didn't answer. I said, "Darrell, look, rice paddies!"

He still didn't answer. His eyes were open, but queerly, as in a trance. I touched him on the arm and pointed at the sight below our window.

With a berserk jolt, Darrell flung out a fist and socked me. Right in the face. Right there, in plain view of all those people. The fist didn't hurt terribly, but its suddenness and craziness stunned me. He slumped sullenly, breathing in gusts, and I couldn't make him explain. (Later, in the hotel, he apologized. He said he'd been having a weird dream, and I'd broken into it. Still bewildered, I told him to forget it.)

27

Now, with this "escort" appearing out of the blue, our trip suddenly seemed a photo reversed to its negative. Did all this attention really signal the importance of our mission? Or the opposite: that we were the purchased patsies, in a sense the prisoners of this gang of rich, brutal strangers?

That's another thing I sometimes do. After looking at something in its best light, then getting jarred into a second look, I sometimes swing way over and scare the hell out of myself, seeing it in its worst light. I didn't want to do that now. This trip was too good to spoil so soon. I restored the negative back to the original photo again.

Seconds after arriving in my room at the Hilton, I had scarcely flushed the toilet when the phone rang.

"You will meet me in the coffee shop?"

"When?"

"Now."

No names. I loved it. How did he know for sure the voice was mine? For that matter, how did I know for sure his was David's?

At a table downstairs, he began abruptly. "Tomorrow morning, I will meet you here at nine."

"The others too?"

"Just you alone."

I nodded. He seemed to relax, as though the business of the meeting was successfully concluded.

Is this why he summoned me downstairs after a round-the-clock, halfway-around-the-world journey? Even for something this simple, he wouldn't trust a phone? I loved it again. This is the international intrigue game I'm in now, and these are the inconvenient rules.

Next morning he was loaded with instructions, with messages, whispered so low I could scarcely hear. Yet he didn't lean forward or look in any way secretive or conspiratorial. Someone watching from another table would never know. I decided to study and master the technique.

"I now have rooms for you at the Jaya Puri Hotel. This—" David's awareness twitched uneasily about the coffee shop, although his eyes scarcely moved. "This place is not good, not secure for us.

Jay-a Pu-ri, you'll remember? First class. Much better for us. This morning, you all check in there."

Directing a taxi driver there would be no problem. In former colonial cities, hotel clerks and most taxi drivers, even many shopkeepers, know the language of the former colonizers. Malaysia had been British.

"Tomorrow night," continued David, "you will meet the boss at dinner. A car will pick you up in front of the Jaya Puri at exactly eight. Eight exactly."

"Will you be in it?"

He pretended not to hear. I must stop asking those questions.

"Saturday evening you will leave for Europe We have tickets for you on Aeroflot to Moscow, and from there to Paris. At Paris you will take a train to Amsterdam."

"To Moscow?"

"Yes."

The sound of it sent a thrill through me. Also a chill. Thrilled or not, I felt it important to offer my best advice.

"I've been thinking about it," I said. "I think we should go back through Copenhagen. I've been there. I know that airport. The customs people are quite relaxed, very much like Holland. And if anything goes wrong, their system is very lenient."

His look was expressionless, patient for me to spill it all.

"Lenient is too late. Our job is to get through with no problems. Moscow is best. We already have the tickets."

Was he closing me off?

"I—I can't imagine Moscow as a relaxed customs point."

"It is not a customs point. Simply a transit point. Your bags will be checked through directly to Paris. In Moscow, you don't even change planes. A different flight number, but same Aeroflot. No inspection, no customs."

"But Paris. You know French customs."

"Better than you do." He tried to soften that jar with his polite houseboy nod. "The French are rigid, indeed, but they know exactly when and where to be rigid. Flights from Moscow are not worth their time. They do not look for our type of business coming out of Moscow. On the day the French start worrying about vodka, then they will worry about flights from Moscow. Besides, they do not pay attention to American tourists. They pay attention to Germans. They pay attention to Turks and Arabs and—and to us. Just be an American tourist. Find a bottle of ketchup and pack it in your suitcase. Wrap it in the same plastic bag as your Right Guard. All will go well. So. In Paris you will get through with no trouble, and you will leave the airport and proceed by train to Amsterdam. That way—well, you know how simple the Amsterdam train station is."

Everything he said sounded true. And he said it with finality. This was the moment to bow respectfully to experience and authority if I wanted to parlay the good impression I'd made into future business with these people. And I had an idea for future business, something clean and practically legal, not based on risky gigs as a courier.

"What are your plans for enjoying Kuala Lumpur?" His face and voice lifted suddenly into a friendly host's. "Do you know anyone here? Something you want to see? I have a friend from India who drives a taxi. He will take you around, show you everything. A few hours, very reasonable. You will enjoy. Would you like new suits, beautiful Malaysian style, made specially for you? Just tell him. He will take you today for measurements. Tomorrow you will have your suits. Very, very reasonable, you will be surprised. Shall I call him? When shall I have him pick you up? Noon? Is that good? At your new hotel, yes? Excellent, very good."

I hadn't responded with a word. But his program sounded fine.

The Jaya Puri did seem more like the place to be: more Oriental and subdued, more wood-carved and velvety, cozier. We gathered in my room and I told Pete and Darrell about our travel instructions.

"Moscow?" Pete was as surprised as I'd been.

I explained the details of David's reasoning.

"Moscow's not the way to go," Pete announced. "The way to go is by boat. I know a guy used to bring stuff into the States. By boat. You buy a ticket to Sweden. In Amsterdam you get off for a day's sightseeing, stuff strapped to your leg or in a shoulder bag, no inspection, nothing, and you never get back on the boat. You ship stuff in a trunk, in a car, to a dock, to an address, lots of ways, and you're not even carrying anything when you get off."

Darrell asked, "How much you think that taxi guy's going to soak us today?"

"A boat takes forever," I said.

"What's the big fucking hurry? The important thing is to get the package there, right?"

"Look, they already have the tickets. These guys know what they're doing."

"I'm going by boat. When do we see them? I'll talk to them."

"Tomorrow night I'm supposed to see the boss."

"*You're* supposed to see the boss?"

"I'll bring it up with him."

"*You'll* bring it up with them? Are we partners or what?"

"He didn't say I should bring anybody."

"Did he say *don't* bring anybody? Are we partners or what?"

"He did say don't bring anybody this morning to the coffee shop."

"I didn't like that, either, but that's different. Tomorrow's with the boss. He wants me to carry his stuff? He'll fucking well take me out for chop suey and give me my say about how I'm going to do it."

"All right, but if he doesn't like your idea, don't push it."

"Why not?"

"Because I don't want to make a bad impression on these people. I think we can do all right with them in other ways, without carrying stuff."

"Like how?"

"We'll see."

"I got some ideas too."

"Okay, then don't ruin it by pushing too hard."

"I go too, don't I?"

Pete turned his face away, grimacing.

"Jesus, Darrell, I'm telling you, I'm not even supposed to bring Pete."

"What'll I do around here?"

"There's a lot to do in this town."

"I'm as much a partner as he is."

I didn't want to get into that. "It's got to be no more than two of us this time, Darrell. Next time we'll make it up to you."

Darrell looked wounded. He sometimes does dumb things, but he's not dumb. I hated to make him feel bad.

When a car, driven by David, pulled to the curb at eight the next evening, Pete and I were wearing our new tropical suits, which the tailors had told us were in the style worn by government ministers: six buttons down the front, flaps and buttons over pockets. Unlike their government ministers, we asked for a bell-bottom cut to our pants. Pete and I had ordered ours in beige; we stood there feeling oddly like twins. Darrell's was navy blue.

David made a show of admiring our new clothes. Then he drove us to the edge of the city and beyond, to a luxurious restaurant where, at a huge round table, we met the boss and his wife. I guess "met" is the right word. David brought us together cordially, with lots of bowing, introducing each of us by his first name to the boss and his wife, but not giving us a name for either of them. Then David disappeared. The boss was as fat and reserved as a Buddha, his wife as bony and perfect as Audrey Hepburn. He spoke no English; she interpreted. Waiters attended us not just with courtesy, but with a subservience that made this fat man seem a lord among lords. He wore a ring I couldn't believe, an oval of jade almost an inch long, set in engraved gold. I'd never cared for jade, but, God, I ached for that ring. Well, not the ring, but the success and power and respect that radiated from it.

He ordered and we talked, the fat man asking, through his wife, about our time in Kuala Lumpur; he didn't seem too interested in my answers. He, too, admired our new suits, then asked if we had been told about our return trip. I said yes. For a moment I thought that was the time to bring up my Copenhagen scheme. But I didn't want Pete to jump in with his boat idea. I didn't and he didn't.

If all worked out well, speculated the fat man, we might have other profitable opportunities. This was the first time his group had employed Europeans as passengers—Americans, he corrected himself with a dip of the head—or, for that matter, any non-Orientals. That was the word they kept using: not couriers, but "passengers."

"If it works well, I can get more," I probed.

The translation puzzled him. More what?

"More Americans in Europe to be passengers. I could line up enough so nobody would take more than one trip. No raising of suspicion. Each one would have just one visa stamp from Malaysia on his passport."

"Yes, that is our thought. Just so."

His encouragement made my breath come faster.

"I could be a kind of coordinator, much more valuable to you than as a—as a passenger. I could find people, screen them for Mr. Lee or whoever. Maybe even escort them here and back, if you want. I wouldn't have to worry about collecting visa stamps, because I'd be carrying nothing."

"That is exactly the possibility."

Then Pete broke in, damn it, and switched it around.

"We could work out ways to move stuff directly into the States. I know people. I'm from Las Vegas. You know Vegas? A lot happening there. I know people, connected people, in L.A., Los Angeles. That's California, Hollywood. I'd have no trouble, no trouble at all, moving stuff . . ."

What the hell did he get into that for? That's not the way we want to go. Not *toward* the heat, but away from it. I half wished he'd barged in with his loony idea about the boat—anything instead of this.

The fat man's wife bit. She asked questions: How would you travel? What routes?

"We'd go by boat. We could buy a ticket—"

33

Without waiting for his answers, she translated Pete's idea to her husband.

The fat man looked hard at Pete and nodded. Then he explained something and she ended it: "He says we are in a different business. Others bring to the States and so on. We bring to—to the distribution point. A different business. Each must do his own business."

The boss switched channels after that, and directed most of his conversation toward me, mostly inquiring as to whether we liked the food. I had sweet-and-sour pork, excellent, but no better than in the good Chinese restaurants of Amsterdam.

The evening made me feel valued, respected, a star—that thrill again, corny as it may sound, of a leading role in a James Bond movie. I never miss James Bond movies. For me, James Bond is the ultimate in sophistication, exotic travel, secrecy, and intrigue, the essence of true adventure. The Russians were soon to say, when they put me on trial, that I was an "adventurist." Their psychiatrist also used that word. They were absolutely right. That was the only detail of the trial that pleased me.

I felt about this host of ours, this Buddha, the way I did about Vito Corleone in *The Godfather*. He seemed partly a tyrant, cold-eyed and merciless; but he also attracted me as a fatherly, benevolent person who would take my interests to heart, and whose confidence I would like to have.

After the meal we strolled together to the parking lot, the fat man leading us to a Mercedes-Benz sedan with Netherlands license plates; a Dutch doll hung from the rearview mirror. Did they divide their time between here and Amsterdam, transporting car and all? That didn't seem too cautious. But, of course, they surely didn't carry anything, so they could do whatever they pleased.

At the rear of the Mercedes, as though guarding it, David waited. He and the fat man exchanged some information in Chinese. The boss grunted a couple of approvals and motioned Pete and me into the back seat. We drove away from the lights of Kuala Lumpur, along a road that led us through a sleeping village, then another, then into an endless moonlit wood. We must have driven for half an hour, saying little, except for the fat man, who repeated that this was the first time they had used non-Orientals for passengers, and that if all went well we could have a profitable future. Then he slowed, looking for a certain landmark, stopped, and backed a few yards into a long dirt driveway. At the end of the path I could make out a darkened house, but that didn't seem to be our destination. We all got out. The fat man opened the car trunk. Its dim automatic light revealed three suitcases, each a different color and shape. They appeared to be of good, thick leather. The trunk smelled of leather. He inspected each one, fingering its corners, tilting it laboriously this way and that. The bags must have been placed in his trunk while we were eating. He seemed not to have handled them before.

"This," he said with hushed pride and an extended palm, like a father presenting an extravagant graduation gift, "is your luggage."

Pete reached first to lift one out.

"Ho-lee shee-yut," he yelped. "Feel this motherfucker."

Damn that Pete. He'll screw up this relationship yet. How can he be so cocksure the fat man's wife doesn't know those words? I should have left this loudmouth at the hotel and brought Darrell.

I reached for a bag. A strain zinged up my arm, kicking me in the shoulder. It was all weight. Dead weight, like a bag of stones.

I whistled. I guess I wanted to restrain my surprise. But I guess I also wanted to assert it. What the hell are they trying to do to us? What's in these bags, anyhow? Do these people know what they're doing?

Stupid question. Of course they know what they're doing. Look at the ring on that guy's finger. Hadn't he bought that from managing shipments like this? But Jesus, how the hell are we going to—? Where's that weight coming from? What is *in* these bags?

"What the fuck is in these bags?" Pete demanded.

The fat man didn't have to get the words. He got the tone.

Unstrapping and unlatching one bag, the fat man arranged his

35

thumb and forefinger to form a caliper, like a letter C. With a sage's smile that said this would explain everything, he showed us, with finger-to-finger measure, how thick were the leatherbound walls of that suitcase. He grunted a triumphant little laugh.

Pete demanded again: "What the hell is *in* there?"

The woman relayed the question.

The fat man looked at his wife, faintly surprised, and muttered something. She, too, appeared puzzled by our question. She said simply, "Heroin."

"Heroin? How goddamn much of it?"

Pete's belligerence no longer bothered me. I was speechless. He was now speaking for at least part of me.

Let me say here that I'm not quite sure what stunned me. The weight of those bags? I felt I was expected to do—committed to do—something that couldn't be done. How could we try to look like innocent American Cub Scouts, hefting all that weight through three customs stations, and walk out free? The sudden reality of our mission shocked me.

But the other shock was of another kind. When she said, "Heroin," a voice in my own head surprised the hell out of me. It said, "I knew it."

I hadn't known it. I hadn't known that I'd ever thought it. I guess I'd never allowed myself to think it. Yet my mind said, "I knew it."

At that instant I remembered the moment when I'd decided I didn't want to know it. It was back at Short's of London, when I asked Mr. Lee what we'd be carrying. I tried now to rerun that tape to retrieve the moment. Actually, he hadn't answered. He'd just looked annoyed, and shrugged and said, Nothing too serious. Had he said it was Thai sticks? No. I'd said to myself it was Thai sticks. I hadn't stopped to wonder—hadn't *wanted* to wonder—how we'd carry enough Thai sticks to justify the fat air express fee he'd just offered. I'd simply settled in my mind that it was Thai, and that was the last I'd let myself think abut it.

On the day Pete arrived in Amsterdam, he'd asked what I thought the stuff was. With certainty I said, "It's got to be Thai sticks." He wondered aloud a couple of times whether it could be anything heavier. I said they would have told us. Then we just left it hanging there. I guess Pete didn't want to know either.

"Ain't no way, no way in hell we're going to get through customs with that kind of weight."

"No problem, no problem," came the translation from this unshakable man. "We have done it many times, luggage just like this. All in how you lift it up and not let the customs man lift. You think of the money and you will have no problem to lift bag." The wife imitated her husband's smile.

"We didn't talk about money for carrying *this* stuff. We never knew this was what we'd be carrying."

"What did Mr. Lee tell you?"

Pete looked at me. My mouth still wouldn't work. I couldn't yet grasp the risk of transporting the stuff. At the same time, I didn't want to ruin the connection with this powerful man who could change everything for me. And more immediately, I didn't want to lose the ten grand, total freedom for months, that would be mine in—what?—four days. Finally I said, "He said it was nothing too heavy. I mean, nothing too serious. So I was sure it couldn't be— I mean, what would that mean to anybody, 'nothing too serious'?"

"Did he tell you you could buy some of this at Malaysia price?"

Pete stayed in charge. "What are we going to do with this stuff? We got to be crazy to deal in this stuff. And how we gonna buy any if we never get there?"

"I tell you no problem to get there."

"With this stuff we *got* to go by boat. No other way. And the hell with buying. We get through with this stuff, we don't buy. We just get a piece."

"Boat is impossible."

"What's so impossible about it?"

"How much do you call a piece?"

"How many pounds in there?"

"Does not matter how many pounds in there. What do you call a piece?"

Pete turned to me. "Hey, Jerry." He startled me, as though I'd forgotten I was there, as though something I'd been watching on television had suddenly sprung to real life. "What do these people call their pounds?"

"A kilo. It's two-point-two pounds."

I couldn't quite trace how it had happened, but suddenly a switch had been accomplished.

Without losing a moment's rhythm, Pete made his bid. "A kilo each. Plus the money."

Even in the dark I saw—I could feel—the pupils of the fat man's eyes contract. This was his country. He had all his people around here. I didn't like this.

He spoke a sentence in Chinese, some really important sentence, like an order to slit a throat.

"You are a courage—" His wife stumbled to rework his words into right English. "You are a man of courage. You will get through without trouble because you have mind and courage. In Amsterdam, you will have one kilo and a half, you divide between you. And the money stay the same."

A pound apiece. More, if we cut Darrell's share. I tried a quick, rough calculation, and my neck got hot. Three pounds had to be worth at least a half-million dollars.

"And you've got to cut that weight in half."

Twice the fat man asked his wife to retranslate that demand.

He wasn't mad. He seemed amused. "You want to cut your share in half? And the money in half?"

"The weight's got to be cut, or won't none of us have nothing."

"We will fix it. Don't worry, there will be no problem. Tomorrow afternoon, about four, you will be in hotel, yes? The bags will come. You will be well satisfied."

We rode the long ride home to the Jaya Puri in darkness and silence.

Next afternoon, Friday, after a hot, sticky, aimless tour of a shopping center, the three of us sat in my room, glum, tired, soaking up the air conditioning and a tray of room service vodka and tonics.

Funny, that shopping center tour. Beautiful things, clothing, jewelry, gorgeous art objects to make a home a palace, all with price tags that meant nothing. We could have it all, any of it, price no object. No matter how I figured our shares—ten thousand American dollars, even as much as two hundred grand—each share was a lot, plenty, without even counting ahead to our bright future with these people. The money was in our hands. My piece of it was as good as in my pocket now. Why were our bosses screwing up a sweet deal by being so greedy?

My feelings about the fat man swirled in confusion. I knew he liked me, had confidence in me, and that made me feel attached to him, respectful. I sensed a future of getting rich through him, a future I always knew would be mine, just a question of when, and through whom. At the same time I resented him. His ears and mind shut us out. He treated us like servants, like prisoners. These people felt free to follow me, spy on me. They knew all about me. They held my life, my future in their hands, and I didn't know the name of a single one of them. Even while he made me feel exalted, this fat man made me feel insignificant, disposable.

Promptly at four, without a call from downstairs, someone knocked at my door.

David? The fat man himself?

I opened the door to a stone-faced, musclebound teenager with a greasy duck's-ass hairdo. An enormous leather suitcase hung from each hand, a third jammed beneath his arm. He entered and laid them on my bed. No huffs, no puffs, no bellyaches about their weight. Pete, always first to be the good guy, flipped a bill out of his wallet, folded it beneath his fingers, as though tipping a Vegas headwaiter, and tendered it. The kid looked at the gift, muttered something in Chinese, and handed it back. He bowed coldly and left.

Pete and I each grabbed a suitcase.

Mine still felt full of rocks. Pete hefted his, put it down, and tried the third. Darrell lifted the one Pete had dropped.

Pete bunched his lips, holding back an outburst, then his look turned dark.

"If they took one feather out of this, just one feather, I'll—I'll eat it. I'll let it tickle me to death. Those bastards."

I lifted my bag to the bed and opened it. It was loosely full of used clothes: a couple of worn, wildly colored shirts, a pair of chinos, a frayed silk robe, underwear, and a detective novel in Dutch. But there was no way that that flea market of stuff, even when the real clothes of one of us was added, could disguise the curious weight of the closed bag.

I sat down to stare at it. Pete sat down. Darrell kept lifting his bag, laying it on the bed, opening it, fingering the false walls, closing it. Every time he closed it, the weight of the lid forced a wind gust, a *vooom*. You couldn't miss it.

"Let's blow this place."

Pete and his ideas. "How can we blow this place?"

"Just blow. They don't own us. We just get the first plane out of here. Tonight."

"We don't have tickets."

"We'll get our own tickets."

"You know what the tickets cost?"

"I got American Express."

"Well, you can't just blow this place."

"Why *can't* we just blow this place? They don't own us."

"What do you mean, they don't own us? They *do* own us. This minute they're watching us."

"How do you know?"

"You think they're *not* watching us? You think they're going to drop off all that stuff and not watch us?"

"Nobody tailed us today. I know how to spot a tail. A CIA guy told me how they do it."

"Did you see David tailing us all the way from Amsterdam? They know how to tail. Besides, we didn't have their stuff then. We have it now."

"If we leave their bags here, just go out and get a taxi, how the hell would they know?"

"You'd never get to the ticket counter. And if you did, you'd wind up in the canal."

"What canal?"

I looked at Darrell. Darrell took the ball like a lateral flip.

"The canals. Amsterdam."

Pete gave Darrell his Darrell look, a disgusted blank.

"That's how the Chinese take care of people. You come floating down the canal. Two, three times a month somebody floats down the canal. Early in the morning."

Pete looked at me for confirmation. "You didn't tell me that."

"What's to tell you?"

"You didn't tell me we're dealing with that type of people."

"I don't know if *these* guys are 'that type of people.' I don't know what type they are. You want to find out? Just leave that stuff on the bed there, and call a taxi for the airport."

Pete twitched his mouth. End of subject.

We all sat there, waiting for the next thought, the next idea for handling this crisis. Then something inside me caught fire and blazed. I was sick of this conversation. Sick of its pessimism, its stink of defeat. We came here for a purpose: a quick ten grand apiece, which now suddenly had become maybe a hundred fifty or more. We had here an opportunity for a future as "coordinators," never getting our hands dirty; a solid crack at a continuing, fat cash flow, practically no risk, practically legal; an opportunity any growing American boy dreams will come along sometime in his life, and here it was. We just had to pay our dues this one time, and it could all be ours—mine. So okay, the stuff in the walls of the bags is something we didn't expect. Let's get the damn thing over with, and we'll never have to touch that stuff again. Here was the big chance

41

breathing right up our noses, and what the hell were we sitting around talking about? Whether we could catch a taxi and sneak out of town.

"Look, the man knows what he's talking about. He's right. It's all in how we handle the bags when we get to Paris. I've gone through a hundred customs counters. The average customs inspector is lazy. He hates to lift suitcases. Darrell, get over there where the customs guy stands."

I hoisted a bag to the bed, careful to disguise the extra muscular effort of my arm and shoulder. I didn't like the way I did it; the strain showed. Returning the bag to the floor, I lifted it again. Better.

"See that? Lift it and swing it forward like this."

That third time felt and looked really good. I did it a fourth and a fifth time, each still easier and still better. From the handle I untied a dangling key and locked the bag so I could unlock it as part of the whole graceful operation. It locked easily enough, but seemed to stick in the unlocking. After a few turns, the lock eased up and responded readily to the key.

"Get that? You've got to loosen the lock and practice it." I looked straight at Darrell. "Practice it. You don't want the inspector to notice you for any reason at all. If your lock sticks and the guy waits for you, he's going to go through everything you've got. Otherwise he feels you wasted his time and kept all those people waiting. He'll put on a show just for them."

Darrell nodded, annoyed.

I swung the bag around to face Darrell and lifted the lid. Its unnatural heaviness surprised me again. Then I closed it. Too fast. *Vooom!* I tried it again. *Vooom!* I held the lid in my hands and eased it down. Too slow, too much effort. Finally I got it just right. Pete wanted to try. *Vooom!* Eventually he got it right, and so did Darrell.

"When we go through in Paris, make sure you open and close the bag yourself. Don't let the customs inspector do it. Make sure you set it down with the locked side facing you, so he can't open it. You have to open it and turn it around, as a courtesy. Get it? We each have to work on that tonight. Tomorrow morning we have to watch each other work on it. We have all day before we leave."

That was it. Not another word about sneaking off to the airport, empty-handed and defeated. Not another word about trying to slip away from the best deal we ever had.

4

SHEREMET'EVO AIRPORT

Saturday, our departure date, was the day Muhammad Ali fought a karate champ in Manila before a worldwide television audience. The phony mismatch of a puncher versus a chopper resulted in a draw, which made it quite forgettable.

But I remember it vividly for three reasons. First, because I'd looked forward to the novelty of seeing it on Far East television. Second, because on that Saturday morning I got so involved in our suitcase practice that I lost my sense of the clock, and turned on the TV just in time to miss the end of the fight. That didn't do a thing for a general jumpiness that had gnawed at me since dawn, connected, I suppose, with our approaching moment of truth at the Paris airport. Third, because, trying to hide my fury at myself for stupidly missing the fight, I grabbed a copy of an English-language newspaper, the *New Straits Times*, that lay next to the TV. There on the first page screamed the news of a Malaysian arrested at the Moscow airport while changing planes. His luggage had concealed seven kilos of heroin.

While changing planes? Didn't he check his bags through to his destination, as we were going to do? If so—if he was simply "in transit" at Moscow—why did they inspect his luggage?

"Hey, Pete, Darrell, look at this."

From their connecting rooms they came and looked. We all studied the article silently, heavily.

Darrell said, "Malaysian. Must've started from here."

"How come they got to his bags? He must've been bringing the stuff into Russia."

"You don't bring stuff into Russia. They couldn't market fifteen pounds in Russia in a hundred years. Anyhow, it says he was changing planes."

"Then how come they got to his bags?"

"How do I know how come they got to his bags?" Pete's insistence irritated me. "With a Malaysian passport, you're always suspect. He must have made the trip too many times, too many visa stamps. Maybe somebody ratted on him. This has nothing to do with us. Nobody anywhere even knows we're— Anyhow, we're white."

Pete read the report again, puffed his lips a couple of times, then looked satisfied. Again, convincing him made me feel better. And I totally dropped it from my mind, more or less.

At the airport that evening, feeling light and sporty in our custom-made Malaysian suits, we arrived an hour before the scheduled departure of Aeroflot Flight 556 bound for Moscow via Karachi, Pakistan.

As he'd instructed me to do, I looked for David, who'd have our tickets. Leaving Pete and Darrell to guard our leaden bags, and trying to look idle about my search, I strolled through shops, the cocktail lounge, the newsstand, then out-of-the-way places, looking into phone booths, empty corners, the men's room. No David. I headed back toward Pete and Darrell, to see if he'd located them. I cut around a large, noisy, baggage-laden crowd of Germans, a group tour waiting to board a charter flight. From nowhere, David appeared, touching eyes with me for the briefest brush, then walking right into the crowd of Germans. I cut into the crowd at a different angle. Damn it, he was gone again. Something slapped into my palm. By reflex, I closed on it. There went David again, the back of him, heading away. In my hand, a thick envelope. The tickets, of course. Neat. A genuine brush-pass. And it had worked. I hadn't screwed it up. Feeling good, I also felt slightly embarrasssed at being surprised, at not expecting the maneuver. So much to learn. I reran the hand-off in my head. Had I really handled it smoothly? Could David tell I was surprised?

Also, so much to unlearn. A deeply bred instinct—something inescapably American, middle-class, I guess—made me feel strange at parting this way from David, the guy who'd been our sort of host and nursemaid for almost a week, without even saying, Good-bye, see you next time around.

Well, business is business, and this is the way the intrigue business works.

Just as well I hadn't said good-bye. As passengers for the flight gathered at the gate, among them stood David, our perpetual escort, paying no more attention to us than to a cluster of five men and a woman who jabbered heatedly in a tongue that sounded Russian. I decided they were Soviet professionals returning from an exchange tour or an international conference. Then, to my astonishment, I beheld the fat man and his wife. Taking no notice whatsoever of David, let alone of us, they waited to board, all patience and dignity, like rich tourists. Trying hard not to look bug-eyed, I just kept my gaze moving. The remaining group was of Oriental young men, about a dozen, standing around in pairs and trios, immaculate in tight, Western-style slacks and knit shirts, wordless, brooding, giving off an aura of fine physical condition and hours spent in the shower room. Clearly an athletic team. What Malaysian athletes would be making an exhibition tour of Russia? Gymnasts, I decided.

And that was the whole crowd, about two dozen. For the flight of a huge jet? No wonder Aeroflot is known for its bargain group rates. And still, their business was lousy.

Soon after we boarded and took off in our plain but comfortable Ilyushin 62 jetliner, Pete headed for the bathroom. He returned to his seat looking stricken, whispering to me, "You remember that tough kid who hauled our bags up to the room? He's here, sitting with some other kid with the same duck's ass. If you ask me, they all look alike."

I strolled to the bathroom to take my own look around. Sure enough, there was our old young friend, whom you could scarcely tell apart from all the other youths strewn about the ship. Gymnasts? The scrubbed athletes all followed me with furtive, icy glances. Were they *all* here for *us?* Why? Who paid their way? At what cost? Again my head bubbled with the importance of our mission. But new sprinklings of puzzlement and uneasiness took over. Was it possible that, except for those five Russians chattering up front by themselves (and for that matter, who could be sure about them?), this whole passenger list, this whole flight, was about us?

Why were they watching us, treating us like prisoners? Would they have us do their dirty work, then do us in? Would they kill us with silenced revolvers between Paris and Amsterdam, heave our bodies off the speeding train, and handle the easy Amsterdam customs themselves? Would they follow us all the way into Amsterdam, then launch our bodies down the canal? Would they go that far just to save a delivery fee? No, not just to save the money, but to rub out three guys who had been useful, but who now knew too much?

Was I coming down with paranoia?

To not a single soul here, except Pete and Darrell, who knew no more than I, could I address a question, a word. Through seventeen eerie hours of almost constant darkness flying westward, I slept little, and when I did, pairs and trios of Chinese gymnasts, who wouldn't look at me, leaped around my brain.

Feeling better at dawn, shortly before landing, I suggested to Pete and Darrell that we go through customs and leave the airport building.

"Go through customs?" Pete's look accused me of going crazy.

"Just walk through. No bags. Our stuff is checked through."

"What the hell for?"

"Maybe see the edge of the city, I don't know."

"You're not going to see any city."

"I'd like to get my passport stamped. This is Moscow. Maybe the only time we'll ever—"

"I don't want their damn stamp on my passport."

I looked at Darrell. Then I realized my plan was no good after all. Without a Soviet visa, issued in advance of our trip, we couldn't get out of the transit area of the airport.

As we dragged ourselves into the Moscow air terminal, my nerves vibrated, heart quickened. Not about the night's tension over our escort, or the dangers of the inspection at de Gaulle, now only four or five hours away, but simply because this was Moscow. For all my weariness and disorientation, the actuality of being here, even if we wouldn't see the city itself—just being able to say for the rest of my life that I'd been to Moscow—was as exotic as landing on Mars.

Then came a confusing instruction. A uniformed official, with a sweeping handwave and incomprehensible words that were all but lost in the echo of the huge, marble-walled air temple, directed those on our flight to fill out declaration forms at little desks and proceed to the customs area, carrying our declaration forms.

For what?

"For what?" I asked him directly.

He replied in a barrage of Russian with gestures.

Why doesn't he say it in English? That annoyed me. English is the required universal language of international airline personnel. Well, maybe not here.

The declaration form asked how much foreign currency we had, and if we were entering the Soviet Union with any narcotics. Ha.

"Hey, guess what," Pete blurted. Turning his back toward the waiting official, he muttered urgently to me out of the side of his mouth, "Our bags are on that conveyor. They took them off the plane. I just saw our bags."

"Those are for people going into Moscow. They go through customs."

"I saw our bags, I'm telling you. You know what that means?"

48

"What do you mean, do I know what that means?"

"It means we go through customs."

I walked nearer to the conveyor and baggage carousel. Sure enough, our bags were circling.

But we were in transit, waiting to proceed on an international flight. Nowhere do customs inspectors interfere with the luggage of through passengers who stay in the transit area.

The earlier moment's pleasant quickening of the heart slowed and churned to a deep, booming rhythm.

Why was I getting upset? There's *no* way they can know we have stuff in our bags. Why are they doing this? We're not going to bother them. We're just passing through. *Why are they doing this?*

"You know what this means."

I didn't want to hear any more of Pete's meanings.

"If we go through customs, it means we go to camp."

"What camp?"

"Camp. Labor camp. Ever hear of Soviet labor camps?"

At the moment his words meant nothing but annoyance, distraction. But for years they were to echo in my head. That was exactly how he said it: "It means we go to camp."

"Let's dump the stuff."

Pete's impulsive first thoughts could drive me nuts. "What do you mean, dump it?"

"Don't claim it. Get back on the plane, just leave it there."

No way. "We'd never take off. They'd come looking for us."

"How'll they know it's ours?"

"The baggage checks."

"We can dump our checks. So how can they match those checks against ours?"

"Then what are we going to show for baggage checks?"

"Who says we got baggage?"

"C'mon, our tickets say we have baggage."

"How they going to prove *that* stuff is ours? We can pick up checks off the ground, and then raise a stink that somebody made off with our bags."

"What do you mean, *prove?* This is Russia, Pete. They don't have to prove. Anyway, what would we do about the Chinese?"

"What about them?"

"We leave those bags there, and even if we did get out of here, we'd never get out of Paris alive."

Pete knew his idea was stupid, and he quit. We knew we had to take our chances.

Instinctively, the three of us—Darrell, Pete, and I—separated, pretended we didn't know each other. The official motioned to us to claim our bags. We shuffled toward the inspection lines.

I was first to reach a counter. A tooth-sucking customs man looked at me for the briefest moment. Just as I feared his look would burn holes in my skin, he lost interest, motioning me to open my bags. That rehearsal in Kuala Lumpur had served me well. As gracefully as I could, I jerked my bag to the counter, careful not to betray a struggle with the weight. Unlocking it, I lifted its lid and swung the bag around toward the haughty Russian. I looked as bored as I could manage, convincing myself that he couldn't hear the pounding in my head.

The inspector inflated to monster-size, radiating hot threat. He towered over me, lifting the corners of my clothes, poking a finger here and there for concealed packages. Then he motioned me to close up and move on.

Of course. There'd been nothing to worry about. A piece of cake.

Leaving the counter, I deeply, silently exhaled. Surprisingly, my breath trembled, as though it wanted me to cry.

And then it wanted me to laugh, to throw my arms around everybody, to fly and sing.

There's something I have to try to explain, even though I've never fully understood it myself. Whenever I go through some dangerous moment like that customs counter, whenever I have to hold my breath like that, suspending my whole life and all my feeling, immediately afterward I'm swallowed up by a rush of exhilaration. It's the rush of, By God, I made it, I put something over, and I'm okay now. It's not a thought or an idea. It's a physical feeling, up my back and across my shoulders, then up into my head and down into my genitals, enrapturing and consuming them like a huge orgasm. Except for me it's better, more immediate, more real, more magnetic—and more necessary.

Everybody knows that runners claim to get a high after a half hour of running, and that researchers have now found that after great physical exertion the brain releases natural drugs, called endorphins, which chemically resemble morphine and heroin. Maybe that explains why runners say their exhausting exercise is "addictive." Recently I read (in the *New York Times* science section) of a new theory about workaholism: that workaholics may be addicts of their own adrenaline; that they may purposely (even though unconsciously) create extremely stressful situations at work, so they can get their daily fix, feel that wonderful "fight or flight" rush of adrenaline to which they've become enslaved.

I'm not a runner, and certainly not a corporate workaholic. But I know there's something about getting through one of those dangerous moments that I need and crave. To feel that ecstasy of winning, I'll take the risk of losing, if there are decent odds. It's not that I tell myself I'm willing to lose. It's that my optimism gets turned on and takes over, muffling that low, cranky voice that wants to moan about consequences. In the coffee shop at the Kuala Lumpur Hilton, when David worked so hard to minimize the dangers of passing through French customs, I was wary, but I also had to conceal my quickening breath. That tingle of anticipation and craving ran up my arms and lovingly teased my thighs so I could hardly stand it.

In the next aisle, Pete, still shuffling toward his inspection, was all nonchalance, except he couldn't unpaste his eyes from me. As I got past my inspection counter, he shot me a quick eye-roll of relief. Eventually he made it through about as simply as I did, and silently joined me. He, too, trying to look routine, was heaving deep, shaky breaths.

51

Meanwhile, Darrell had somehow switched to the tooth-sucker's line, maybe after seeing my trouble-free experience. Good move.

"Damn it, I wish he'd shut his mouth," Pete muttered urgently. Pete still couldn't stand Darrell's missing tooth. In fact, right now that hole in Darrell's face didn't fortify my confidence.

Next thing we knew, Darrell was fumbling in his pockets—for his key! I'd warned him! Finally he found it. Now the customs man was poking into Darrell's bag, continued poking intently, then— *good God, Darrell was emptying his bag!* Emptying it of every stitch.

The customs man left the counter, carrying the empty suitcase, tilting slightly from its weight. Darrell, all his pants and underwear piled before him, remained at the counter, trembling, twitching, darting uncertain glances at us. We looked away, turned around, anything to avoid his eyes. Then the customs man reappeared and ordered Darrell to follow him into an office out of our sight.

Another official strutted out, announcing in Russian words and universal gestures that everybody was to line up again for reinspection. *Again?* I'd never felt more like a sitting duck: through our employers' stupidity in giving us new leather suitcases and encouraging us to buy identical clothes (my cool suit now felt aflame on my skin), Pete and I were announcing to this entire crowd, to the whole Soviet government, that that scared kid with the air-leak under his lip, the one in big trouble, was one of us—the Three Stooges.

Waiting in the re-formed line, I tried to rehearse an aura of calm, to anticipate official questions, to figure out explanations, excuses. I looked around for the fat man and his wife. There they were, perfectly cool, looking annoyed, absolutely unflustered over Darrell, whose downfall they must have seen, absolutely unconcerned about Pete and me, giving us not even a split-second glance.

My head began screaming nutty things at me: that the fat man simply *had* to step forward and take responsibility for what was happening. He's the professional smuggler, not us. What do we— Pete and I—know about all this, about what to do next? This heavy monster pulling down my right arm was taunting me so loudly I

52

could hear it: The bag, the bag, you sucker, you jerk, he's leaving you holding the bag.

When my turn came at the counter, the inspector looked at my suitcase. He must have noticed its similarity to Darrell's. He looked at me, at my condemned man's uniform of a Malaysian suit. He swung my bag around, unlatched it, felt the thickness of its walls, and motioned me to follow him. I reached for the bag. He lifted it first, shot me a freezing look, and carried it, straining.

He put me in a dank room, empty except for a plain table and two chairs, closed the door, and walked out with my suitcase. After a long, hollow wait, which every moment more and more transformed me into an unprotected, helpless kid—minutes? hours? I don't know—he returned and led me to a larger room. No Darrell, no Pete.

But there on a table, surrounded by a committee of grave, silent customs officers, lay three suitcases, empty of clothes, their double bottoms chiseled open, revealing plastic bags of gray, lumpy meal. I'd often heard that Asian stuff was not the well-known powder of fine, pure white, but that it came in gray lumps. There it was, sure enough—and good God, bags and bags and bags of it.

Twenty-eight kilos—about sixty-two pounds—I soon learned.

Two officials took me back to the small room. One spoke English, the other muttered in Russian for the first to translate. They questioned me, questioned, questioned. Yes, I admitted, we'd been hired as couriers, but I insisted that we'd thought we were carrying gold. A third customs man entered, said something in Russian, and disappeared. My English-speaking interrogator digested the message, looked at me, organized a question in his head, and stated it:

"We now find if you tell truth. When you arrive to Amsterdam, they promise to pay you money, but also promise to pay you kilos of drug. How many kilos?"

The question stunned me. Darrell or Pete, or both, had begun spilling.

"We know answer, so you tell truth."

My gold story was dead.

I wanted to scream at the fat man with his fat jade ring, riding that plane to freedom, abandoning us here in this enemy country with his stuff, his rap. I wanted more than to scream. I wanted to kill him.

"The top man," I heard myself shout at my interrogator, pointing to the transit area. "The top man is out there, getting on the plane right now. He's traveling with us. We are nobodies, just carriers. He's the one you want."

He glared at me coldly. "Plane flying now. He already go."

"Doesn't it stop at Leningrad?"

He consulted with his colleague. The colleague slipped out, returned with an older official, clearly more authoritative. The older man asked in English, "Your China comrade, he carry drug in luggage?"

"No, of course not. I mean, I doubt it."

He shrugged with disinterest and ambled out.

(Many weeks later, traveling in that Soviet prison train, our Malaysian fellow prisoner, named Lim Guat Beng, turned out to be the one we'd read about in the *New Straits Times*, arrested with eight kilos at Sheremet'evo. He spoke fairly good English. When I described the fat man to him, he countered by describing the fat man's wife and David. He also knew a surprising amount about our mission. I told him of the "athletes" on the plane.

"Thirteen," he said flatly.

"Why?" I asked.

He shrugged. "To make sure you delivered their merchandise."

The cost of the air fares alone astonished me. "Lim," I asked, "in the end, would they have fucked us?"

"Oh no," he assured me, "they would pay you. They are honorable people, like your Mafia. They don't cheat their own. Only rivals, who they kill for winking an eye.")

5

LEFORTOVO

That day at the airport was one long stretch of worry. What would happen to us? Did we have any rights? Could a Russian lawyer be trusted? Would they let us bring a lawyer from the States? What would that cost? Could we notify anybody? What could the American embassy do to help us? Could we trust them to do it?

From out of those blurry speculations, from out of the fog of waiting, from out of nowhere, there appeared before me the face of a woman. The startling blur focused into the face of a lovely woman: golden hair, joyous dancing eyes (enhanced by rimless specs), full of caring. Young, maybe twenty-three, twenty-four. Petite, say, five feet two. Well, not so petite. Voluptuous, actually, for a compact kid.

"I am Tatyana," she said, twinkling. "Your interpreter."

"Oh."

I tried to shake myself back from wherever I was. Habit made me want to do something, smile brightly, stand up, offer a chair, say something gallant, winning, boy-to-girl. But I did none of those things.

"What happens now?"

"They will come to talk with you."

"Who?"

"To ask you information."

"I've been giving them information. All day."

"Maybe a little longer. Not much longer."

She sounded like an American with a foreign accent. Like home. My heart reached out.

"Then what?"

"They wait for some people from city."

"Who?"

"From, how you call, from *Ka*, from K, mm, G, mm, B."

The size of my trouble took on a new order of magnitude. I wanted to ask something. I didn't know what to ask.

"Are you from the KGB?"

"Uch, no. Uch, no, no, no. Intourist, Soviet travel agency. I am translator, only translator."

"What's going to happen?"

"Soon they come."

"Then what's going to happen?"

"They, mmm, ask questions. They come soon."

"Yeah, but then what's going to happen? What are they going to do with us?"

"Aaahh." It was the sound of her now understanding my question. "Ah, you don't worry. You are nice man, good man. Don't worry, in Soviet Union you won't have problem."

Her words flowed through me like warm chicken soup. I absolutely believed her.

"Look, I'm very thirsty. Water. Drink. Can I get—?"

"Of *course*."

She took my arm. Not like a guard, but a friend. I really liked her.

"You have rubles, kopecks?"

"No, but I have money. I can exchange—"

She held up a silencing hand, and led me out of the room and down the corridor.

56

Are we allowed to do this? Who's guarding me? Could she be armed? If those customs men back there see me, what if one of them whips out a gun and fires? What if I just break away?

What if I did? Where the hell would I run to? Moscow? Go racing through the streets, asking everybody in English, "Where's the American embassy, I want to defect"? Maybe I could tear out to the runway and hijack a plane to Cuba.

She took me to a dispensing machine, sure enough, coin-operated. It bore a picture of a cut-up apple. I'd have been happy with anything, but, accustomed to choices, I asked, "What kind?"

I must have been pointing to the big word on the front. She translated, "Means clean. Mmm, pure. It is, how you say, automatic, so no hands touch drink. Pure."

She put in a coin, her own money, and out poured a reddish fluid, into a drinking glass. It was a glass made of *glass*, left there by the last drinker, presumably unwashed, and I'd leave it for the next. (The fascination of this stayed with me, and later I asked Russian prisoners about it. Yes, those machines are common in the Soviet Union. No one I asked saw anything strange—or amusing—about drinking pure apple-flavored soda water, never touched by human hands, out of a communal glass.)

After more assurances that I am good man and in Soviet Union I have no problem, Tatyana's quitting time arrived. I hated for her to leave. Didn't she understand I needed her? She didn't. I was alone again in that bare room.

Eventually two young, alert, civilian-suited fellows entered. With one of them, who had black hair and friendly eyes, I quickly established Spanish as our common language. I guessed he'd been a KGB spy in Spain. Maybe Latin America. Maybe an aide to Fidel.

He informed me in a tone of friendliness, but also of an official announcement, that I was being detained by the KGB, and that later in the evening I would go to the city for interrogation.

Later in the evening? It was now 7:00 P.M. We had landed thirteen hours ago.

"Am I under arrest?"

"Detained. For interrogation."

I was glad to hear that again. It had a promising sound.

"Would you like something to eat?"

I couldn't say it fast enough. "Yes, I would."

"We have dining room or place to serve yourself."

Feeling too fluttery for a sumptuous, sit-down meal, I chose the cafeteria. I picked a plateful of small open sandwiches laden with melted cheese and caviar, both black and red, surprisingly inexpensive. Flutters or no, caviar seemed right. This was, after all, Russia, and I should get the most out of the experience while I was there. The two agents bought nothing, but just sat, trying not to stare at me eating.

"Am I going to some kind of prison?"

"Yes."

"Can I buy some cigarettes, in case I'm here for a few days?"

Fidel's man looked at me oddly.

"Yes."

They took me to the duty-free shop. I bought four cartons of Marlboros. Then I remembered that Darrell had left Kuala Lumpur with only three dollars and change left in his pocket. I bought four cartons of Winstons.

"Can I bring these to my friend?"

"No."

"Can you give them to him?"

"No."

They took us into the city, each in a separate van. For a brief moment at a distance I saw Darrell, then Pete, for the first time in more than twelve hours. I ached to talk with them, find out what they had been asked, what they had said.

My sense of time had been twisted out of shape. For almost sixteen hours we'd flown through darkness, our jet racing the westward movement of the night. Now, sixteen hours after dawn, the city of Moscow, farther north than the Aleutian islands, still basked under a high summer sun.

The van sped us through a short stretch of muddy suburb, many of its bunched dwellings surprisingly old and dumpy. Suddenly blocks and blocks, actually miles and miles, of high apartment houses engulfed us, all apparently new, all the same height, about ten stories, all the same design, plain, all the same color, a listless yellow. In spaces between the apartment buildings and beyond, in every direction, cranes stood like long-necked sleeping birds, waiting for Monday morning, to resume building again.

The streets hummed with bicyclists and strolling Muscovites. No, not strolling, *walking*, charging forward, going somewhere. (Actually, they're usually not going anywhere, I soon learned in camp. It seems that all those new apartments, although people are glad to get them, are small, crowded, conducive to family tensions. Where do you go for release? You walk. Why so fast? In a country that is frigid eight months a year, you learn to walk fast.) We passed a lovely green stretch with glens, trees, benches, and lots of walkers. My Spanish-speaking KGB man broke his silence to identify Gorky Park.

"Where are we going?"

"Lefortovo."

"Where is that?"

"Not far."

"What is it, a city?"

He spread his palm and pouted to express something hard to explain. "A prison. KGB prison."

"I'm now under arrest?"

"No. Interrogation."

"For how long?"

Again the spread palm, the face of uncertainty, of hard-to-explain.

At the gate of a broad hulk of a red brick building with barred windows, we slowed. A guard in a kiosk, recognizing the van and my companions, grimly signaled us in.

Lefortovo. Stony, dark, smelling of ancient dampness.

Inside, a guard, recognizing my escorts, shoved a huge key into a door, ground it around, then pushed a button to ring a bell. After a while the face of another uniformed man appeared at the door's small, grated window. He inserted a second key from his side, unlocking the door. This second man, wearing an armband, led us to a further door, inserted his key, and rang a bell. Still another guard, on the other side, unlocked the door to let us through. Every door had two locks, two keys, two guards, two separate approvals to admit, one always by an armbanded officer of the day. (Only one man, I later heard, has ever escaped Lefortovo, and no doubt he had inside help. The man was Felix Dzerzhinsky, a high-born Pole arrested for assisting Lenin and the Bolsheviks. Soon after the 1917 Revolution, Dzerzhinsky founded the Soviet secret police, which evolved into the KGB. Thus he became, ironically, the ruler of the prison he had fled.)

We marched down a corridor to a desk and a guard, eerily lit by what seemed a halo. The man at the desk presided over what appeared to be the entire prison. Four banks of cells fanned out from him like the spokes of half a wheel: one to his left, one to his right, and between them, one branching diagonally to his half-left, and one to his half-right. The dim lights of each bank met and overlapped at his desk, resulting in the creepy angelic effect. More dramatically, each bank rose four tiers high, rows of closed-door cells atop rows of more cells. Either directly or assisted by mirrors, this all-powerful control guard could see every cell door along every walkway.

A simpler way to describe the layout of the prison would be to say that it formed the shape of the letter **K**, the guard sitting where all the lines converge. Actually I hadn't noticed that letter-shape at first, although the prison's builder had intended me to. The shape was to honor the name of Katerina, Catherine the Great, who built Lefortovo as well as the notorious Vladimir (in the city of the same name) and others in an eighteenth-century spree of prison-building, every one of them, deck upon deck, shaped as a **K**. In every wing, each deck was hung with a metal net across the open space from walkway to walkway. Thus, a desperate prisoner leaping from the highest, or fourth-floor, walkway would never make it even to the third, let alone to the bottom. He'd have to find another way to kill himself.

That night I spent alone in a tiny room, shut off from the world by a wooden door, alone with a slab and a thin mattress for a bed, and a hole in the floor for a toilet. I'd never known such aloneness. Maybe I dozed a few times, but mostly it seemed like dark, empty waiting. I didn't know what I was waiting for, except morning.

Twice during the night I banged on the door until a guard opened a hatch and peered in. I asked in English, spreading my hands to express the question, "What's going to happen?" He must have understood. Ignoring his cranky Russian, I made out his sign language of eight fingers and gestures: eight o'clock, someone come, you talk.

At seven or so, a clatter at the door. A hatch in the door opened and a hand tried to shove a tin cup at me. "*Chai,*" grumbled a voice. I tried to squeeze the cup through the opening, scalding my fingers. Soon another clatter, another voice: "*Sakhar.*" Sugar. Then, "*Khleb.*" Bread, a black, hard chunk. Then a spoonful of kasha. I ate none of it, but sipped a bit of the sour hot water that passed for tea.

At eight, promptly, a voice at the hatch commanded, "*Ahmstairr!*" My name never sounded so sweet. I existed. Someone wanted me. He would take me somewhere and I'd learn something, *something*, about my fate.

The guard led me toward the hub of the **K**, then motioned me to stop. Ahead of us at the intersection another uniformed man, who a moment ago had held up a green flag, had now raised a red one. Around a corner we heard footsteps. The guard muttered something to me. Annoyed that I hadn't obeyed what he said, he grabbed my shoulders and jerked me around so I faced the wall. Soon the footsteps came and went. The guard commanded me to get going again. The flag ahead was green.

61

I soon learned that in a KGB prison, where almost all inmates are subjects of investigation or awaiting trial, insofar as possible no inmate is supposed to see another's face. The other guy might be under interrogation for the same crime as mine, perhaps someone arrested later. I wouldn't know they had him, let alone what he might be spilling. That's why there's no mess hall, no work routine, no group activity. That's why the red flags and green flags.

The guard led me up a staircase and down the entire length of a second-tier walkway, through a door (two locks, two keys, two approvals), then another, and another. We were now in the annex, the investigational part of Lefortovo, where there are no cells, just interrogation rooms and offices. The prisoners mockingly call it Lubyanka. Lubyanka is really the name of a fearsome bureaucratic palace near Red Square, the central headquarters of the KGB.

A trim, blue-eyed fellow in shirtsleeves and open collar showed me to a chair opposite him at a table, and declared, "Aleshkoi."

"Aleshkoi," I replied.

I assumed the word was a greeting. It turned out to be his name. Lieutenant Aleshkoi (I never learned his first name, even after seeing him almost every day for two months) was my investigator. He was something like all the KGB men I had seen the previous evening: athletic, alert, a college-trained look, businesslike but not brusque. In fact, he was something like every FBI man I'd ever seen on television.

Beside him sat an even younger, even better-looking blond fellow named Alex (I never learned his last name), a KGB translator.

On the wall hung a portrait of Stalin. That surprised and confused me. I'd thought Khrushchev had put an end to Stalin worship. But apparently, since the fall of Khrushchev and the rise of Brezhnev, Stalin had made a comeback, especially with the KGB.

For Aleshkoi I had to review my recent adventure still another time, answering questions and more questions. Everything I said, Alex translated and Aleshkoi typed. After a while he stopped to make a pot of tea, laying out three cups and saucers, sugar, and a dish of wafers, like social tea biscuits. I must have gone at those wafers like a tiger. Aleshkoi asked if I'd had breakfast. When I said I couldn't eat it, he refilled my teacup, opened a whole box of wafers, and put them in front of me. Like a worried mother, he said, "You've got to eat."

As long as he was being that friendly, I asked if he could get the four cartons of Winstons to Darrell. He puckered his lips in deep judgment and said, "Possible." After the lunch break in my cell—during which I still couldn't bring myself to swallow their hard crust and dry kasha—I brought the cigarettes back to the interrogation room. Later Darrell sent me a thank-you note.

The next day and the next and the next, Aleshkoi chastised me about the reports reaching him that I was not eating. He warned that if I didn't eat the prison food they'd have to force-feed me, and I wouldn't like it. Meanwhile, Aleshkoi kept putting those tea biscuits in front of me, and I kept devouring them.

Actually, by this time I was eating pretty well, but through strictly unofficial channels. After the second day of interrogation, they'd assigned me to a new cell, on the second floor, which I shared with a Russian named Volodia. The Russians usually require a prisoner, after an initial day or two of isolation, to have a cellmate, who must be an absolute stranger. One rumored reason is that either prisoner, to improve his own situation, might offer to inform on the private, late-night confessions of the other. Second, either one would be held answerable for the other killing himself in the cell.

Anyhow, this guy Volodia, handsome and slick with a meticulous Ronald Colman mustache, took a deep interest in my nutrition. His mother paid him visits, and every two weeks (as long as he was under investigation, not yet a convicted prisoner) she was allowed to bring a package of five kilograms, eleven pounds. The first time he offered me food, I accepted gratefully, but felt guilty about it. Soon I learned that in a Russian prison the rigid custom is that when one cellmate has something, he shares. So every night I shared a small feast of cheeses, kolbasa, real white bread, tomatoes, and parsnips, a sweet and meaty vegetable I had never tasted. In those nightly treats, the sharers have to restrain themselves to make the treasure last through two weeks, till the next visit. If I got timid and took too little, however, Volodia would insist, "Vitamin"—in Russian, pronounced *vee-ta-meen*—"vitamin, vitamin, you need vitamin."

Volodia spoke a little English. His crime had been that of accosting tourists (mostly in English) for illegal currency transactions, a very serious offense. His English greatly speeded up my mastery of Russian, both through conversation and through translation of newspapers, which guards gave us.

Actually, Volodia's sharing of food didn't all spring from generosity. He knew the American consul would soon come to see me. Sure enough, the consul came, and brought me two plastic bags of goodies, purchased, I suppose, at the embassy commissary: M&Ms, small Mounds bars, Life Savers, chewing gum, raisins, and, treat of treats, miniature Baby Ruths. That night I broke open one of my bags, took one item, and bade Volodia take one. With elaborate appreciation, he did. Then he wouldn't open it. Next night, same thing. He tucked his candy away, refusing to open it. I felt bad, wanting him to enjoy it, wanting to watch him enjoy it.

"Oh no," he said. "After trial, I bring to camp. Look, confection from America, from American consul. I big man."

I pleaded with him, even doubling my nightly offerings, one to eat, one to save. He'd accept both—and save both.

Later, in camp, I learned that the value of my goodies was not only prestige. One of those miniature Halloween-size Mounds bars or M&M bags, just one of them, worth about a dime, could be traded for five packs of Prima cigarettes—worth a ruble, roughly a dollar, in earned credit at the *magazin*. Actually, most cigarettes are brought in from town by guards for cash. Cash, in turn, is smuggled in by visitors. For anything the guard buys, he charges a prisoner double; a ruble's worth of cigarettes costs two rubles, or two dollars. Two dollars in Primas is a pretty impressive turnover for a ten-cent treat.

Those candy bars stick in my memory for another reason. The vice-consul who brought them to me was a pleasant woman who asked lots of questions to make sure I was okay. A few weeks later I saw her picture on the first page of *Pravda*. She'd been arrested in a Moscow park as a CIA spy. The Russians claimed her clothing concealed a tape recorder, camera, microfilm, even a cyanide capsule. After the routine dramatics of declaring their shock, the Russians expelled her.

Four days after my arrival at Lefortovo, I got a wonderful surprise. My guard brought me, a little later than usual, to the investigation room. On Aleshkoi's right sat another KGB man, one I hadn't previously seen. Aleshkoi was looking serious. I didn't care, because to his right in Alex's chair sat not Alex but beautiful, blond, radiant Tatyana. It seemed Alex was sick that morning, so Aleshkoi had gone to fetch her from the airport to translate. Tatyana twinkled and glowed through those rimless specs as though just seeing me lit up her life, as though she'd really missed me. My heart, my whole chest blazed up like a match thrown into gasoline. I realized instantly I was in love with her.

Aleshkoi stood up.

The other guy stood up.

Tatyana stood up.

Aleshkoi said something.

Tatyana said, "Please stand up."

I stood up.

They were going to send me home. They had apprehended the Chinese fat man in Amsterdam with the cooperation of the Dutch police, and now they understood that he and he alone, as the international capitalist financing my mission, was the one responsible for this heinous crime, and they now wished to extend a formal apology to me and my government.

I waited.

Tatyana stood so elegantly, so primly, expectantly watching Aleshkoi, trying to look so solemn that I felt Aleshkoi was going to pronounce us man and wife.

Aleshkoi began to say something, the way a clergyman recites the vows from memory, trying to sound spontaneous. He went on and on.

Then Tatyana translated.

The Komitet Gosudarstvennoi Bezopasnosti (KGB), the Committee for State Security of the Union of Soviet Socialist Republics, was placing me under arrest. The charges against me were, one, taking part in a conspiracy to transport contraband into the Soviet Union, two, making a false declaration to a customs officer of the Soviet Union, and, three, entering the Soviet Union with contraband in my possession. Then a lot of other stuff about a lawyer who would be assigned to defend me, about the importance of telling the truth, and the consequences of not telling the truth.

Immediately after his speech, the two men took me out into the corridor, Tatyana following behind us. Joined there by two uniformed guards, we marched to an unfurnished, absolutely empty room. They faced me toward the far wall, which had a tiny, high window as its only source of light. Aleshkoi said something to me in Russian that I didn't understand. He made gestures. This time I thought I understood, but couldn't believe it. He was telling me to take off all my clothes. I glared at him. Wasn't Tatyana still behind me? Was he going to make me do this in front of her? I stood paralyzed.

Annoyed, Aleshkoi said something to someone behind me. Then, good God, I heard Tatyana's voice.

"He wants you to take off all clothes."

What is this bare room, their persuasion chamber? Is this worst of all possible humiliations the beginning of their torture?

Really, nudity doesn't bother me. But for some weeks I'd been living pretty well. I was fatter than I like to be. I didn't give a damn how I looked for them, but of all times, *now*, with Tatyana there! Why did they have to do this to me?

I hated Aleshkoi. I wanted to turn and tell him that all his endearing little friendly acts, those cookies, the cigarettes for Darrell, were the most despicable kind of hypocrisy. I'd heard and read all about the KGB and its ruthlessness. In America, in the most depraved of prisons, they wouldn't do this.

I began to unbutton my shirt. Then I started at the other end, removing my shoes and socks.

Behind me something shifted, moved. I barely heard it. Was it the quiet opening and closing of a door? Was it just my imagination? To turn around and look, admitting my concern, would be even worse humiliation.

Off came my shirt. Then my pants. Then my underwear.

One of the guards took each piece, scrutinized it, frisked it, practically fondled it, showing particular interest in the zipper and crotch of my pants. Jesus Christ. Then he went at my shoes, fingering their soles and heels, poring over them as if they were state-of-the-art high-tech secret devices.

The guard said something and gestured by flopping his hand.

No. He can't make me do that. Not here. Not with her there. He *can't.*

He insisted.

I bent over.

The monster, flashlight in hand, stepped behind me and the other guard spread my buttocks. Were they all huddling back there, heads pressed together, gaping up my entrails in defense of the Marxist-Leninist state? What the fuck did they expect to find when for four days I've been under *their* lock and key? A stash of coke? A new way of snorting it? Why were they putting me through this?

The guard released me.

Aleshkoi mumbled something and a lot of feet shuffled out. Only the two guards remained as I dressed.

Had she been there during my disgrace?

Should I ask the guard? I couldn't. I didn't know how to ask in Russian. And if I had known how, I wouldn't have.

How could I go back to that interrogation room now and face Tatyana? How could I ever face her again anywhere?

They didn't take me to the interrogation room, but to my cell, for meal break.

And the fact is, that morning was the last time I ever saw the heavenly face of Tatyana.

The following Sunday, which marked exactly a week that I'd been a Soviet prisoner, Aleshkoi sent for me.

I couldn't figure out his schedule. Sometimes after a long day I'd go back to my cell, assuming we were finished. I'd be dozing off for the night and, bingo, the door would open, the guard calling.

"*Ahmstairr. Sledovatel'!*" Investigator! And I'd have to go back for more questions.

Anyhow, on this first full Sunday at Lefortovo, which I had assumed to be Aleshkoi's day off, the call came, "*Sledovatel'!*" So the guard and I took the long trudge to Lubyanka and the interrogation room.

Uh-oh. Aleshkoi, holding a piece of paper, and Alex were standing again, looking formal.

This time, what? Last words? Firing squad, no trial?

Aleshkoi began to read from his piece of paper.

I didn't like this.

Alex, standing practically at attention, translated Aleshkoi's two-sentence pronouncement.

"Today is fourth day of July, one thousand nine hundred and seventy-six. On behalf of investigation unit of KGB, we wish to congratulate you on bicentennial of your country."

The Fourth of July. The two hundredth. They knew and remembered, even though I'd forgotten. My chest tightened, partly from homesickness, partly from gratitude at the generosity of these two guys, at this country, for so touching a remembrance. The moment threw upon me a diplomatic responsibility, and I was at a loss to know how to fulfill it properly. Also, it filled me with a sense of opportunity. Maybe their gesture was a signal of leniency, of forgiveness, of détente. This prospect brought words to my lips.

"I hope on this occasion, I hope—on this occasion, I hope our two great countries will come closer together and be good friends. I also hope you understand that I respect your country, and that my comrades and I meant the Soviet Union no harm, and that you will send us home."

Aleshkoi nodded. He muttered something to Alex.

Alex said, "Who knows what will happen in world affairs? But next year, sixtieth anniversary of our country, don't worry, will be big amnesty."

That was the first time I'd heard that from official lips—in fact, from anyone's lips except Volodia's, and I didn't consider my cell-mate the best predictor of Soviet policy.

I felt good about these guys again.

Sandy-haired Alex became a kind of friend. I always felt he translated accurately and fairly, never playing KGB investigator or prosecutor. A couple of times, when I came up with inconsistent details, even before translating for Aleshkoi he'd say to me, "This makes not good sense with what you said before."

When Aleshkoi would leave the room and we had to wait, Alex would talk frankly as a friend. He asked about the United States. He showed me his leather jacket, sort of French-style, which, out of sheer pride of ownership, he sometimes wore to work even in July. He told me how much it had cost him and how much he earned (the former a lot, the latter not much; I don't recall the numbers). He showed me his leather attaché case and his KGB pass.

Sometimes he even confided in me about Aleshkoi. After weeks of interrogation, when our trial date was near and he had to wrap up all the details, Aleshkoi stayed a lot of nights, pumping me, organizing notes for the prosecution. One night his phone rang. By this time I understood ordinary Russian conversation.

"Hard to say . . . I'm just not in a position to say . . . I told you I can't tell you. Look, I don't like it any more than you do." Then his face tightened, and he exploded, *"Ëb tvoiu mat'!"*

He smashed the phone down so hard I thought he'd break his

hand. Whatever the cause of his fury, I was sure he'd now take it out on me.

Instead, he stormed out of the room.

I glanced at Alex.

As embarrassed as I was, Alex shook his head. "He married a tough one."

I'd heard the words of Aleshkoi's oath often, from Volodia, from guards, from KGB men talking among themselves. I'd even heard an American consul employee say them (in Russian) on a prison visit when he couldn't find a certain paper in his briefcase. The expression, used apparently by everyone of every class, seemed a harmless and generalized exclamation, like "damn it."

Then one night Volodia told me it means "I fuck your mother."

Now Alex explained that there are two ways to say it. By emphasizing the *ëb*, a vernacular form of *ia* for "I," one is saying the oath impersonally, inoffensively. That's the way it's almost always said. Sometimes he might shorten the whole oath to "*Ëb tvoi*," denying Mother the honor of even a mention. But when you inflect it the way Aleshkoi did, pounding each syllable equally, you're not simply making light profanity. You're saying literally and explicitly to a particular person, "I fuck your mother."

"That is real insult," Alex intoned. "For saying that, some people might kill you."

Despite Alex's excellent translations, I kept having a basic failure of communication with Aleshkoi. Well, maybe not really with Aleshkoi, but I guess with the KGB, of which he was a perfect exemplar.

He couldn't comprehend a crime of an international nature without something political about it. He couldn't be satisfied with simple evidence that would close the case in any Western court of law: Here's the bag of narcotics. Here it is, concealed between false walls of my baggage, with my baggage check stapled to my airline ticket that has my name and passport number on it, and here's my passport, and here's my confession of the whole thing.

No, he had to probe for more. Did Mr. Lee or David or the fat man mention anything, *anything*, about the People's Republic of China? Did Pete or Darrell ever mention any connection with right-wing causes? Have I ever had any association whatever with any right-wing causes? Did I ever attend a meeting of the Ku Klux Klan?

"What the hell for? I wouldn't know where to look for a Klan meeting."

"We will get along better if you don't try to fool me."

"Fool you about what?"

"You can try to tell me you are not Klan, okay. But don't try to tell me you don't know where, because then I believe nothing you say. We know America. We know anywhere you can go to next streetcorner, you find drug for sale, and you find Klan."

Aleshkoi was sure he had me because in my attaché case, which contained all my papers and portable junk, they'd found a medal with a dangling bronze swastika.

He didn't even ask me to explain it. Wordlessly he just laid it down in front of me, its message of condemnation complete.

"That's from World War Two," I told him.

"Of course. But why do you have it? Where did you get it?"

"In East Berlin."

"Who gave it to you?"

"I bought it."

"Oompossible." To Russians, I kept finding out, anything improbable is declared impossible. When said in English by a Russian, it's so consistently said "oompossible" that even when it was said in Russian I heard it that way. "Oompossible. In East Germany they don't sell things like that. This is Nazi."

"It was an antique store."

"What?"

"Antiques. Old things."

"But they cannot sell things like this."

"Maybe they can't here. But I found this in Berlin. East Berlin."

Aleshkoi glared at me, not believing. Then, with a look of dismay and hopelessness, he fingered the papers he'd found in my attaché case.

"How can one person have so many papers about himself? Don't so many papers make you crazy?"

When bouncing around Europe I always took my letters, receipts, legal bits of paper, with me. But their sheer number seemed proof to Aleshkoi that my life was enmeshed in mysterious and ominous connections. Two items that especially baffled him were plastic cards embossed with my name and a long series of numbers, obviously code.

He asked me what they were.

I told him.

He asked me again.

I told him again, a different way.

"But what do you do with it?"

"You buy things—meals, airplane tickets—and you don't have to have money with you."

"Why would anyone give you meal or airplane ticket if you have no money?"

"You pay them later."

"How do they know you'll pay them later?"

"If you don't pay them, you lose the card."

"But if you buy airplane ticket, you go to other side of world and you take card. They can't chase you. Why would you pay them?"

I tried to explain the importance of maintaining a good credit rating. Then I explained that anyway you don't pay the restaurant or airline. They collect from their bank, and later you pay your bank, after they send you a bill.

"Then your bank must pay their bank?"

"Yes."

"So much work for money of one lunch?"

"It's not so much work. We have computers."

He nodded with deep, sad wonderment at our folly. "We have also computers. But we have important work for computers. We fly in space. You—you pay bank for lunch."

I know he didn't believe me about other items in my attaché case. Poor Alex had to translate every item, every scribble, every letter. I had a document from my father's lawyer in New York, explaining in legalese that I could hardly understand myself some technicality about an escrow account for a small trust fund that still remained of my father's estate. Alex pleaded with me to explain sentence after sentence, saying *he'd* be in trouble with the KGB if he couldn't make better sense of it than he had. I tried. But how do you explain what an escrow account is to a Russian? He wanted to know what the escrow was made of, how it looked. I tried to explain it's not really a thing, but just, well, just a way to figure, to hold money aside for a special purpose. He was convinced I was lying. How could it not be a thing? It said right there that they would open the escrow account on such-and-such a date at such-and-such bank. Why was I misleading him?

Letters from several of my old girlfriends around Europe aroused Aleshkoi's worst suspicions and caused Alex still more grief. Especially one from a girl named Gretchen in West Berlin. Aleshkoi knew, of course, that West Berlin, supervised by the military of four Allied governments, was a nest of spies, as well as a minor dope capital.

He kept pumping me about Gretchen. I didn't know what to say about her. She wasn't all that terrific. Actually, she was too prudish for my taste. Long after I would totally have forgotten her, she kept writing to rehash our frustrating, boring sexual experiences.

"To where you traveled with Gretchen?"

"We didn't travel anywhere."

"For whom you traveled with her?"

"I told you we didn't travel anywhere."

"For whom you wanted her to travel with you?"

"What do you mean, for whom?"

"For which government? For what organization? What?"

"Look, I told you—"

"Then not for political reason. You traveled to transport narcotic, contraband, for money."

73

"I didn't travel with her."

Aleshkoi gave Alex an instruction in Russian. From his pile, Alex pulled a letter from Gretchen and read. Like many young Germans, Gretchen spoke and wrote impeccable English:

"I want to go with you, whatever you do, wherever you go. I will sacrifice *anything* to continue going with you, my life here, my job, my security. But your price is too high. I am not ready to go all the way with you. I am what I am. I cannot become someone else just like that. Your insistence is more than I can handle. At least for now. Please, Jerry, take me as I am. I will make you happy that you did. But please do not insist—for the present—on my going all the way."

Like the swastika medal, like the credit cards, this too I tried to explain. Gretchen's plea not to "become someone else" had nothing to do with identity papers; her refusal to "go all the way" had nothing to do with travel. But I don't think Aleshkoi, or even Alex, believed me.

Early in the investigation I had an inspiration that changed its entire tone and course.

I *had* to find some way to get Aleshkoi's sympathy, and through him the KGB's, the whole Soviet Union's. They couldn't just put me away as a common smuggler, some run-of-the-mill lawbreaker. I had to save them from that awful error, and save myself.

They had to see that I meant no premeditated evil, that I had scarcely thought about the seriousness of my act, that I'd had some pressing personal problems, most specifically that my money was running out, and that my judgment was thereby distorted. That, in fact, my infraction wasn't really voluntary because I wasn't really in my right mind.

I *had* to make them see that.

And then, from out of nowhere, my lips, as though governing themselves, began to form the perfect explanation of this imperfectly executed crime.

"You've got to understand," I heard myself appealing to Aleshkoi, "that I couldn't help myself. Because, you've got to understand, I'd slipped into addiction to a drug."

Aleshkoi looked at me long, and in a totally new way.

"Uh-huhhh," he intoned, drawing it out. "Uh-huuuuuuuhhh," he repeated, nodding his head. With obvious sympathy. Or at least with some deep new understanding. Something important in our relationship, in his whole approach to the subject of his investigation, had changed. I had hit a bull's-eye.

He sat back and folded his hands across his trim belly and rocked gently. "Uh-huhhh," he said still again, waiting for me to tell more.

I did.

Two years earlier, in Amsterdam, when I was just starting my European travels, I had met a German girl. Not Gretchen, another one. She was passionate and racked by trouble in ways that appealed to me. I moved into her place. (Aleshkoi didn't flicker an eye. These young Russians are probably no more prim than we are.) It turned out that she needed something every day. Heroin, actually. At the oddest times she'd run out to get it, which annoyed me. Then she began sending me out to get it. I didn't like getting it for her. I didn't like buying it or carrying it or handling it. I didn't like her using it. But she was a very magnetic and satisfying woman, with great power over me. So what could I do?

Well, as everybody knows, one thing leads to another. When you share a roof with a lover, fix meals with her, take your clothes off with her, wake up with her, and she does something as important to herself as what she daily did to herself, well, needless to say, I had to become a little curious. A few times, I doubt more than a half-dozen over a period of a couple of months, I put a dab of her white powder on my knuckle and sniffed it, just to get a whiff of her experience.

Let me emphatically set something straight right now. What I have said so far is true. The rest of what I told Aleshkoi, and later testified at my trial on this subject, is false. Despite what I told him, I never became an addict, and never injected a drug into my body. I find the thought repulsive. I am repelled by needles and by the

75

thought of addiction. When I want kicks, my usual drugs are moderate quantities of vodka and beer. I don't blame Christopher Wren, who covered our trial for the *New York Times*, for taking my testimony at face value, nor other newspapers that have since repeated as fact his account of my false testimony. (I should probably apologize to Mr. Wren for duping him, but I think I'll pass up the opportunity. In the same story he also described me as "ferret-faced.")

Anyhow, I told Aleshkoi that I'd soon begun shooting heroin, and had become enslaved by a serious habit, which was why I had leaped at Mr. Lee's proposition, because I needed money so desperately. I knew exactly what his reaction would be, *had* to be. And it was exactly what I wanted it to be. I had heard about it over and over again in Holland, in Denmark, in Sweden, and certainly in the United States, in all the humane countries that sided with the unfortunate, the wayward, the stricken and helpless. A confession of addiction gives the prosecutor a chance to be humane himself, to become the understanding good guy. He's no longer dealing with a criminal, but with someone who's ill. He asks the judge not for iron bars but for group therapy, to which the prisoner tearfully consents and surrenders himself. The prosecutor goes home and basks in praise from his wife and children for having given way to compassion.

That was the gift I now offered Aleshkoi. Let him unburden himself of my fate. Let him throw me to the psychiatrists.

Of course, no Russian psychiatrist in his right mind would keep me around. What would the Kremlin have to gain by the restoration of my mental health?

"Uh-huhhh," Aleshkoi intoned once more. He looked at me a very long time, eyes full of softness and pity. Even Alex lowered his tone as he translated. "Do you realize what this means?"

I looked at Aleshkoi, saying nothing, waiting for what I knew he'd say next.

"This means Article Thirty-eight."

I just looked glum and said nothing.

"You force me now to call in a psychiatrist."

I tried to drop my eyes in remorse over his loss.

"Why are you telling me this, Amster? Did I ask you? Why are you making me give you up this way?"

I had no idea our days and evenings together had meant so much to him. I was genuinely touched.

"I don't understand you, Amster. No matter how hard I try, I cannot understand you." His voice was rising. He was truly upset with me. "Number one, all right, you need more money. We all need more money. So where do *you* go to get more money? To Malaysia." He threw up his hands and slapped them to his thighs. "Malaysia! How many countries in world do you think give death penalty for contraband? Three? Five? At *most*, five. So you need money, *you* choose Malaysia."

"What death penalty?"

"Death penalty, death penalty." He flipped open his big looseleaf book to a page with a printed table. "Here, narcotics contraband, Malaysia, in or out, either way. Penalty, death. You didn't know that?"

I guess I barely breathed my response. "No."

"You can thank—" He reached his hands heavenward, tautly, almost saying what I couldn't imagine he'd let himself say. "You can thank *somebody* for Soviet Union. Thank somebody that customs agent discover you not in Malaysia, but in Soviet Union. That is number one. So now comes number two. Now you tell me you are addict. I don't see, mmm, dead man's eyes. I don't see hands shake. I don't see you on floor in pain. Why you tell me this? Did I ask?"

I couldn't make sense of his upset. Yet I had to keep looking innocent, not show the advantage I had just maneuvered. "It's the truth. You said I have to tell the truth. What difference does it make?"

"What difference? Whole different book of laws is difference. Now I must call psychiatrist. If psychiatrist examine you and sign paper you are addict, is whole different crime. Contraband is nothing. Now you put yourself in class of parasite on socialist society. Whole different class. In Soviet Union, addict—of narcotic or vodka, same thing—is not only parasite, but person who lives whole life to escape socialist reality. Parasite, no amnesty, no parole, finished, good-bye. Article Thirty-eight. Different laws."

Again the slapping of the thighs, the deep, disgusted sigh of frustration.

My little inspiration had clearly screwed me up. But anything I'd slipped into that easily couldn't be too hard to get out of.

Within a few days I fell into the possession of my Soviet shrink. I expected him to look exactly like my mental image of Sigmund Freud, with pince-nez specs and a little goatee that he forever stroked. Instead she was a motherly woman of about fifty. (The great majority of medical doctors in the Soviet Union, I soon learned, are women, including psychiatrists.) She could have been, in fact, the mother of Tatyana, emitting exactly the same rays of sunshine and sympathy. Actually, she was a relative, all right, but someone else's: the daughter—Alex told me this, so impressed that I knew he wasn't pulling my leg—of Felix Dzerzhinsky, the father of the KGB. Sure enough, her name was Margarita Felixievna (daughter of Felix) Dzerzhinskaia.

For the next two months the Soviet medical establishment devoted their state-of-the-art resources to "detoxifying" me. Every day about noon they served me a fat capsule containing some synthetic narcotic, maybe something like methadone, I don't know. I asked once if that was what it was, and they didn't know what I was talking about. I never learned the name of the stuff.

All I know is that every afternoon, all afternoon, I lay happily in my cell, high as a helium-filled purple balloon.

That was one result of my "confession." The other was that two or three mornings a week, Margarita Daughter of Felix listened to me. She asked about everything and I told her as much about myself—well, almost as much—as I thought she could grasp, considering that not everything about American life is graspable by the Soviet mind, and vice versa.

Rerunning my life that way fascinated me, all the time it must have been puzzling the hell out of her. Margarita Felixievna, who'd never seen America, listened and listened, as though she'd never had a patient anything like me. And she probably never had.

6

PATERSON

I've said I don't like to think about my father. But I had to tell Margarita Daughter of Felix at least this one thing.

When I was, I guess, about ten, I tagged along with some school-mates one afternoon for Little League tryouts. Being chubby, I didn't feel as loose and coordinated as I imagined other kids felt. In fact, I was scared that if I tried out I'd wind up shamed. But when the ball was pitched at me, I flung that heavy bat around and, by God, I hit it. Hit it good. Kids cheered Then the coach threw the ball at me. Hard. I wanted to flatten on the ground, but I shoved my glove up at it. The ball stuck in my glove. I couldn't believe it. The coach told me I'd made the team. He said I should bring my father Saturday morning to sign me up.

I said my father might be busy. My father was always saying, "Don't bother me now, I'm busy," even when he wasn't doing anything.

The coach said my father had to sign a paper or I couldn't play.

I imagined myself becoming a star among my schoolmates. They'd all see me sock that ball mercilessly till it split. They'd see me hurl myself at line drives, at soaring flies. They'd all marvel at a heroism no one suspected lay hidden in me. They'd cheer me, talk about me, want me for their friend. They'd love me.

I ran all the way home and told my father about Saturday.

"If I'm not busy," he said.

That night I prayed. I didn't know anything about praying except that sometimes, usually during a tearful argument with my father, my mother covered her heart with the flat of her hand and swore that God would hear her voice. So I knew you had to talk to pray. That night I talked to God in bed, loud enough, I figured, for Him to hear, but not loud enough to reach my father, sitting with his newspaper in the kitchen. I prayed that my father would not be busy on Saturday.

Saturday I reminded him what day it was.

"I'm busy," he said.

My mother put in a plea.

He glared at her, at her insolence. "You heard me say I'm busy."

That was the end of Little League for me. Years later, looking back at the tragedy of that day, which I've never put fully behind me, I did realize my mother could have taken me to the field and signed the paper. But that's not what my mother would do. She didn't go out. She was afraid to, except to go to the store. She didn't know where anything was, didn't feel she belonged there if she did know. She'd be afraid to face that coach, certainly afraid to sign the paper unless my father was there and told her to. So it didn't occur to me on that awful day that my mother might come with me.

I'm continually surprised at new realizations of what my mother didn't know how to do. A few years ago, as I sat in a smart outdoor restaurant in Geneva, surrounded by glamorous diners, I realized that in all my childhood my mother never made a salad. Ever. I don't think she knew how.

My father was strict, greedy, and determined that I would not have anything he hadn't had as a child. I never got a Christmas gift, at least not at Christmas. He'd wait for the clearance sales in January

81

and then get me some cheap thing. When school opened the day after New Year's, kids would ask me what I'd gotten. I was dumb enough to tell them my father was waiting for the sales. Then I'd feel the humiliation I could have avoided simply by lying to them.

Often I yearned for the old days, for the first nine years of my life, when my father wasn't around. My parents had split when I was an infant of six months. My older brother (ten years older, far too occupied with his own important affairs to pay attention to me) and I moved with my mother into the home of her parents. Really, I was brought up by my grandfather and grandmother. I'll never understand why my parents reconciled, but they did when I was in third grade, just about the time my brother was setting out on his own as a boxer. (He soon became New Jersey's Golden Gloves middleweight champion.) I guess my mother still needed someone to control and abuse her, and my father still needed her to control and abuse. Their excuse, of course, was that resuming their marriage was better for me.

I'm sure my father's income was important in luring my mother back. As a skilled factory worker doing something or other with animal hides, he didn't earn a hell of a lot, but the work was fairly steady. The stock market fascinated him. He'd study Wall Street listings by the hour. During slack periods of work, when he'd get half-days off with no pay, he'd go to a broker's office and watch prices sweep by on the board. No matter how little he earned, no matter how he deprived us, he always sank a piece of every paycheck into stocks. Later he took a stockbroker's exam, quit his job at the factory, and went to work for a brokerage house, building a modest following among the factory workers he'd known.

Once they reunited, my father's miserliness tortured my mother exactly as it had before they'd split. They quarreled constantly. In every quarrel, without fail, one or the other would say they had reunited "only for the sake of Jerry." That stabbed me like a knife every time, each stab pinning me with another piece of blame for my mother's suffering. I felt evil, cursed, and helpless. Yet for all my central importance to their disastrous lives, I couldn't get either of them to notice me, to believe that anything I said or did or thought had the slightest worth. The confusion sometimes made me feel crazy.

One summer day when I was thirteen, they were at it again.

"With pleasure," he threatened loudly from their bedroom. "You wish I'd leave? I'll leave!"

"I wish to God," my mother shouted from the kitchen sink. "If not for Jerry, I'd tell you this minute, go."

She covered her eyes with a wet hand and began to sob.

Her back was turned to me. I was standing by the window, which was opened wide to catch the breeze. We had iron casement windows, actually pairs of windows, each opening outward, controlled by turning a handle. A metal bar separated each pair down the center.

I should explain exactly how I felt at that moment. But I don't remember. I should analyze the reasons why I did what I did. But I can't. I don't even remember the act of doing it.

All I remember is, moments later, hanging down the outside of that high apartment building, feet dangling six stories above the sidewalk, my white-knuckled hands clutching the center bar of that window. I don't remember climbing out there and can't bring myself to believe I did it. I'm terrified of heights. To this day I cringe at stepping out on a fire escape.

All I remember is the thrilling terror, mostly in my groin, as I looked down and saw nothing but an unobstructed drop. I couldn't stand the fear. Yet I couldn't contain the exhilaration. I needed to stop it. But I wanted to stretch it out. I wanted my mother to see me before my screaming fingers had to let go and I hurtled straight down. I didn't want to call her. I wanted her to discover me. I wanted her to save me. I wanted her to wail out loud and grasp me and lift me up through the window and press me against her bosom. I wanted her to know my terror through her terror. I wanted her to feel my feelings, to know all the corners of my existence.

I couldn't hold on much longer. My hands burned from the grip, and the flames ran up my arms. Next thing I remember, I stuck the toe of one sneaker into a groove between two bricks. It caught. Then the other toe. The weight of my body lifted from my arms, shifting to my toes. I was light. I could just stay like that. I had full control.

I looked down. An awesome tickle surged up into my guts.

I had power.

What power.

I didn't need anybody's help. I could just stay like this as long as I wanted. I was in charge of my life. I had full control. I could let go and kill myself, or I could stay there and let a breathless world watch me.

Or I could climb up, toes between bricks, crawl back through the window, and end this. Something inside made me want to cry with a strange regret. If I did that, if I just climbed inside, I might never again feel this overpowering exhilaration. I wanted it to be part of me, something I could feel and know, again and again and again.

The kitchen telephone rang. I heard my mother gasp, almost shriek, and I heard the phone drop. In a moment I saw her face at the window, so close to me I could almost stroke it with my hand, if I could release my hands. She was frozen, stricken, afraid a word, a sucked breath, would frighten me and send me plunging.

The next thing I remember is her fingernails dug into my shoulders and my back, transmitting thankfulness and anger at me as I slid over the sill. And I remember, after it was all over, my father finally heeding her calls and coming out of the bedroom.

They both badgered me to explain why I had done it. I couldn't explain. A police car screeched to a halt downstairs and two cops banged at our door. They tried to get me to explain. One of them urged, practically ordered, my father to "take the kid in." Going to jail impressed me as important. My father put on his hat and the cops took us in their car.

Not to jail, it turned out, but to the hospital.

That too seemed important, but a little disappointing.

A doctor with an oddly soothing voice tried to get me to talk about myself, mostly to explain how I'd been feeling and what was worrying me. He told my father he wanted me to stay in the hospital a few days, for observation. My father went home.

In my ward, the psychiatric ward, I met this girl named Cindy, thirteen like me, who'd laugh one minute and cry the next. I liked her unpredictable spirit and we played a lot of Parcheesi in the solarium. A kid named Tony, who was fifteen and talked like a foreigner, always wanted to play the next game with her. That was fine with me, except Cindy would ask me to play her again so she wouldn't have to play Tony. She was afraid of him.

I slept in a room for two, but had it by myself. One night I was blasted out of my sleep by a sock across my face. The assailant was on top of me, ranting angrily, practically frothing at the mouth. It was Tony. The best I could make out in his part-English, part-foreign language was some kind of accusation that I'd been fucking Cindy. At thirteen, I'd never clearly learned what that vile act was, but I had some idea. In any case, he was certainly mistaken and I denied it, which made him angrier. Then I felt him squirt my abdomen and chest with a scalding fluid. I looked down and couldn't believe what I saw. He was stabbing holes in me with a hunting knife. The whole front of me was running with blood.

I must have screamed. A couple of orderlies raced in.

The point of my telling this has to do with the next scene in my memory: lying on a wheeled bed in the emergency room, where they took me because, with eighteen major stab wounds and thirty-eight cuts, I was too dangerously hurt to wait for the operating room.

I don't remember whether they were about to begin on me or had just finished. I just remember that, through my pain and dizziness from anesthesia, I felt a hand take mine, tenderly, caringly.

I opened my eyes. There was my father. His eyes looked right

85

into mine, as though pleading with me, and sure as hell he was crying. I felt his tears on my face, tickling my nose and cheeks.

In my deep, swirling dopiness I felt them, and realized something surprising. And I realized it later when I woke up and thought about it. I can't be sure of what it meant to me. But it surprised me, deeply surprised me, and it kept surprising me.

When all was said and done, my father loved me.

7

NEW YORK

My father's new career as a stockbroker eventually took us to live in an apartment in northern Manhattan, near Columbia University. I enrolled as a freshman in the evening school at Columbia, not because I revered its Ivy League greatness, but because I could walk there, and because they offered me a daytime job in the School of Library Services. I had no clear idea what I sought from school, except that I yearned to break out at the first opportunity into some wider world of excitement and glamor that I had never seen but knew existed.

The approach of summer vacation brought the first opportunity. It stared me in the face from a school bulletin board: a student charter flight to Paris. *Paris.* The fare was so low the adventure could actually be mine, and I'd still have three hundred dollars in my savings account for spending money. My hand practically trembled as I signed up.

In Paris, I took a course at the Sorbonne—a crash course in French for students visiting from other countries. It excited me more than anything at Columbia. I felt cosmopolitan, almost a Parisian. If I could speak French in a city of Frenchmen, nobody had to know me as a kid from Paterson with a Scrooge for a father, and a mother too scared to walk to the Little League. Then I took another course at the Alliance Française to refine my act a little more. Meanwhile I lived in a colony of international student residences, drinking wine and staying up late with young people from all over the world.

Paradoxically, I never felt as much at home, as confident of belonging in my surroundings, as I did on this foreign continent. I awoke every morning with a fierce appetite for new foods, new sights, new people, new words, new adventure.

In August I went to Berlin, found a cheap room in a *Studentendorf*, and signed up for a course in German for foreigners at the Free University of Berlin. I quickly got the hang of German as well as of the freewheeling life-style of Berlin, and decided that this was better than returning to Columbia. Here and there I picked up an odd job or a deal—reselling a used Volkswagen or a war souvenir— and didn't go flat broke until midwinter, in Frankfurt.

I threw my problem at the U.S. Consulate, and it didn't faze them. They cabled my parents, and I soon received a money order for fifty-seven dollars. (Later I found out my mother had scraped it up. My father, who had disapproved of my "bumming" for a summer, something he'd never done, favored letting me rot.) The consulate advanced a little more money and booked me on a troop transport out of Bremerhaven. Then they stamped my passport invalid for further trips until I settled with Uncle Sam for the transportation and the advance. I hitchhiked to Bremerhaven and boarded the USS *General Patch*, loaded with soldiers—and four civilians stranded in Europe without funds.

Back in New York, I missed the good times I'd had in Berlin, the fun of making my way in a foreign language. In fact, what I hated most about coming back was the ordinariness of talking English to everybody, all the time. One day in midtown Manhattan I walked by the Berlitz School and, on impulse, went in and asked for a job. I said I could teach German. They hired me and sent me to their training course. I didn't mind too much that instead of teaching

88

German I was to teach English as a foreign language, through their "total immersion" method.

In one of my Berlitz classes I met a girl who was a native of Hamburg but had lived most of her life in Brazil. I began seeing her outside of class until we became a case of total immersion ourselves. Young as I was, just turned twenty, I asked her to marry me. Our engagement soon broke up, but not before she introduced me to a Brazilian travel agent who offered me an unusual job. That job led me, in an indirect way, to my first experience of—well, lawbreaking. I don't want to say *crime* because I don't consider myself a criminal, and besides, what my employer forced me to do to him I do not consider a crime under the circumstances. But it wasn't lawful either.

In the normal course of his perfectly normal business, this guy received a steady stream of Brazilians, most of them to buy airline tickets to Brazil. But a few came right after returning from Brazil, to see him about his other business. They'd bring him pocketfuls of semi-precious stones—aquamarines, topazes and the like—that are relatively cheap in South America. Also, these stones are simple as gumdrops to run through customs, sewn into clothes, into laundry bags—undeclared, of course, which helps keep them cheap. These visitors would solemnly file behind my boss into his back office, where they'd whisper, whisper, and leave their haul behind.

My job was to call on jewelers in Boston, Philadelphia, and other cities in the Northeast, display his elegant wares in a plush attaché case, and sell for cash only, no written receipts. He never told me in so many words how he got his stones or why his business was so secret, and I never explicitly asked.

I had to pay for my own travel and lodging, but my commission rate was satisfactory and the stuff sold well. What was far from satisfactory was that every time, *every time*, I returned from a trip and dumped a bundle of cash on him, my employer would weigh and scrutinize every unsold stone I brought back, "discover" a microscopic scratch on this one, a karat missing from that one, deduct

89

from my commission for this, deduct for that, and I'd wind up, after my expenses, with next to nothing.

I realized this guy was crooked. He was stealing from me right and left. I could have just quit, but by the time I was ready to, my blood was already at full boil. I had to get back at him. Should I just take his suitcase full of goodies next time, sell it for cash, and not come back? Clearly that wouldn't work. He knew my girl, knew where I lived. I didn't know what revenge he might take.

So I thought out a more subtle plan. When I wasn't traveling, I usually called him every morning to see if there was something for me to do. More often than not there was, and I'd drop by for a while in the afternoon. On one of those afternoons I feigned stomach distress and asked for the key to the bathroom, which was down the corridor, high up in a busy midtown skyscraper. As he always did, he singled out the bathroom key in a collection of about ten, handing me the whole bunch. That collection also contained, of course, a key to his front office door, another to his private office inside, and still another to the locked file cabinet in his private office in which he kept the attaché case full of jewels. I didn't know, of course, which key was which.

Around the corner of the corridor, near the elevators, I'd stationed an accomplice, a compliant kid whom I could depend on to drop everything when I said I needed him, on the assurance that I'd give him some money. I was learning young that it's always good to have that kind of potential helper on call. That's why, years later, I didn't mind Darrell's proposition to tag along with me to Europe. Before ducking into the bathroom, I removed three keys from the ring and dispatched the kid downstairs to get them duplicated, fast. For ten minutes or so I sat nervously in a booth, then went out to meet him at the elevator. Next day, and the day after that, my abdominal emergencies persisted until I had the boss's entire key ring duplicated, three keys at a time.

On the morning after that, as soon as the building opened at eight o'clock—neither my boss nor his secretary ever arrived before nine—I showed up at the front office door with my keys and a pair

90

of surgical gloves. One of the keys slipped into the front door and opened it. His private door opened just as easily.

Now for the prize. One after another, I tried the keys to find the one for the locked file drawer. The more my hands wanted to tremble, the steadier I worked them. I began to sweat. I heard footsteps in the hall. In the silence, I heard someone arrive in the next office. I wanted to run. Even more, I wanted to stay and get it done and get even with this guy. That fizz of danger, that tingle and thrill seized me, first in my head and chest, then in my genitals, just like hanging out that window in Paterson or years later in that customs line in Moscow. It was fearsome and exquisite, like keeping full control over an urge to let go, like the finely balanced sweet moment of holding back an orgasm.

Damn! None of them worked. None of the keys came close to slipping into the file-drawer lock, let alone opening it. I tried them all again, quickly, with concentration. None worked. What the hell could be wrong? Whatever it was, I had to get out of here. I clicked the inner office door locked, went out the front door, clicked it locked, and headed for the bathroom. Damn it, the bathroom key was the only one I hadn't sent down for copying. I pressed for the elevator and thought I'd die before it arrived. The time wasn't yet 8:20, but I kept seeing the grotesque face of my boss stepping out and glowering at me. The elevator opened, took me down more than twenty floors, and I marched out of the lobby as composed and dignified as a bank examiner. God, how I wanted to run!

I knew that both my boss and his secretary walked from a subway west of the building, so I headed east as fast as I could without running. Finally, in the entranceway of a garage I felt safe in stopping to look at those damn keys, comparing one against another. Sure enough, two were identical. Either through my error or the key-maker's, he'd made two copies of one key, while one had gone uncopied—the one that opened the file drawer. I cursed my luck—and called my young accomplice to hang out by the elevator again that afternoon. So, again, late that day I developed cramps, until finally I got a copy of that precious missing key.

Next morning, return engagement, gloves and all. And this time it went like opening night on Broadway, rehearsed, broken in, just perfect. The attaché case was loaded with gorgeous rocks, far more than what he would send out with me on a road trip. By this time I knew values. This stuff must be worth—*what?* My fast figure came to at least a hundred thousand dollars! My insides trembled. I thought of putting the case back. Then I thought of the explosion in this guy's heart when he discovered it gone. Again, careful about locking doors behind me, I took off.

In midmorning, just as I did every day, with a voice as routine as a switchboard operator's, I called in to see if anything was doing.

"Hi, this is Jerry. Anything doing?"

"Can you come down right away?" He sounded agitated. Worse. Like he was struggling for breath. I loved it.

"Sure. Something doing?"

"Come down. Right away."

"What's doing?" I figured I'd taunt him.

"Can't talk. Come down. Soon as you can."

"Okay, sure. I just have to—"

"Right away, right away. Somebody wants to talk to you."

"About what?"

"I told you I can't talk. Come *down*."

I didn't like that last part. What "somebody"? There was no way it could be the police. No way. I'd figured all that out carefully. How would a travel agent explain a suitcase full of jewelry in his safe? He couldn't show where he got it or what he intended to do with it. He might as well walk into the front door of the federal courthouse, unroll a scroll of smuggling and income-tax offenses, and ask for a pen to sign it. That's why I'd felt safe in lifting it.

No way he could call the police. Then who the hell was it?

Curious and nervous as I was, I didn't think I ought to hurry, and I didn't. I got there about 12:45, when he'd normally be at lunch.

The place looked ransacked. Even *he* looked ransacked, sunk behind a desk, vest askew, collar open. Two sour-faced guys, one of them Italian-tough, the other Irish-rednosed, slumped into chairs as though in a waiting room, looked me over.

My boss nodded to them, saying nothing.

The Italian tough got up and flashed a badge. "Detective Rosenblatt," he said, and thumbed toward his rednosed partner. "This is Detective Perrone."

I looked as puzzled as could be. And surprised and nervous, I'm sure, because I really was. What could they do to me for looking surprised and nervous?

"We want to ask you some questions."

I guess I nodded.

"Whyn't you come out with us?"

"Where?"

"Just ride around a little. That's all."

Their car was out front, in a loading zone. And they weren't kidding, that's what we did. We just rode around. Perrone, the quiet one, drove. I sat next to him in front, Rosenblatt in back, leaning forward, breathing right into my ear.

"You know what your boss keeps in his locked safe?"

What a trick question. Of course I knew. And they knew I knew. But if I knew, and said I knew, was I playing into their game? Would I make trouble for myself by admitting to selling his smuggled jewels? Would I make trouble for *him*? The hell with *him*.

"Jewelry."

"It's gone."

"It *is*?" Did I say it too soon?

"Where is it?"

"Hey, wait a minute. How do I know?"

"Where is it?"

"How do I know?"

"You knew it was there."

"A lot of people knew."

93

"Name one."

"Matilda. The secretary."

"She didn't know."

"She must have known."

"She didn't know."

"How do you know she didn't know?"

"We're asking the questions, kid."

"How about the people who brought the stuff? The people who sold it to him?"

"We're not interested in who he got it from."

"Do you know how he got that stuff?"

"I said we're asking the questions."

"You ought to look into how he got that stuff. He—"

"We're looking into how *you* got that stuff."

"I don't know anything about it."

Perrone stopped the car. Maybe he sensed I was running out of nerve. He sounded more understanding than Rosenblatt.

"Tell me, Jerry, you got a record?"

"No."

"Never been arrested for anything?"

"Never."

"Well, then, maybe we could arrange something. My partner and me, we got a very busy day. We can't fuck around with this. We can take you in right now and you get yourself a lawyer to arrange bail."

"How much is bail?"

"That's up to the judge, when you get around to seeing a judge. Tomorrow, the next day, when my partner and me got more time, we'll get a warrant and search your place, and we'll talk to your mother and father and every friend you got, and we'll have our case. You want a record for the rest of your life, you can have it right now."

He stopped talking and looked at me. What was he getting at?

"You got another choice. Now tell me, Jerry, you're not leading us on. You got no record?"

94

"No, I swear."

"Well, we don't like to see a kid like you get a record. Take us right now to where the stuff is. Right now. And we'll forget the whole thing."

Should I open this door or not?

"I didn't do it, I'm telling you. But if I give you a good lead to where the stuff is, you'll forget it?"

"If it's all there, right now, it's a deal. We never knew a thing about it."

"How can I be sure?"

Perrone's eyes hardened. Then he looked hurt. Then helpless. He turned to Rosenblatt.

"Do you go along with that deal, Rosie?"

"He has our word."

"You have our word. What more can we give you?"

I didn't get it. My head was racing fast. Why would cops do that? They *were* cops, no question. I'd had a good look at Rosenblatt's badge, a genuine city shield. Trouble was, the attaché case of stuff was in my own room. I was going to bring it somewhere else this afternoon, maybe to my grandfather's in New Jersey. If they took me in now and got a search warrant, they'd find it, sure, and I wouldn't have a prayer. This thing had gotten too big for me. Before I opened that case from the safe I had no idea it was full of stuff worth more than a hundred grand! Christ, that's too hot. The main thing I wanted was just to get even with that crook, just hurt him enough to get even. But this is—Christ, they could get me for grand larceny. The trial, the headlines, the talk around the neighborhood—a jail sentence, maybe—would disgrace my mother, my grandparents. My father would go crazy and make my mother suffer for it. Were these guys leveling with me? If I showed them where it was, would they—no, unbelievable—would they just drop it, forget it? Even if they figured out I had done it?

My body ached with a wish to undo this whole nightmare, just erase it, make it not have happened. And now these guys were saying I *could* undo it. Why would they do that?

95

"Even if I did know where the stuff might be, why would you forget it?"

"You ask too many questions, kid. We told you we'd forget it."

"The deal is this," soothed Perrone. "Your boss is a friend of ours. We're not out to hurt anybody. We just want to help him out, just get his stuff back. You can count on it."

It all snapped together. My boss's brother-in-law, his wife's brother, was a police officer. So the boss came to work, found his satchel gone. What's he going to do? He can't call the police. So in a panic he calls his brother-in-law to ask, "What am I going to do?" The brother-in-law asks who he thinks did it, and my boss says, "My salesman, Jerry. But how am I going to prove it? And if I could prove it, what can I—?" I hear his voice fade out. The brother-in-law thinks a minute and says, "I'll line up a couple of detectives. They'll grind the kid down. But they'll have to do it on their own time, like as private consultants, you know? If they find the stuff, you'll have to take good care of them. You'll have to give them a piece."

"Okay, it's a deal," I said. "But no questions. I mean, I don't have to answer any questions."

"Deal," said Perrone.

I took them to northern Manhattan. How would I make them stay in the car? I didn't want my mother asking who those guys were.

They didn't get out.

When I returned downstairs, I handed Perrone the attaché case. He snapped it open, glanced inside hastily, and shut it.

"Okay, kid," he barked, and gunned the car away.

I felt strangely empty-handed. Not only of the attaché case, but of the episode itself. Exactly as I'd wished, the happening had been made to unhappen. And somehow I felt robbed of it.

Looking back, all I can say about the event is that I would never do anything like that again. I was an inexperienced, naïve kid, I can't understand whatever made me do something so stupid.

It was absolutely idiotic to cave in under the intimidation of those cops.

I could have kept those jewels with no problem. I didn't yet know anything about the law, about police procedures. They had no fingerprints, no witnesses, no evidence whatsoever, except my boss's guess. They couldn't even prove a crime had been committed. How could I steal something that my boss couldn't—or wouldn't—prove existed? If they'd brought me to trial, I'd have his life in the palm of my hand. I could have destroyed him, and those cops too—flashing an official badge in the private service of a smuggler. Today, if I found myself in a spot like that, I'd just keep saying till they were blue in the face, "I don't know what you're talking about."

Well, all was not lost. On the way downstairs I'd slipped a small fistful of stones into my pocket. That kept me solvent for a while. After all, I was in no position to convert the loss of my job into unemployment insurance.

That adventure left me jittery, unsure of myself. I decided that what my life needed was some corporate stability, so I answered a call from General Motors for young men interested in public relations. They said that only college graduates need apply, so I applied as a graduate of Columbia. There was a certain truth to it. If I'd gone to Columbia full time and stayed, instead of going part time and leaving after one year, by this time I wouldn't be far from a B.A.

General Motors selected the ten of us who looked most qualified, and flew us to Pontiac, Michigan, for a six-week training program, mainly to memorize the specifications of the Pontiac engine: dimensions, output, gas mileage, and so forth. Then they flew us back to New York, dressed us in red jackets with the corporate emblem on our breast pockets, and installed us at the New York World's Fair to answer questions from tourists at Futurama, the most popular exhibit and ride at the entire fair.

I was given a special assignment because I looked so good to them. I was assigned to the VIP lounge as an escort for celebrities. On one of Jacqueline Kennedy's first ventures back into the public world following her husband's death, she took my arm to climb into our special cart. I drove her around and explained everything, including the Pontiac engine's size, output, and gas mileage, then escorted her on the famous Futurama ride into the World of Tomorrow. Not just Jackie, but, at other times, Governor and Mrs. Nelson Rockefeller, and more movie stars than I can remember.

Even if the World's Fair hadn't closed soon, I wouldn't have lasted there. Life hadn't trained me for the predictability of putting in scheduled hours for scheduled, fixed pay. Even my paycheck, with its exactly predictable amount and exactly predictable deductions, bored me. I couldn't see the point.

I tried other jobs, mostly in sales, payable by commission, but never did well at them. For example, one was with a high-powered Florida real-estate developer, selling land, sight unseen, to couples saving for retirement. Near the Everglades, we were told to tell them. Our inside joke was that we sold the real estate by the acre, and they resold it by the gallon. My problem with selling has always been that I can't sit down face to face with an ordinary man, look him in the eye, and try to get him to invest in something when I don't have real belief in the product myself.

"My son, the big wheeler-dealer," my father would mutter whenever he tried to talk with me about my future.

Being a failure in his eyes was the worst humiliation I knew. I carried this picture in my head of some night coming to his house, maybe just for a home-cooked meal, and pretending to look for something in my wallet. To search for it, I'd empty the wallet and spread out a wad of hundred-dollar bills, plus a few fifties and twenties for small change. I wouldn't explain how I'd made it. Just the cash being there would prove my success. In that daydream, I then presented my mother with an expensive necklace, and my father's eyes popped. I'd give him maybe a flashy, diamond-studded tie pin. Maybe nothing. In the dream, I never decided about that.

Not long after that, my father got cancer. I was twenty-seven.

On my last visit to him at the hospital, I found him in a respirator. The doctors had cut a hole in his throat to admit air through a tube. He couldn't talk. He looked at me mournfully, urgently, as though talking. His body was skinny and dead, but his eyes shone with life.

I had a powerful urge, before he sank away for good, to tell him things, ask him questions, make everything okay, ask what fathers know that boys and young men don't know, ask what I needed to know for living the rest of my life. But I didn't know what to say or what to ask.

His fingers twitched near a pad and pencil that lay by his side. I handed them to him. Slowly, shakily, he scrawled:

"Be my son."

I couldn't help it, I just let loose an outpouring of tears. And I did something strange, before I had a moment to think about it. I moved my head so it was right over his, my face directly facing his face. And my tears fell all over his face, filling his eyes and slopping down his cheeks. His eyes blinked, and I knew he began crying himself, and I couldn't tell my tears from his.

Helpless and speechless and half-dead as he was, I knew the warm drops on his face were good medicine, even though he died the next day.

8

MOSCOW CITY COURT

Soon after she recovered from those tales of my life in America, Margarita Daughter of Felix pronounced me recovered from "addiction." I could now be tried as an upstanding lawbreaker, not as a Section 38 fugitive from socialist reality.

That left another question unsettled. Even if I was no longer an "addict," was I otherwise a candidate for a loony bin? I picked up from some discussion between them, and from questions each of them asked me, that that was a subject of some controversy between Margarita Daughter of Felix and my law-enforcement interrogators—both Aleshkoi and a grim-faced new man in my life, Gennady Vazhenin, who was to be my prosecutor.

As best I could put it together, Margarita felt sorry for me. Also, she felt she had a case for recommending that I be sentenced to psychiatric care. What a soft alternative to a labor camp that seemed! I signed a waiver so that she could receive, through the U.S. State Department, all my childhood medical records. They included a file full of stuff I had told that shrink at the Paterson hospital: about my father's cruelty to my mother; her threats to kill herself, and my urges to kill myself because I felt responsible for her wanting to kill herself; my craving for my father's attention any way I could get it, even while I hated him; my boyhood dreams of surreptitiously feeling up little girls in crowded places, and daytime fantasies of running into the girls' locker room at school and catching them all naked. That Paterson shrink hadn't batted an eye at my admission that naked girls ran through my mind a lot, which made me a little less worried about myself. But now Margarita seemed to stiffen her neck and bulge her eyes every time the notes led her to question me about my preoccupation with girls. Later I learned that Soviet psychiatrists are not big fans of Sigmund Freud, especially not on the subject of sex.

I wasn't surprised that Margarita wanted to hospitalize me. Whenever doctors diagnose trouble, their impulse is to heal it. But similarly, whenever cops and prosecutors uncover trouble, their impulse is to punish and make an example of it. In this case Aleshkoi and Vazhenin relished the rare opportunity to make an example of a greedy, corrupt capitalist American. So this daughter of the KGB and these sons of the KGB fought over my soul.

Their subdued, polite struggle kept me awake at night. Knowing I could influence the outcome, I tried to figure out which way to go. But I couldn't decide. Margarita had kept pulling out of me layer after layer of personal embarrassments. I couldn't keep myself from telling her everything, or almost everything. She listened with enthrallment, with sympathy, with more sheer attention that I'd ever known from anybody. It was wonderful. I just kept digging and talking, just to keep her listening, even forgetting that between us sat a total stranger of a translator.

Then she'd shock me back to remembering what was going on here. Almost in tears, she'd moan with my pain, and say, "I'll ask you about that in court. You'll tell that in court?"

"No! I can't tell about that in front of everybody."

She'd shake her head in pain again and say, "Then I'll have to testify that you're competent."

We must have gone through that dialogue a half-dozen times. And each time I wondered if her conclusion was a loss for me or a

101

victory. I'd think of clean white sheets in a psychiatric hospital, of good food, of Margarita—or some woman, probably a motherly woman, but maybe a young, beautiful woman, like Tatyana—listening to me, every day, closing her eyes and shaking her head at my misfortunes, listening, listening, and finally saying one day, "You're all cured, Ahmstairr, you can go home now."

Then my thoughts would turn cold and realistic, and I'd get scared. Commitment to a psychiatric hospital has no time limit. Would I ever get out? Sure, I could make a pest of myself, make them want to get rid of me. But that might make them keep me longer. They might just ship me off to a worse hospital, keep shunting me around forever. I'd have no control over my fate.

At least punishment has a fixed sentence. A year. Two years. Five years, God forbid. But with time off for good behavior. And then all those assurances from my cellmate, from Aleshkoi, that I'd soon get amnesty. God, I wanted to get out of this alien, rude place. No question about it, the smart way to go, even if the tougher way, was to a labor camp. I'm a survivor. I'd survive it.

Then again I'd think of those white sheets, those women listening to me every day . . . and I'd remember what I'd have to do: display my most humiliating psychic wounds in court, like dropping my pants in front of Aleshkoi, in front of Alex, letting these Russians mock me, laugh at me, maybe turn away in disgust. I'd have to display the most sensitive shames of my childhood in front of Darrell and Pete, for them to take home to America and tell and retell anywhere, anytime, to anybody they pleased, without my control. I couldn't stand the thought of it. It was worse than serving a sentence.

When I finally learned that Margarita was to testify that I was competent to stand trial, I felt liberated, I felt condemned, I felt confused, I didn't know how I felt.

In mid-August, our trial date less than a week away, Larry Napper, a vice-consul at the American embassy, visited me to make sure I was okay. Larry was the most helpful American I met during my whole time in the Soviet Union. When an aunt of mine flew to Moscow to visit me a few days after the trial, Larry and his wife invited her for dinner at their home.

At our meeting, Napper told me the trial would be publicized widely in the States. The Soviets, relishing a display of their three American captives, invited the international press, an extremely unusual move.

When he told me that, my insides crumbled. Until now, the press hadn't even known our names. The embassy identified us only as three Americans.

Even his warning didn't prepare me. On Tuesday morning, August 24, when they marched me into the Moskovskii Gorodskoi Sud, the Moscow City Court, the blue walls shone with television floodlights. The crowd filled every seat and spilled over into standing room. To get to the prisoner's dock, I had to step across cable after cable of TV cameras, lights, and microphones.

And there in the dock, blinking and just as surprised and befuddled as I, gleamed Pete and Darrell. We hadn't seen one another since the day of our disaster at Sheremet'evo.

I believe that was the first moment the thought hit me hard: I want to kill myself. I can't face this. I am not strong enough to survive this. I don't have the will to keep living, to keep being myself, if I am to be stripped bare for these people, to be flashed all over America, all over the world. I want to be dead and not know about it.

If, in fact, we had been carrying gold, I wouldn't have felt that way. But I saw the disbelieving face of my dead father, the bewildered face of my mother, now also dead, their lips forming a dreaded word, *heroin*. I saw my aunt, who had always protected me, and her husband, who had always disapproved of me, and my tough older brother, now a fight manager, glaring at me, asking how I could be such a jerk. I tried to find the words to explain to them that the heroin really had nothing to do with me, that really I hadn't even been sure that that was what it was. But I couldn't change the shock and the shame on their faces. Except to erase myself. Then I would not have to know what I'd brought down on us all.

Funny, just a few days earlier I had been thinking about my strength. I'd lie awake trying to figure whether to lean toward Margarita and the nuthouse, or toward Aleshkoi and the labor camp. One of the attractions of the labor camp was imagining how terrible it must be. No matter how cold, how long the working days, how sadistic the guards, if others had survived it, I'd survive it. There was something thrilling about knowing I'd get through it, knowing that no matter what hardship life brought after that, I'd have survived worse. I loved that idea. It made me feel powerful and ecstatic, like those moments hanging out the window, when I knew I could hold on and my whole existence felt under my control.

But now that strength was gone, as though they'd zapped me with a ray gun.

Suddenly I knew the answer to a question I'd wondered about, idly but often. Back in the States, on the TV news, I'd be watching some South Bronx jerk in handcuffs who'd stuck up a bank, or hijacked a truckload of designer dresses, or raped a schoolteacher. The guy is probably a habitual criminal, his whole life wrapped up in his game, whatever it is. He'll take risks like crazy for his goal, and take the consequences without complaint if he loses. He's fearless and tough, probably spending every moment of his life working on his toughness and fearlessness. After he pays his price, if he pays one, he'll probably go out and do the same thing again, because that's the life he knows. What always struck me, though, and never really made sense until this minute, was that one thing did terrify him: being seen by the TV camera. He'd turn his head away or cover it with his black leather jacket, or duck it down low, twist it around, hide it behind the cop he's cuffed to, anything to hide his face. Suddenly I sensed what this guy is so afraid of: that the camera will expose not only his face, but somehow his real identity, the shame he secretly knows about himself that brought him to this point.

He's not strong enough to bear that.

And right now, in this Moscow courtroom, I did not feel strong enough to bear it, either. A sentence in a labor camp, okay. But not naked exposure of my life, my family, my childhood, my most embarrassing secrets.

I caught Larry Napper's attention, then cast my eyes, like pointers, around the crowd. He crinkled his face and nodded, to express understanding and helplessness.

With exaggerated clarity I moved my lips to form the word *page*, and held up my index finger. I felt sure he caught my silent question:

"Page one?"

He nodded again, sadly, as though it hurt him to have to tell me.

An electric shock crackled through my system. I am cooked, finished, exterminated. Every stupid little mistake will come out and everything will connect with everything else. I am beyond saving.

I have to explain something in my past that I had thought was over with, buried forever, that was never important to begin with, that would now probably finish me.

About six years earlier, a couple of guys had knocked on my door. Would you believe, from the U.S. Secret Service? They pulled out a clipping about me from the *New York Post*. Oh my God, they knew.

What had happened was that a couple of years before, King Faisal of Saudi Arabia had visited New York to attend a big function at the Waldorf-Astoria for Arab and American oil tycoons. For political reasons, Mayor John V. Lindsay publicly refused to attend the function, which stirred up a storm. The king whipped it into a hurricane when he remarked that he understood why Lindsay was staying away: because·the city was dominated by Jews.

I had a prank-loving friend named Philip who got an idea based on my knowing languages. We planned it out and rehearsed it. I put on my most dignified clothes, and outside the Waldorf-Astoria meeting room, right near the stakeout of reporters, I approached the king's personal secretary, whose picture had been in the paper, and addressed him in French with a German accent. I told him I was first secretary to Ziegesmund Von Braun, head of the West German observer group at the United Nations, and that Dr. Von Braun wanted to know if the king was going to apologize for his remarks about New York. Don't ask me why I posed as a German. I guess because I'd been to Germany and it seemed clever at the time. Anyhow, the king's secretary was surprised as hell, and stammered his "no comment," and then Philip, introducing himself as press secretary to the German observer group, held an impromptu press conference about it. The reporters absolutely fell for it, and questioned us and scribbled notes furiously. After Philip felt we'd conned them enough, he asked me a question that, by prearrangement, I answered in English with no accent at all. We then revealed our hoax. Most of the reporters refused to the see the humor in it, but the guy from the *Post* at least took our names and addresses.

I was glad he did, because there we were in the paper the next day. I'd never had my name in the paper. I felt powerful and mischievous. But the thrill turned sour when I had a big fight with my mother. The paper had come out on a Saturday, when she didn't have to go to work at her office job. Her boss called.

"Do you know what your lunatic son has done?"

"What happened? What?"

"Go buy the *New York Post*."

She went almost insane and threw me out of the house. I didn't mind being thrown out, but I hated making her suffer.

I think what actually drew me to the prank was that I'd hoped to show I was as clever as another friend of mine, a Canadian named Steve, who pulled lots of capers like that and got lots of publicity. In Atlanta, he once presented himself to someone on the governor's staff as Lester Pearson, Jr., son of the Canadian prime minister, and he wound up riding in a motorcade, sitting beside Governor Lester Maddox. His hoax got him on television and into *Time* magazine, and I really envied him.

Anyhow, when those Secret Service men startled me with that clipping, I don't remember what I mumbled.

"Do you know we could put you away?"

"Put me away for what?" I laughed, explaining that my friend and I were just having fun.

These guys were grim, totally lacking in humor.

"Please, I got a job. I don't want any trouble."

"Where you working?"

I could have bit my tongue. What the hell did I mention that for? "First National City Bank." That's what Citibank and Citicorp used to call itself. "I'm a trainee, overseas operations."

"How long?"

God, did I have to tell them? This would finish me. "Today was my first day."

These Secret Service guys knew other things about me, too. Like the time in Los Angeles when I was mugged and called the police to report it. They caught the guy who did it, because my description was good. But as criminals often do, he got off. During the questioning, however, I had made the mistake of letting the cops look around my place, and they'd found a smidgen of marijuana in my refrigerator, just the tiniest pinch in a plastic bag. After plea-bargaining a possession charge, at that time a felony in California, down to a misdemeanor, "being present in a place where marijuana in used," I—the victim of the crime they had come to investigate—I had to pay a fine, while the mugger got off.

But all these foolish mistakes were in the past. Why the hell was the Secret Service coming after me now?

One of them pulled out a picture of a middle-aged woman, a dead ringer for Golda Meir.

"You recognize her?"

"No."

"You sure?"

"I don't know anybody like that. She looks like Golda Meir."

"That's right."

I glared at him.

He glared back at me, hard. "Do you know she's coming to New York next week?"

107

"No, I didn't know that."

"Where you going to be next week?"

"Working."

"You better be working. You call me Monday morning, this number, and tell me where you'll be all day Monday, and again on Tuesday, and every day next week until you read in the paper she's left New York. Got it?"

I promised. And that's what I did. And that was the last I heard of the Secret Service.

But now in that prisoner's dock I knew, just knew, that when this trial hit the world press, all that stuff was going to come up again, maybe with my face on the cover of *Time*, and behind mine the shadowy silhouettes of King Faisal's and Golda Meir's, and a headline, TRIAL IN MOSCOW. And I knew, just knew, what the consequence would be. Some American agent would meet secretly with some Russian agent, maybe in Moscow, maybe in Washington, and say, "Look, King Faisal, Golda Meir, pot in the refrigerator. We've had enough of this guy. Keep him. Throw the book at him. Let him die there. Make an example of him. Anything, but don't let him back in America."

Beneath the somber perch of a three-judge panel, a court employee read the charges, and our translator, standing at the prisoner's dock, repeated them in English. I pleaded guilty. Pete pleaded guilty. Then Darrell pulled a surprise, pleading not guilty to one charge, the technical one of conspiracy—planning with Pete and me and our employers to carry contraband into the Soviet Union. (Later he explained angrily to Pete and me that all we did was order him around, that we wouldn't let him come to the important meetings, and that therefore he was not guilty of conspiring with us.) All three judges turned to look at Darrell. The middle one, the chief judge, asked if his investigator had made clear to him that if he pleaded not guilty and was later found guilty, according to Soviet law he must then receive the maximum sentence for the crime, with no possibility of clemency.

"Yeah, yeah, he told me."

Darrell has a talent for picking the worst moments to be surly and defiant, to show off his machismo. Why does he switch on his brain and throw his imagination into gear only at a chance to make his life worse than it already is? Poor Darrell.

The prosecutor, Gennady Vazhenin, uniformed, blond, muscular, started his opening statement in a low key, as though bored, then slowly warmed up. Without bothering to turn his eyes in our direction, he waggled a scolding hand at us as he said:

"In the society where they were born and brought up, everything can be purchased, even human souls. . . . The crime being investigated here is unusual for a socialist society, but is characteristic of a capitalist one."

On hearing that, Larry Napper either lost control of himself or felt he had to show a reaction as a diplomatic duty. He let out a pained laugh, then turned away as though to hide it. I hoped it didn't hurt our cause.

In the opening testimony that he drew from customs officials, Vazhenin brought out information that was new and surprising to us. They said that the Russians had become aware about a year earlier of the shift via Moscow of much of the world's opium traffic. The shift had resulted from the United States pressuring Turkey into clamping down on poppy cultivation, and the French police severing the "French connection" at Marseilles. So the main source had moved from Turkey to Southeast Asia, and the packaging and wholesale center from Marseilles to Amsterdam. That had opened the "Moscow connection," partly encouraged by low fares on Aeroflot, but chiefly by the fact that there was little suspicion of drug traffic flowing through Moscow. Within the past year, Soviet customs agents at Sheremet'evo had quietly arrested about twenty foreigners carrying commercial quantities of drugs, among them British, Australians, West Germans, Dutch, Swiss, Italians, Malaysians, and Singaporeans. What was most surprising was the testimony that about a month earlier the Soviet customs bureau had issued new declaration forms specifically asking about drugs. Also, it had ordered inspectors to pay particular attention to flights from Southeast Asia. I was surprised that the fat man and David and Mr. Lee, professionals at this game, hadn't known about that.

Something else that caught my ear was the repeated mention of the role in our adventure played by the *Kitaetsy*. Vazhenin repeated that word a lot, and so did his customs witnesses. They talked about the *Kitaets* in Amsterdam, the *Kitaets* in Kuala Lumpur, the *Kitaets* named Lee, the *Kitaets* named David, the *Kitaets* we called "the fat man."

In Russian, *Kitaets* means Chinese. Vazhenin never missed an opportunity to label a person or an act as *Kitaets*, implying, I suppose, that the drug commerce of the world was somehow masterminded by the hated government in Peking. The fact is, of course, that most of the expatriate Chinese in Amsterdam and Southeast Asia were individualistic, entrepreneurial types who, after World War II, had fled the oncoming wave of Maoism in China. But the hammering away by these Russians at the international criminality of the *Kitaetsy* made me nervous. It gave me the feeling that our prosecutors were out to prove more than the simple fact of our guilt, that we'd been caught in a political current that was far bigger than the three of us.

At the end of the opening day, a squad of internal security guards escorted the three of us as they goose-stepped down back stairs, stony and endless, to a deep basement of the court building. We entered a gloomy corridor lined on either side with a row of solid doors, each with a peep-slat that could be opened only from the outside. They locked Darrell behind one first, then Pete, a few doors down. Finally, still another few doors down, me. Even at this late date, they seemed intent on keeping us out of touch with one another. The room wasn't a room, but a box, no more than a yard wide and maybe five feet deep. Along one five-foot wall stretched a board, for sitting and sleeping; at the end of the other wall there was a hole in the floor for a toilet. From the ceiling dangled a light bulb that gave off a faint, dingy yellow light.

The instant my door slammed shut, the isolation choked me.

Compared to this, Lefortovo was a busy, crowded hotel lobby. There at least I had had a cellmate, even if I couldn't understand him half the time. What if I banged on a wall? Would one of the guys hear me? No, this wall was of unbangable stucco, gritty enough to rip the skin off your hands.

The goose-stepping tramped the length of the dungeon and faded up the stairs. Surely they wouldn't leave us alone down here. The silence droned. This was going to be one hell of a long night.

I heard a distant moan. No, it wasn't a moan, but a muffled voice.

Then a deep answering voice.

After a brief silence, I heard them both again.

"Hey, Pete! Can you hear me, Pete?"

"Tisho, tisho." That's Russian for *quiet*. I'd heard it plenty from guards at Lefortovo. So there was at least one guard out there.

"Hey, Darrell. That you?" I could just make out the muffled blasts. They were shouting through their locked doors.

"Tisho! Tisho!"

"Where's Jerry?"

I didn't feel like answering. I didn't feel like yelling at the top of my lungs in this tiny, gritty box, especially since useful conversation seemed impossible.

This time, another guard's voice. This guy knew some English. "Dun't tuck! Stup tucking!"

"Hey, Jerry."

"You there, Jerry?"

The hell with it. I kept my peace.

"Dun't tuck! Stup tucking!"

"Hey, Pete. I hear the KGB is out to fuck Jerry."

"Yeah? What you hear?"

"Tisho! Dun't tuck! Stup tucking!"

I could have killed that guard for interrupting.

" 'Cause he's the ringleader, the brains. We might get off."

"Who said that?"

"My investigator."

111

"Brains! Jerry's brains got us here." In mock baritone: "We did it *his* way!"

I couldn't take that.

"What do you mean, *my* way?" My bellow, resounding against the stucco, almost split my head.

More extra-rich baritone: "We did it *yo-o-o-our* way."

"Tisho! Tisho!" This was the first guy, whose tight voice suggested he was the one of the Asians in the squad. By now he was picking up his own smattering of English from his buddy. "Dun't stup tucking! Dun't stup tucking!"

"Yo-o-o-our way."

"What do you mean, my way?"

"Hey, you hear that guy?" Darrell began to laugh weirdly. "He said, 'Don't stop talking.' You hear that?"

"We did it yo-o-o-our way."

"What was my way?"

"Moscow was your way."

"That wasn't my idea."

"I wanted to take a boat."

"The Chinese said no."

"Why didn't you say, 'Fuck you'?"

"We'd be dead."

"You're as good as dead now. We did it yo-o-o-our way."

The strain was great, on both the throat and ears. We stupped tucking. For a while.

"Hey, Jerry." That was Darrell.

I didn't feel like answering. "What?"

"So it was really twenty thousand. You were fucking me out of ten."

"That's not true."

"It is so true, you motherfucker." That was Pete. Christ, they're both on me. I was about to yell at Darrell that Pete was in on that, too, but arguing that now seemed hopeless and pointless.

And the instant I saw the pointlessness, I saw the point.

Pete couldn't have turned Darrell against me like this. They never saw one another. It had to be the investigators, the KGB. That was why they kept us out of each other's sight, unable to exchange a syllable. That was the reason for the red flags and green flags, the meals in a cell instead of a mess hall, the total isolation, except for cellmates, total strangers, each hoping for a break, in exchange for playing the rat. And that was why the three investigators had spent so much time between our interviews, day after day, night after night, for two nonstop months, meeting together. Comparing every scrap of what I said against what Pete said, against what Darrell said, then turning what each one of us said against the others.

That explained Aleshkoi's peculiar repetition of some questions that had puzzled me. Especially about those Nazi medals. What was so important about them? One of the souvenirs, for goodness sake, was what was called a "mother cross." A mother got it for producing seven children or more for Hitler's war machine. Was there any way I could have obtained that, except by buying it as a souvenir? Could anyone deny its historical interest? Its value in the collectors' market? Much later—in labor camp—I finally understood their peculiar interest, when I brought it up with Darrell and Pete. The investigators had asked both of them, separately, why I was carrying the medals around. Pete had apparently shrugged it off. But that damn Darrell!

"I told them you like Germans."

"You told them *what?*"

"Well, you do, don't you?"

"But those were Nazi medals."

"That's German, isn't it?"

"Do you know what Russians feel about Nazis?"

"What should they feel about them?"

"What do you mean, what should they feel about them? Did you ever hear of World War Two?"

"Well, they both believed in dictators, didn't they? I mean, what's the difference?"

There was no point in starting to explain. But he wouldn't quit trying to explain:

113

"I mean, I was trying to make it look good for you."

So that was why my investigator never stopped trying to link me to the Nazis, and failing that, to the CIA, to the Chinese, to terrorists, to something—*anything*—political and sinister. Finally I had a glimmering. The funny thing is, much as they had tried to turn Darrell against me, and in many ways succeeded, in this instance I think Darrell actually meant to do right by me. His problem was that as a political analyst he didn't score too high.

For the next three days, Vazhenin dragged us through every microscopic detail of our encounter with Mr. Lee in Amsterdam, our trip to Kuala Lumpur, our apprehension in Moscow, in fact, every detail of our lives.

One surprising moment for me occurred when Pete was on the stand. For most of his testimony, he was pure Pete, all brass and bravado. Pete stated he'd had absolutely no experience with narcotics. Vazhenin pressed him to explain why, on one day's notice, he'd agreed to cross a continent and an ocean for a proposition that clearly smacked of smuggling.

Pete shrugged and said, "I thought it might be a good idea, like a Hollywood movie."

Vazhenin dragged Pete through his childhood. Just like Darrell and me, Pete came from a broken home. I hadn't known that. As a kid on a farm near Philadelphia, he had had to work at seven years of age, slaughtering chickens for market. I hadn't known that either. I did know a little about the big tragedy in his life; a couple of years before I'd met him, his wife and sister were killed in a car crash. He had since found himself a new wife who helped him take care of his four kids and his sister's kid, as well as his aging mother, all living together and depending on him for support.

What surprised me weren't the details of that story, but that Pete suddenly burst into tears, real sobbing tears, talking about those kids. He took pictures out of his pocket and, without asking permission, just handed them to the translator to give to the judges. They took them and passed them from one to the other. Each judge looked at each one, as though the pictures really mattered. Russians were

114

suckers for kids. I learned about that later, in camp, when consistently I saw the toughest toughs, the tattooed guys called the *blatnye*, turn to mush talking about their children, or listening to other toughs talk about theirs.

Finally the trial ended, and the judges disappeared for two hours, to make a show of "deliberating." At 9:30 P.M. they returned with their verdict and sentences.

I got the worst of it: eight years in labor camp on *usilennyi* or "strengthened regime." That's the second most lenient of four penal categories. My head replayed the reassuring echoes of Aleshkoi and my cellmate, saying, "Amnesty. You'll get amnesty."

Darrell got seven years, the judge making a point of scolding him for his plea of "not guilty," and reminding him of his ineligibility for a reduction of sentence. Those Russians want a show of humility and remorse, of beating your breast and saying, "I was wrong and I'm full of regret." That was all they wanted out of Darrell. Poor Darrell.

And Pete got only five years, out of the judges' "sympathy for his family responsibilities." Not so dumb, that Pete.

9

THE LAND OF KASHA

I said earlier that the Soviet Union could have done nothing worse to me than impose the penalty of constant hunger. In fairness, I want to clarify that.

Not long before I began writing this, an American newspaper reporter interviewed me for a feature article on my experiences. After the interview, he dogged me to let him write a book about them, but we soon had a falling out. He said he didn't mind my stonewalling for his newspaper story, but for the book he wouldn't go along with my holding back.

"How did I stonewall?"

"You wouldn't tell me about the brutality."

"What brutality?"

"About the torture, the guards, the beatings."

"But I never saw any torture. I never once saw a guard beat anybody."

"You must have heard stories, first-hand, from other prisoners."

"Never."

"You've got to be lying."

"How can you say I'm lying? Were you there?"

116

"They'd never let me in. I know too much about the Soviet Union."

That short acquaintanceship, and particularly that short conversation, increased my lack of trust about what I read in the papers.

He couldn't bring himself to accept that the worst suffering, the torture I endured at Soviet hands, had nothing to do with deliberate brutality. It resulted from their national overdependence on kasha.

There were times when I suspected that kasha, three times a day, was their secret means of exterminating us. When I landed in the prison hospital camp, the only place a foreigner could meet and mingle with Soviet prisoners, I heard a different point of view. They might complain that the kasha was overcooked or stingily spooned, but never that they got it too often.

As civilians, these Russians had grown up eating kasha at least two, often three, times a day. For breakfast, kasha definitely, or it wasn't breakfast. Maybe with a dab of butter or margarine, or a bite of fish or meat to flavor it, and probably with tea, in a glass. For the civilian family's lunch, always soup, but probably followed by a heap of steaming kasha. At night, potatoes might replace kasha, but would more likely accompany it.

The amount of food we got did meet international legal standards for prisoners. It was enough to keep us alive. My biggest problem with it was that I wasn't Russian. I'd never seen or eaten kasha in my life.

So what were they supposed to do? Send out to McDonald's for hamburgers just for me? After all, the whole country is poor. Even in Soviet life outside of prison camps, the average civilian rarely has good beef or fresh fruit or cheese, or any of those nice things that we produce in surplus in America, giving our farmers economic headaches.

The fact remains that their kasha diet almost killed me.

Hunger first began to bother me at Lefortovo as we approached the day of the trial. On my left side, just above the bottom rib, I felt a dull pressure, a gnawing, not quite a pain unless I pressed a finger on it. I didn't pay it much mind, being worried about the trial itself, wondering if they might suspend my sentence and send me home, or if they'd clobber me with the maximum. Starting a day or so before the trial, the worry kept me from eating, and for the three nights during the trial I didn't sleep a wink. When the sentence finally came and they returned me to Lefortovo late Friday night, three Russians in white awaited me at my cell door. One of them, an elderly woman with the stoniest eyes I'd ever seen, whom the prisoners called Ilse Koch after an infamous Nazi personage, gave me a shot in the arm, a sedative. I wondered how they knew I felt sick. Later I learned that this committee routinely meets and sedates every prisoner after a verdict. None of them have eaten; none have slept.

Starting the next day, between meals I got surges of heartburn and sour regurgitations. At night I'd twist and turn, the hours would stretch, and my mind would tease me with thoughts of food, food, food.

I don't remember the first of my egg fantasies, but they started driving me crazy. I'd see a bowl of eggs, then a ring of eggs dancing in air, then, worst of all, a single egg. One tantalizingly real egg seducing me under my nose. Hard-boiled. To crack its shell, I'd drop it on the table or on the floor and it would bounce back into my hand, ready for stripping. I'd start to peel it, slowly, respectfully, delicately. Then I'd hear the Red Army orchestra, the one that played the national anthem on Radio Moscow to wake us every morning, blaring erotic bumpy and grindy striptease music. Peeling that egg down to its moist, silky whiteness, I'd strip it of every speck of shell, then I'd hold it aloft on my fingertips, all bare, and behold it. That wasn't yet the egg down to its true nakedness. Oh no. For that, I'd sink into it with my gentle loving mouth, big front incisors first, then press my lips into its precious secret, its most private treasure, the yolk.

Oh God, if only I could see, touch, lick, suck, bite into one hard-boiled egg. Oh God, if only I could stop thinking about it.

I guess my mother, although she never made it as the salad queen, had cultivated my taste for hard-boiled eggs. She'd chop an

118

egg and mash it with mayonnaise. After I grew up and learned to live on my own, I chopped eggs and mashed them with mayonnaise exactly as she'd done. In Europe, when I traveled on trains, at the station I'd buy a snack to take along: two hard-boiled eggs, maybe three or four for a long trip, and tiny fresh rolls.

If only I could stop thinking about, tasting, hearing the crumb-crushing crunch of those tiny rolls.

Funny that I should have thought of hard-boiled eggs as I did. During all those weeks before the trial, I can't remember the faintest sexual urge or impulse. Not even for Tatyana. What set me afire about her was her face, her sweetness, her loving glow. I wanted her to care about me, understand me, hope for me, moan for me, put her face on my shoulder, and maybe make me some soup. But I don't think I once thought about Tatyana with her clothes off.

By the time I got to the camp, four months after my arrest, my sexual instinct was a dead fish. I didn't think of it unless someone else brought it up. I couldn't remember why it ever was important, didn't know if it could ever be important again, and didn't care.

My mind played a lot with the idea of ending it all by dying. Yet, paradoxically, the only instinct that stirred me was surviving, particularly through food. I remember cravings for chocolate, for a juicy, melty cheeseburger. Soon, however, even those cravings withered away. All that stayed, reminding me I was alive, was that teasing hard-boiled egg.

Many times I said to myself—and said openly to others—I'd rather do my full eight years in this place with a satisfying diet than half the time living like this. The pain, the heartburn, the regurgitations got worse until the medics finally admitted, after I made innumerable trips to the camp dispensary, and spent several stays at the hospital, that I had what was called gastritis. Almost a year after that they said I had a pre-ulcer condition. I have little doubt that my ulcers—I eventually wound up with two—were there earlier. Anyhow, the pre-ulcer designation entitled me to a special diet, which amounted to an extra smear of gravy on top of my kasha.

All my suffering came from those hated meals. Yet I can't say that I resented my treatment. Since coming home to America, I've told people of those reluctant diagnoses, that awful "special diet." They shake their heads, finding my story hard to believe, then ask if Soviet doctors are that incompetent, or if they're just cruel. I don't see them as either.

This was a prison. In many ways I think the Soviets have a clearer idea of how to run a prison and how to treat prisoners than Americans and most Europeans do. They did not owe us kindness or comfort or consideration. All of us there, in one way or another, had looked at orderly society and laws and said, "Fuck you." So now society was repaying us in kind, saying "Fuck you" back.

In the Soviet "free" world outside of labor camp, if you complain of symptoms that suggest an ulcer, a medical person will jump to attention and care for you. But the prisoners around me had made it clear that *they* didn't care about others. They stole or raped or smuggled harmful substances, and the nicer guys among them cheated with pen and ink or currency values. Why should society repay them with caring and kindness?

I know my saying that a tough prison is right for these guys sounds crazy when you consider that I ranted and lied and connived to stay out of their prison. I say throw the book at lawbreakers, yet I knowingly broke the law. I'll also say I think there are two kinds of lawbreakers, and one should be treated far more harshly than the other: those who physically threaten and harm people and those who cleverly improve their own situations while scarcely doing any perceptible harm to others; the latter includes most white-collar crime against large institutions, which spreads loss to individuals so widely and thinly that nobody's really hurt. But having said that, I know perfectly well that mine was no white-collar crime. Sixty-two pounds of heroin threatens real harm to real people, a lot of real people. I've thought about that a lot. In camp and afterward I carried a heavy, lousy burden of moral guilt. But I'm not copping a plea. Before the crime I refused to think about who'd get hurt, simply because I knew I wouldn't like what I thought.

120

But getting back to those ulcers, almost every Russian long-term prisoner I met in hospital camp had ulcers, or pre-ulcers, or gastritis. (I suppose fewer guys in 5–1, the foreigners' camp, had damaged stomachs simply because of the Russian aversion to keeping foreigners around; thus their frequent amnesties.) So far as I could tell, none of these Russians had ever heard of any commercially made antacids, like Maalox or Tums. What they did know about was baking soda.

Baking soda was to the prisoner what fine caviar was to the civilian Russian. You always wondered how the owner got it because there was practically no legal way of getting any. The *magazin* had none for sale, the kitchen none for baking. That left only the dispensary, which could dispense it only when it was prescribed, which it rarely was. And even when it was, the dispensary was usually out of it, at least officially.

Which left only one last remaining possibility: the *fel'dsher's* private stash. The *fel'dsher* was a prisoner who had the job of non-professional medical assistant at his camp's dispensary. He had considerably autonomy there, because doctors and nurses came and went, rarely bothering to dawdle long in one dispensary on their rounds of all the prisons in the archipelago. His status was something like that of the medic in the infantry: while given only the most cursory medical instructions, he was the guy who often saved the day, or saved a life, simply because he was there. The *fel'dsher* had the best job in the camp, for reasons I'll get to. And only one of its rich bundle of privileges was conducting a small private commerce, a black market in baking soda.

Among the world's most active centers of private commerce—capitalism, if you will—is the Soviet labor camp. Somebody once said (I think it was my high-school economics teacher, who was a Marxist) that capitalism thrives on scarcity. I know just where he could prove his thesis. In Mordovia he'd find everything he was looking for: assumption of risk in the hope of potential reward; direction of extraordinary intelligence, creativity, and entrepreneurship into the narrow channels of materialism, greed, and corruption. And at the root of it all he'd find scarcity. A superabundance of scarcity. More scarcity than he'd know what to do with.

The best place to observe Soviet capitalism is in the hospital camp, which offers the most scarcity. For one thing, prison meals are stingier, actually smaller in the hospital than in labor camp.

How cruel, say charitable Westerners, how awful to deny the sick. But is it cruelty? In the Soviet view, it's simply socialist logic, and I dare anyone to try to disprove the logic. You want more prisoners to claim illness, even be tempted to inflict deliberate injury on themselves? You want them to abandon the productive work they perform in labor camp that benefits society and go and malinger as parasites in the hospital? Easily done. Reward them for going. Feed them better food and more of it in hospital camp, and you have an absolute guarantee that more prisoners will turn up with convincing complaints. On the other hand, make any complainer pay for going— shrink his meals—and you have an absolute test of whether he legitimately feels sick.

The policy of scarcity goes further. The *magazin*, or commissary, in the hospital opens only twice a month, and when it does it has almost nothing to sell, even less than the depleted store back in camp. So when a prisoner is ordered to the hospital, he's to be pitied. He goes to his friends and co-workers, also to every *zemliak* he knows, prisoners from his part of the country (in the foreigners' camp, to prisoners of his nationality), and asks for gifts to sustain himself. He'll get a hundred grams of margarine or, more commonly, a pig-fat lard called *zhir*, because sometimes the store is out of margarine for six months at a time. The store lady wraps the margarine or *zhir* in a piece of newspaper, so if you spread it carefully over your chunk of stony black bread you might be able to read the news over breakfast, backwards. Or his friends might give him two or three tins of conserves, some moldy sourballs, whatever. Now, if he happens to be in the right labor camp, he can also arrange better than that. If he works, say, in the camp that performs sewing for the whole prison system, and if he has a little nerve, he slips a new work uniform on his back just before his hospital trip. A good-looking new uniform is a high-status item. At the hospital you might get a good quantity of tea for it, and that tea, in turn, has high trading value.

The tea flows into the hospital sewn cleverly into a *shliapka*, a hat, or the lining of a *telogreika*, a prisoner's coat. To keep it from getting too loosely distributed and lost, the batch of tea may be folded in a piece of newspaper, although the crackle and stiffness of the paper involves risk. Better than newspaper is a used scrap of cellophane, if the prisoner can get one. And there's commerce in cigarettes (sometimes imported), valued trinkets like ballpoint pens and civilian combs, even an occasional piece of strictly illegal chocolate.

How did prisoners get their hands on all that stuff? That question leads to another layer of Mordovian capitalism: involvement of our MVD prison guards.

Naturally, every economy needs to be fed with fresh supplies of consumable goods. The most obvious source of our new goods, of course, was the routine junk from the *magazin*, purchased with work credit, in my regime six rubles (roughly six dollars) a month, plus two more for making *norma*, the work quota. But the best stuff for trading came through *posylki*, packages of five kilos of goodies that a prisoner was permitted to receive from relatives after serving half his sentence. He may get them once a year, or twice or three times, depending on the severity of the regime he's been sentenced to. Not having yet served my half-sentence, I was not entitled to a *posylka*, but only to a *banderol'*, a one-kilo package, twice a year. The American consul would send me a *banderol'*, bought with money deposited with the embassy by my aunt. Now, either the consul didn't know the exact weight limit and what goodies were forbidden, or he understood the system well enough to pretend not to know. For example, I'd get chewing gum, strictly forbidden. I'd just have to hand over one pack of gum for each one I kept, and everything was fine. Russians are crazy about American gum, and I'd trade it for food. The consul sent me Mars bars and Baby Ruths,

123

covered with strictly forbidden chocolate, as well as packages of cigarettes, American soap, and Kool-Aid, all of which are permitted and have extraordinary bartering value. Of any forbidden articles, the guard kept half. I'd rarely keep my half of those luxury items. If my fellow foreigners wanted them so much, they could pay for them. And they did, with what I wanted most: food, food, food, never enough food.

To Russian prisoners, relatives from Moscow and other big cities brought spicy, moist kolbasa. This delicious Russian-style salami was forbidden to prisoners, of course, but had the accompanying advantage of being difficult to find in the village stores of Mordovia. So it was craved by guards as well as prisoners. That made it a natural for the half-and-half rule. Sometimes I heard of visitors paying a guard cash to allow a prisoner his kolbasa or vodka or Armenian cognac, unavailable in Mordovia.

Then there's the matter of cash gifts to prisoners. Naturally, cash gifts from the outside are strictly forbidden, but a prisoner gets to know a guard and establishes a trust. Next time his family visits, they hand the guard some money. He gives half to the prisoner, keeping half for himself. Thus two economies are helped, that of the camp, and that of Mordovia. Mordovia needs this outside economic assistance. A guard doesn't earn much. By the time he feeds and clothes a wife and a child or two, he's hard put to finance a man's normal weekly ration of vodka. This extra income makes all the difference.

Of course, the prisoner's half of the cash is strictly forbidden in camp. His own funds have been confiscated as part of his sentence or put away for him until his release, and all work is paid for in *magazin* credit. So, since rubles officially don't exist in camp, spending them is risky. There are three things to do with rubles: First, you can buy something from another prisoner, thus passing to him the risk of getting rid of the rubles. Second, you can ask the old woman who peeps at you through the tiny sliding window of the *magazin* to buy something for you in town, perhaps fresh bread, or real margarine, or cigarettes with real tobacco (her store variety, called *makhorka*, is mixed from plants and herbs, with a reputed base of wood shavings). For whatever she procures, she charges double. But she could get into a lot of trouble for procuring, so she deals with only a few favored prisoners. And finally, you can deal through a guard, probably the same one who received and split the money in the first place. The main obstacle here is psychological. The prisoner doesn't like a guard to know too much of his illicit activity, and the guard certainly doesn't like a prisoner to know too much of *his*. A guard, too, doubles the price of everything.

So the price structure in Mordovian capitalism is fixed and simple. For everything you want to buy for cash that costs one ruble, your relative has to send you four. The money is halved on the way in, and again on the way out.

In the camp for foreigners, guards felt they had to be especially wary, more so than in camps for Russians. Most prisoners in Camp 5–1 had been arrested and investigated by the KGB, the state security police, and continued to be regarded as KGB prisoners, occasionally visited and interrogated by KGB men. We were turned over to the MVD, the internal security militia, which runs the camps. Those who have read *Gorky Park*, or seen the movie, have an idea of the jealousy and mutual distrust between the MVD and the KGB. On the other hand, our MVD guards knew none of us was likely to finger them to the KGB, because, even under a four-to-one profit system, we needed their procurement services at least as much as they needed our profits.

I conducted commerce with guards more than most, partly because I was American and partly because of my generous aunt.

I had arrived in camp carrying a huge duffel bag stuffed with provisions and gifts from my aunt, who had flown to Moscow to visit me right after the verdict. By camp standards I was a millionaire, possessor not of mere valuables, but of *American* valuables. Soon after I got the hang of how commerce with guards works, I understood more clearly why that baby-faced receiving officer of the day, Ramashin, had sniggered with such friendliness at me, at my being American, and why he had offered his assurances that prison would be a snap if I stayed out of trouble. He was first among his colleagues to see my treasures, peering and grinning as, item by item, I emptied my bag for inspection in the *sklad*, the storage room.

His move on me came later, and subtly.

"Ahmstairr," a Bulgarian prisoner I hardly knew propositioned me one day, "how much *magazin* you want for dark eyeglass?"

How the hell did he know I had sunglasses? When Ramashin had informed me at the *sklad*— with a regretful grin—that I couldn't wear them in camp, I had left them in the duffel bag.

"How do you know I have dark eyeglasses?"

"I want dark eyeglass. How much?"

"How would I get them out of the *sklad?*"

"No worry. I get. How much?"

"Six rubles *magazin*." I figured that would end it. How could he have accumulated a store credit of a month's unspent work allowance?

He pursed his lips as though to say he'd have to consult his accountant, and walked away.

Next day the Bulgarian announced, "Okay." All trendy Europeans on either side of the Iron Curtain like to say "okay" to Americans "Okay, six rubles *magazin*."

He astonished me. "You have six rubles credit?"

"Six rubles. I said okay."

I didn't want to offend the guy, but— "How do I know you have six rubles?"

"I tell you okay. You ask lady at *magazin*."

"Okay."

"Wait, don't ask lady. I tell you when ask lady."

"Okay."

That was the end of it, I was sure.

A couple of days later the Bulgarian said to me, "Now you ask lady."

That afternoon I asked lady.

"No," she responded crankily. "He has no six rubles. He give them you."

"I now have six rubles?"

"*Da, da*, you have, you have."

I couldn't figure this. I went to the *sklad*, asked for the sunglasses in my duffel bag, got them with no trouble, signed a receipt, and gave them to the Bulgarian.

A few days later, from a distance I saw Ramashin in the observation tower above the *shtab*, the MVD headquarters building. When he saw me he turned the other way. I was sure it was Ramashin, although he looked different. His face was masked by a sporty pair of sunglasses.

Suddenly I got it. If he had approached me directly, he'd have increased ever so slightly the risk of exposure to his superiors or the KGB that he was dealing with a prisoner. So he dealt roundabout, through a trusted "cutout," to use a CIA term. Subsequently, several mysterious offers like that came my way, and I made deals without asking too many questions. Afterwards, I'd often catch sight of a familiar object in the possession of an officer or guard.

One gift from my aunt that sent guards and prisoners alike into frenzies of envy and desire was the Gillette twin-bladed disposable razor, the one marketed in the States under the name Good News, but sold in Europe at that time as G-2. They'd never seen a razor with two separate blades, both unremovable from the razor. But what do you do after a few shaves, when it wears out? I'd let them test it. Even with cold water, or no water at all, it would cut close, and keep cutting close, for a week, even a month. Sometimes I'd use one for three months, six months. But what sent them into spasms of disbelief was that it was *disposable*. Americans just *throw these away?* They absolutely couldn't believe such a marvel of luxury and waste.

Fortunately, my aunt packed several G-2s and the consul later sent more. Guards, of course, were delighted that razors from outside

127

were forbidden, so they could grab for their cut, no pun intended. Sometimes I'd give one to a guard whose eyes bulged covetously, just to buy him. But I gave them away reluctantly, because they could be traded for food. For one razor, worth a fraction of a dollar, guys gave me a month's allowance at the *magazin*. I'm sure I was the only man in the Soviet sphere who used disposable Gillettes to fight hunger and reduce the pain of ulcers.

10

FROM TSEKH TO
SANCHAST'

For my first two years in Camp 5–1, I worked six days a week, nine hours a day, in the *tsekh*, the factory. Our factory manufactured chess pieces, sitting stools, and glass fittings for chandeliers, which were shipped throughout the Soviet Union to supply the regular civilian economy. My friends are surprised when I tell them that the most brutal work was making chess pieces, which required standing all day at a lathe, maintaining terrific speed and precision. The job was so awful that the MVD assigned the work only to Orientals, usually North Koreans or Chinese. Orientals qualified in two ways. First, they had the best stamina for work. Second, the Russians despised them.

Not only ours, but all labor camps produce for the regular civilian economy. A Soviet citizen doesn't stop contributing to society simply because he committed a crime, the way many American and most Western criminals do. One camp of Soviet prisoners in Mordovia made railroad cars. Another painted the railroad cars. Another cast wheel trucks for the railroad cars. Still another shaped chassis for TV sets. Only the most dangerous criminals were locked in prison cells away from work, where society supported them expensively, getting no return.

I worked at the *tsekh* helping make *taburetki*, wooden stools. For two years, my job was to sandpaper each part and correct its imperfections by filling every scar and hole with putty. I did that all day, every day. My *norma* was thirty stools a day, later increased to fifty.

One of the main problems in accomplishing the *norma* was that at least a couple of mornings a week we had to stand around waiting for parts, because of someone's poor planning somewhere. If a prisoner failed to complete his *norma*, he lost his extra two-ruble credit at the *magazin*. If the whole *tsekh* fell short of its *norma*, we worked all day Sunday. We could not complain to the camp commandant that the shortage was caused by delayed parts. Russian officials, whether low or high, do not admit errors.

That trait puzzles and confounds foreigners, who often misread its meaning. For example, no public announcement was made at first when, not long ago, a huge riverboat crashed into a Volga bridge. The boat plunged to the bottom, drowning hundreds of tourists and sightseers, mostly Russians. The Soviet news media reported nothing. The West picked up rumors of a riverboat calamity so huge that some thought the story must be an anti-Soviet hoax. Then thousands upon thousands of relatives and friends of those hundreds of victims, who were told no details, spread such wild speculations that finally the accident was acknowledged—days after its occurrence.

An American official told me during a moment of relaxed conversation on the day of my departure for the United States that Aeroflot had never had a fatal accident.

I squinted at him, not sure I had heard right.

Then he explained. "We've had calls from the foreign ministry to notify us that, say, two Americans had been lost 'in transit.' We'd happen to know that the Americans were flying, say, to Tashkent. We'd ask when the crash occurred. Always the same answer: 'No crash. They were lost in transit.' One of my colleagues and I were driving one day past Sheremet'evo airport and saw a big jet, tail sticking up in the air, still in flames. We called and asked, 'Any Americans aboard that crash?' Answer, the same as always: 'What crash? No crash.' This has nothing to do with their being Communist or arrogant or deceitful. In the Russian culture and in many cultures throughout Asia, it's extremely humiliating to confess that something went wrong, and very impolite to press someone into having to do so. In the American culture, we consider it brave and commendable to admit mistakes. We have our hangups with other kinds of failures, like admitting poverty. Ask any real-estate agent in our richest counties, like Fairfield and Westchester, to tell you about people who buy expensive homes with lovely shutters and grand lawns, then put no furniture on the second floor because they can't afford any. The kids may live on peanut butter, but the neighbors will be entertained with the best Scotch, no matter what. That's the American peculiarity that helps explain this Russian peculiarity."

As matters would soon turn out, that Russian peculiarity was to take on a central importance in my getting out of the Soviet Union. But I had no glimmering of that as yet.

But to get back to unadmitted mistakes at the *tsekh*, the working prisoner had no one to complain to when he was screwed by the late arrival of parts. As though that weren't trouble enough, some were also systematically screwed by their foreman, a fellow prisoner whose main job was to drive men to make their *norma*.

A worker's *norma* was, let's say, fifty pieces. If he was an easy mark, the foreman might inform him that ten of his fifty were rejected. So the worker had to do another ten, or lose his *norma* credit at the *magazin*. He stepped up his work and did them. Meanwhile, the foreman now had ten pieces he could credit to someone else, because nothing was wrong with those pieces in the first place. A worker could double, even triple his weekly *norma* payment of two rubles by producing substantially more than his fifty pieces. So the foreman "sold" the sucker's extra work to a trusted friend for a

131

split in the extra *magazin* credit. On *magazin* days, a procession of prisoners passed the bed of a foreman, wordlessly handing him packages of tea, cigarettes, sourballs—payoffs for chiseled *norma*.

This form of screwing your buddy was not a violation of the prisoner's code, like stealing food from his *tumbochka* or welshing on a bet. Minor corruptions were tolerated, expected, as the perks of power. In a deprived society, how else could a fellow rise a mere inch above simple survival, except at the expense of those around him?

I loathed my work. I hated every day of it, every moment. For one thing, doing anything repetitive drives me to the edge of insanity. Second, the working environment couldn't have been more miserable. The factory had no heat and we froze. The electric saws and cutting machines, screaming all day, deafened us. Fine sawdust cut into my skin, burned my eyes, and crept up my nose, somehow intensifying my constant heartburn and hunger. Because men had to scramble and compete for parts, fistfights broke out. Third, my nervous system was allergic to sandpapering. The sound and feeling of it were like a fingernail scratching a blackboard, shooting quivers up my spine. I never got used to it.

One day the commandant of the camp came by, on inspection. Impulsively, I took the risk of addressing him. I told him I couldn't bear to do this work anymore, but there was another kind, a harder kind, I'd gladly do.

"What kind that?" he asked suspiciously.

"Loading and unloading trucks."

I think he was surprised. That work was harder. But I did prefer it. No matter how cold, it was in the open air. No matter how heavy the boxes, it was not deadly monotonous. He glared at me.

I detected indecision. Maybe I was halfway there. I pushed: "Look, I never did work like this. I am a *pedagog*."

"Ahmstairr, to me you not *pedagog*. You contrabandist."

He strutted away haughtily.

I hoped I wouldn't get some extra punishment for the direct appeal to him.

132

A week later I was transferred to the loading dock.

That experience, plus others, taught me that in the labor camp, just as in capitalist America, the better jobs don't fall into your lap. You have to go after them.

I went after an even better job during one of my stays at the hospital camp, and got it. The medical doctor in charge of my ward was a prisoner, on a fifteen-year sentence for murder. He was a Tajikistani, from the Caucasus Mountains near Afghanistan, an ethnic identity at which Russians spit. But this doctor had full power over our ward, including the authority to recommend that a prisoner remain hospitalized. I cultivated his good will, and he recommended that my medical condition required continued hospital care, and that I be given a job at the hospital, which could mean a long stay. The recommendation was approved.

My job was to serve the food and wash the dishes in the kitchen of the medical ward. Cooking was done elsewhere. I worked under a ward *zavkhoz*, a prisoner in charge.

Each morning I got up earlier than others to start heating two huge pots of water for tea. For the whole ward of sixty prisoners, we got a fifty-gram package of tea, less than two ounces, the amount used for making a small pot of *chaffir*, the illicit concentrate. Before handing me the tea to dump in the water, the *zavkhoz* skimmed some of the dry leaves for himself, some days as much as half. The men complained of the colorless, flavorless hot water we served them. They knew the *zavkhoz* was routinely cheating them, but had no way of proving it. Sometimes he gave me a cut of what he stole.

Then I had to unlatch the thermoses of hot kasha or whatever, getting them ready to serve. The *zavkhoz* always watched that procedure to make sure I didn't steal any. When I opened the small pot of gravy that we spooned out to dampen the kasha, together he and I skimmed it of morsels of meat and fat, saving them for our own portion. Then we opened a package of butter. Real butter. In certain items the hospital diet was better than camp's, even though portions were purposefully smaller. Each man's daily allotment of butter was thirty grams, about a spoonful. We weighed the pats,

133

putting them on small scraps of newspaper. Instead of thirty grams, we weighed them out at twenty-five. The *zavkhoz* took more than half of the total skim and threw the rest on the table for me, sometimes to be shared with another helper. He stole—and shared with me—similarly from the daily sugar allotment.

My morning kasha, with a chunk of butter and a sprinkling of sugar, tasted like real food.

That job lasted two months. I never knew for sure why it ended. One morning I'd started work as usual. The tea water was just starting to boil when the *zavkhoz* arrived and said, "You're going back to camp today."

"To camp? Why?"

He shrugged.

I ran out of the kitchen and found my ward doctor. He knew nothing about it. I went to the chief medical officer, to the camp commandant. Once you work there, it's no great breach to approach these people. But nobody I saw could rescind the order, because none of them knew where it came from.

I figured the KGB wanted me back among the foreigners, where I belonged. Suppose someone attacked me. How would some little KGB man explain my being there in the first place? Heads might roll. The American embassy might protest that I was supposed to be in the camp for foreigners, protected under international law.

Then I began thinking that maybe a *pomilovka*, an order for my release, had arrived at Camp 5–1. Some nights I dreamed of that order. In those long, sawdusty, screeching hours at the *tsekh*, every time an official entered, especially someone I didn't know, my first thought was that he was looking for me. President Carter had demanded of Brezhnev that I be released, and this guy had the order in his briefcase. If ever I saw a stranger arrive on my day off, I'd wonder, Would they bring a *pomilovka* on Sunday?

I never did find out why I was transferred out of that wonderful job, with its skimmed gravy and morsels of fat, its sugar and lovely chunks of butter on my kasha.

Although that job suited me perfectly, other work at the hospital appealed more to some guys. In fact, there was a widespread opinion that the luckiest job holder of all was the *zavkhoz* of the morgue. For one thing, he was the only kind of prisoner in the entire Soviet labor camp system given free belts of vodka—almost daily, and *legally*.

He got his shot every morning there was to be an autopsy. Soviet doctors are not crazy about cutting up corpses. So the *zavkhoz* gets to the morgue early, slugs down his allotted vodka to stabilize his nerves, lights a fire, and starts to slice the dead. Then the doctors arrive. With hands clasped behind backs, they just lean over the stiff, peer at its parts, then decide, "Aha! Infection of this, and cancer of that."

But vodka is not the job's main attraction. Before the doctors come, even before he heaves down the vodka, the *zavkhoz* pries open the mouth of the corpse to inspect for dental gold. One of the first skills he learns on the job, although it's not included in his formal training, is to yank out the gold—neatly, so the doctors won't notice.

Fencing the gold is not simple. The *zavkhoz* has to pass it to the hospital dental technician, also a prisoner. Then the technician has to pass it to one of the civilian dentists who make the rounds of the camps. The dentist knows where to sell it. Each of these participants gets a piece of the sale price—that is, each except the original owner.

You don't have to be dead to have your gold passed through those channels. Over lunch one day, the dental technician, a skinny Ukrainian named Yuri, once caught the glint of my shiny gold crown, installed a decade earlier in Greenwich Village. He stared at me all through my potato soup, then nabbed me on the way out.

"Let me see mouth."

I opened wide.

He scrutinized critically, and made me an offer I couldn't refuse. "For gold, two *magazin*."

A hospital *magazin* is five rubles. Ten rubles is five *norma* bonuses back at camp, or the spending value of a smuggled twenty-ruble cash gift.

"What would I do for a crown?"

"I take out gold nice. You come to dentist, tell him you lost, he make new."

"Make a new one out of what?" Silly question. I knew the answer.

He shrugged. "Steel."

I accepted his deal, but he screwed me. He had less than five rubles coming to him at the *magazin*, and said he'd give me the rest as soon as he built his credit. He never did.

But I got even. Yuri had a bitter enemy named Sergei, an educated former customs inspector serving serious time for taking bribes. Sergei had taken over as *zavkhoz* of the psycho-isolator, and became a good friend of mine.

When I told him of Yuri's betrayal, Sergei beamed with devilish savor. He made me repeat the details: what Yuri had offered for my crown and what he'd actually paid me. This was a substantiation of what everyone knew, that Yuri trafficked in gold.

Next day Sergei presented me with a piece of paper, my story of Yuri all written out.

"You sign here," he said with a leer. "I wait. When your *po-milovka* comes—after you leave Soviet Union, not before, I promise—I use letter to finish Yuri."

I signed Sergei's paper, trusting him not to use it before I was gone, but feeling nervous about it. The way matters turned out, however, Sergei didn't need it. On a subsequent stay at the hospital, I learned that Yuri had gone berserk one day and killed himself. Suicides at the hospital were fairly common.

Back at camp, the best general kind of job was the kind that served the operation of the camp itself, such as cooking, doing laundry, making repairs. Those jobs escaped the incessant pressure of work quotas. You did what had to be done, and that was it. The assignment many prisoners craved was repair work, carpentry or electrical chores around the barracks. But whenever possible our Russian keepers gave those desirable jobs to the Chinese and other Orientals, despised as they were. A repair worker moves around the whole camp, so our jailers could use him to spy on other prisoners. Thus at one stroke the authorities made use of Orientals while, at the same time, deepening the hatred between them and Caucasians.

There was one job I coveted above all others in Camp 5–1, but one that I realized was silly for me to dream of getting. That was the job of camp *fel'dsher*, the medic at the *sanchast'*, the camp dispensary. The *fel'dsher* was practically in business for himself. He slept alone in a room of the *sanchast'*, mainly to guard its drugs. The room had its own furnace, and even though he wasn't supposed to, the *fel'dsher* could heat the room as much as he liked. He had his own sink for washing, and a pail that made it unnecessary to go out in the snow in the middle of the night. If he got his hands on extra food, he could use the dispensary hot plate. All in all, a luxurious pad.

The duties of the job made it even more desirable. Early each morning, before the *tsekh* opened, and in late afternoon, before the second shift, he had to conduct *priëm*, sick call. Guys came with complaints, and the *fel'dsher* had to decide whether they required being seen by a nurse or doctor who usually visited in late morning. Other than that obligation, the *fel'dsher*'s job was easygoing and fairly independent.

Maybe the job appeared especially privileged because of the prisoner who held it during my first couple of years at 5–1. He was, in fact, the most privileged person in camp, and maybe the most privileged any camp had ever had.

Walter Haefelin was the first prisoner I'd met on arriving at the 5–1 barracks, when my head still burned from that humiliating haircut. He stepped out of the group, a stocky man about my age, with eyeglasses, a thick head, and the look of a well-fed intellectual. He stuck his hand out toward me confidently, saying in perfect English, "My name is Walter."

I took him first for an Englishman, but soon detected a trace of

German accent. I switched to German and he was delighted, as he had been unable to speak with anyone else in German in the whole camp. Walter was Swiss, a multimillionaire who had had big contracts with the Soviet government for building prefabricated factories. For five years he had traveled freely into and out of the Soviet Union. On his exit trips he smuggled icons, valuable religious artifacts from the days of the tsars. The KGB knew it, and he knew they knew it, but he also knew they wouldn't bother him. He was much too valuable to the Soviets as a builder.

What the Soviets did get him for, a crime they don't forgive, was bribing a high Soviet official with tens of thousands of rubles to nail down one of his contracts.

Although an economic crime against the state is among the most severely punishable, prisoners and guards tend to respect the guy convicted of it as a high-class prisoner. And Walter had other advantages going for him. When he was still at Lefortovo, awaiting trial, he mouthed his first dab of dry kasha and announced, "I will not eat this food. I refuse. I will starve myself and I will die." The Soviets got scared because he was conspicuous. They and the Swiss embassy had a quick negotiation, and Walter began dining on food brought in especially for him from the outside.

Once he was convicted and sent to Mordovia, however, there was no way for such privilege to continue. But Walter managed anyway. The legend of his catered food, and of his high importance and great wealth, traveled with him from Lefortovo to 5–1. The commandant fired the prisoner then serving as *fel'dsher*, and gave the coveted job to Walter.

While the *fel'dsher* cannot send someone to the hospital, he can influence the visiting doctor to send or not send a would-be patient. In camp, that is power. Perhaps more important, while the *fel'dsher* cannot prescribe drugs, he dispenses them on the doctor's prescription. That means that he controls the supply. So what if this guy, who's supposed to get these painkillers, misses out on a few, and that guy—who may be a prisoner, or may be a guard—gets them instead? That is power.

Walter was no novice in trading the uses of his power for other valuables. In camp, he continued to live like a millionaire, relatively speaking. On good days the camp kitchen received a six-ounce cupful of tomato puree to dab on the kasha. The whole camp of a hundred or so prisoners got about five ounces, a tiny smear apiece. A full ounce went to Walter. On good days our greasy broth had an ancient fish head floating in it for flavor. No, Walter didn't get the head. From somewhere—I never did find out where—Walter sometimes got a real, whole fish, broiled or fried.

Sure, other prisoners resented him. But they also respected him. He was royalty. Anytime he walked by, men asked obsequiously, "Dobroe utro? How are you?"

After every visit to a prison outside Moscow to meet his consul, a privilege each of us had every three months, and after every conjugal visit from his girlfriend every four months, Walter's room at the dispensary was loaded with treats, most of them illegal for prisoners, including the Swiss brand of Ovaltine, which they call Ovalmaltine.

In the two languages we shared, Walter loved to while away time telling me about his adventures among the Soviets. He told me about dealing with corrupt Soviet officials, about prostitutes who specialize in rich foreigners at Moscow hotels. I had confidence in his stories, because he was not a showy guy, not an admiration-seeker. He didn't need it. I've had opportunity to verify some of his stories. They always checked.

The way Walter got out—and, in fact, the way he got into camp in the first place—reveals a lot about the special uses the Soviets make of their foreign prisoners. I mentioned that the KGB knew he'd been smuggling icons out of the Soviet Union, but never bothered him for it. One day two East German spies, a married couple, were arrested in Switzerland. I doubt that Walter connected that occurrence with his own fate at the time. But some strange things began to happen. He arrived in Czechoslovakia from Budapest, Hungary, when he received a phone call telling him to meet somone at the certain hotel where this person was registered. He went, and the hotel knew of no such person. On the way back to his own hotel, someone followed him. Leaving Czechoslovakia, he was detained at the airport for a search. When the tail, whom he assumed was KGB, clung to him all the way to Moscow, he knew he was to be arrested. He was.

He assumed the bust was over the icons, a relatively minor offense compared to the charge that hit him: high-level bribery. For more than a year the KGB held him at Lefortovo, delaying the trial, delaying his transfer to camp, as though they were waiting for something, he didn't know what. At his trial he refused to admit guilt, stating that he'd rather serve to the last day of his sentence than lie just to please the KGB and the court. He got ten years. The Soviet official who had been accused of accepting Walter's alleged bribe was shot by a firing squad.

He didn't serve the full time, however. Four years later the woman of the East German spy couple was ill with cancer in a Swiss prison sanitarium. The East Germans, and therefore the Soviets, wanted that couple back. So they ignored the gravity of the charge against Walter Haefelin, ignored his refusal to plead guilty, and traded him for the spies. It may be that his arrest had been a response to *their* arrest—a setup for the trade to come. I remember Walter telling me that the KGB permits a lot of irregular activity by foreigners, just keeping an eye on it without interfering. They simply wait until they might need a certain kind of person to arrest for a certain kind of potential trade.

Even after his release, Walter's extraordinary influence continued in camp, in the form of the corruption of the commandant, Yevgeny Ivanovich Khrushchev. (No relation to what's-his-name. Khrushchev is a common name in the Ukraine.) Khrushchev was head and shoulders above most commandants in one important skill, that of playing one prisoner against another, especially playing on their ethnic differences. He was a tireless investigator and snooper, knowing everything going on in camp. He knew who was making *chaffir*, but didn't order the making of it stopped. Instead, he'd mention it to the offenders so he could hold it over their heads. He

140

knew who was trading American cigarettes for credit at the *magazin*. But he was a pragmatic man. Why prevent *chaffir*-making if it energized men for work?

Khrushchev always struck me as looking oddly like an American bureaucrat, squat and officious, with black plastic eyeglass frames of the kind commonly seen in the fifties, especially on George Reeves playing Superman, except that Khrushchev's frames never fit him quite right. They tilted. One day he strutted around with gorgeous new frames, a perfect fit, stylishly shaped. Soon everyone in camp knew where they came from, because Willie Schaffner couldn't keep a secret. Willie Schaffner was Walter Haefelin's special friend, being the only other Swiss in camp. During his three-year sentence for contraband, he was Walter's faithful dinner partner, bodyguard, valet, ego-booster and yes-man. Walter was grateful. Before his release, he and Willie worked out a little code so that Willie's letters would keep Walter informed as to how Khrushchev was treating Willie. The eyeglass frames, of fine Swiss make, had come from Walter. Later came a watch. All Willie had to do was signal that the good treatment had turned sour, and Walter's gift-of-the-month club would close down. Khrushchev knew that.

When Walter left, I fully expected that Willie would get Walter's dream job. But I decided to go for it. I put in a plea to the *opershas*, number-two man to the commandant. He said he'd talk to the commandant, which I took to be a dodge. So I took my life in my hands and talked to Khrushchev myself. I didn't have to remind him that I was not among the rebels and troublemakers when most of the Westerners in camp pulled a strike, an episode I'll describe.

When I saw a doctor arrive in camp, which one or another did every couple of days, I broke the rules and approached her. I made sure doctors knew about my grasp of languages, especially German, French, and Spanish, as well as English. They knew without my reminding them that the most frequent complainers at *priëm*, sick call, were Westerners. I would be a reliable screener and translator of their complaints. In dispensing medications, I'd be a dependable transmitter of instructions.

That strong point was also my vulnerable point. Every literate prisoner in camp coveted the *fel'dsher*'s job, or at least resented the guy lucky enough to get it. As soon as they learned I was lobbying hard for it, some of them grumbled loudly, usually making sure a guard was nearby. "Amster the smuggler? They're going to put him in charge of all those drugs?"

The administration was grateful to me, all right, for trying to help cool the strike. But Khrushchev himself told me they wondered if staying out of it reflected a certain weakness of character that might lead me into corruption, were I in charge of the baking soda and all those pills.

The nerve of them! Corruption? Who, me? Why, I'd be every bit as incorruptible as anyone else who had ever held that job.

To my absolute astonishment and elation, I got it. I couldn't believe I had become the successor to Walter Haefelin.

11

STRIKE

After we arrived at camp, Pete, Darrell, and I rarely went out of our way to indulge in comradeship. We still smarted from the wounds of the pretrial investigation, the way our KGB investigators had used each of us against the other two. Besides, both Pete's and Darrell's talent for getting into pointless trouble made me want to stay away from them. Pete's American entrepreneurial instincts helped him get by quite well under the Mordovian system of capitalism. Darrell became a foreman at his *tsekh*, which earned him *norma* bonuses. But when he had something of value, he'd almost never offer any, so I stopped sharing what I had, and we drifted apart.

In the late summer of 1977, almost a year after we arrived at camp, Pete had an inspiration. He remembered seeing on television back in Las Vegas that a famous Soviet dissident, probably Solzhenitsyn, had protested his imprisonment by refusing to eat. Through his network of fellow dissidents who were not imprisoned, word of the hunger strike reached the outer world. His protest, enormously publicized, made the Soviets extremely nervous. In a gesture of humanitarianism, they soon booted him out of the country.

I don't think Pete saw clearly that he was not exactly Solzhenitsyn in Soviet eyes. But that didn't diminish his enthusiasm. Even without confederates in the outside world, he went on a hunger strike too. His protest movement spread to Darrell, who also stopped eating. When their hunger got really bad, they gave up the strike.

But they had touched a nerve that made other prisoners jump. A couple of Englishmen and an Italian, upset about working Sundays, deliberately slowed their work pace at the *tsekh* and persuaded a few others to slow theirs. This was followed by numbers of prisoners complaining to their consuls about camp conditions. The consuls, in turn, complained to the Soviet Foreign Ministry. In response, a commission from Moscow came to 5–1 to investigate.

On a previous visit by a commission from Moscow, Western prisoners, always more unruly than the rest, walked right up to colonels and generals and boldly announced their complaints. Unheard of. That would never happen in a camp of Russian prisoners.

Commandant Khrushchev wasn't going to let that happen again at his camp. At a Friday morning formation of prisoners, before the Monday arrival of the commission, Lieutenant Ramashin announced that all those whose names were called were to get their things together to go to the hospital that day. The names were practically a full roster of all Westerners, more than a dozen. Everyone knew that the Friday transfer convoy was for the hospital.

The befuddled men, usually eager for a hospital vacation, called after Ramashin: "Hospital? What for?" "Hey, I'm not sick." "I didn't go on *priëm*. I didn't complain."

"*Prikaz, prikaz*. Orders, orders, that's all I know about it."

After the commission left, the Westerners suffered a mass attack of wellness, and Khrushchev recalled them all to camp.

When the men learned that they'd have no work holiday on Christmas Day, they broke out in hives of dissatisfaction again: a hunger strike here, work sabotage there. Khrushchev struck again. He ordered the troublemakers to gather their things and go to the isolator. First among the names was that of Pete Benack.

When he heard his name at formation, Pete didn't go into the barracks to get his stuff. Instead he turned to Ramashin and ran the

144

backs of his fingers down the middle of his abdomen, from his chest to his crotch. That's the *nakhui* sign. Roughly translated, it means, "I give you cock." The thinking prisoner doesn't give that sign even to a guard; it takes an idiot to give it to an officer.

"To isolator immediately," sputtered Ramashin.

Pete turned toward the barracks.

"Immediately! Go now!"

Pete stopped like a freeze-frame and—I'll never forget this—just lay down on the road in front of the barracks steps. He folded his hands across his belly and stared up at the sky.

"Benack!" the officer called. He dug his toe into Benack's hip, not a kick, but a sharp wake-up nudge. Pete lay there, as passive-resistant as a Selma marcher.

While I and other prisoners watched the drama, Ramashin flipped his hand in an instruction to a guard. Two of them disappeared, and returned with a stretcher. They loaded Pete's huge, meaty, limp body on it, and carried him away. Later our Australian prisoner, who worked in the kitchen and delivered food to the isolator, told us that the guards had steered the stretcher into an isolator room and flipped it, as though dumping a load of wood. When Pete's hulk hit the ground, his bones crunched.

Pete stayed in the isolator fourteen days, one less than the maximum sentence. The other Westerners got out in seven.

The trouble continued off and on, because the discomforts continued: kasha too often, portions too small, work too hard, *norma* too high. The Westerners who kept the pot of trouble boiling, besides Pete, were five Englishmen, a Swiss (not Haefelin, but his attendant, Willie), a Frenchman, an Italian, a Spaniard, two Australians, and a Belgian. At their fringe stood seven or eight Lebanese, a couple of Iranians, a handful of Malaysians and Singaporeans, and an African or two. Almost all were there for carrying contraband, some for dope, some for diamonds and gold.

When officers and prisoners found themselves in confrontation, I usually served as translator. I liked the job. It kept me useful to both sides and out of the crossfire. I'd try to go beyond literal trans-

145

lation and convey the intent of words, which sometimes got me into trouble. For example, Khrushchev might say they'd better do as ordered, or they were going to the isolator. I might add, "And it looks to me like he really means it." The prisoners wouldn't like that.

The most outspoken prisoner, besides Pete, was an Englishman named Parkins. Actually, he was a black Jamaican with a British passport. At his consul meetings, he was always demanding that the British charge the Russians with antiblack racism. It was true, the guards did pick on the blacks more. Also, the prisoners taunted and excluded blacks. Those poor foreign service officers would duly note the protest. Whether they transmitted it to the Russians, I'll never know.

One day Parkins stared Khrushchev right in the eye and called him a fascist son of a bitch. Then he looked at me, waiting for me to translate. My eyes beseeched his, but his glare didn't budge.

"I don't think you really want me to translate that," I begged.

Parkins pulled himself up with haughty diplomatic dignity. "You trahnslate every mothafuckeen word."

I guess I did. To save my life, I can't remember.

Khrushchev, knowing that I wasn't part of the revolt, began greeting me by name, like a friendly suburban neighbor. Prisoners noticed, and I didn't like it. Then Khrushchev struck up conversations with me, once inviting me to his office. To stay in his good graces, I would tell him what he already knew.

The men then began accusing me of cleaning Khrushchev's ashtrays, a remarkably unobscene metaphor, as Russian metaphors go, for licking the commandant's boots. One day I lost my cool and let them have it.

"You guys are crazy, thinking you're going to bring the Russians to their knees. The Tartars couldn't do it. Genghis Khan couldn't do it. Napoleon couldn't do it. Hitler couldn't do it. And you guys think you're going to do it."

"If you're not for us, you're against us," said a fellow named Kennett, a blond, nasty English smuggler in his twenties.

146

"All I know is, most of you guys are here for like three years. You know you'll be out in a year and a half, and even before you got to camp, half a year of that was already gone. They gave me eight years, *eight years*, for doing the same thing you guys did. They want to make me serve the whole eight. I don't know if I can survive eight years. I'm not going to make my situation worse over your nonsense."

That finished me with the strikers.

One late summer afternoon a Syrian named Fuad Sago approached me. He was a pleasant guy, always friendly to me, who had been arrested for currency exchange while a graduate student at Lumumba University.

He said, "I want to talk with you about something, but not here."

His manner, perfectly friendly, seemed odd. He led me to a spot between the bath house and the kitchen, an area not visible from the rest of the camp. About thirty prisoners sat in a circle on the grass, gaping at me ominously. I couldn't figure out why he'd brought me here. All I knew for sure was that my whole body was trembling, and I hoped the others didn't see it.

Little Willie the Swiss spoke up, solemn, dignified, carrying great responsibility. He told me this was a court, that the men had leveled certain accusations against me. And that I was on trial.

"What charges? What did I do?"

Fluttering his eyes like a judge who refuses to be perturbed by a prisoner's interruption, he proceeded with the charges. "You have spied for the administration of the camp. You have spied for the KGB. You have sucked up to the authorities, trying to get early release. You have cooperated with the administration to break our hunger strikes. You have stolen food and cigarettes from prisoners."

And more. I can't remember the whole list. Some of it was true, some partially true, some not at all true.

I denied it all.

We haggled for at least an hour. Out of the corner of my eye, I saw guards walking this way and that, at a distance. They knew

147

something was going on, but they always stayed away from what they called "internal matters." That was consistent with Lenin's teaching that prisoners will do away with each other, thus solving a problem for socialist society.

The kangaroo court sentenced me to isolation. Nobody was to talk to me. And for about two months, nobody did. I had never experienced anything like that feeling of being a total outcast. But it gave me a lot of time to think. The isolation had as many plusses as minuses. Most of those guys were weaklings and losers, and I didn't like talking to them anyway. My highest priority was not social intercourse and acceptance. It was food, and getting out of there. None of those guys could write my *pomilovka*. Guards and officers observed that I was avoided by the troublemakers, and I suppose it made me look better in the eyes of officials who could do something about my fate. Now and then an officer would furtively ask, "Ahmstairr, everything okay? Anybody bother you?" I always said no, but felt protected and elevated by their asking.

Before long, one of the kangaroo court's not-so-true charges against me began coming true. One day a guard told me to report to headquarters. I assumed Khrushchev wanted me for one of his little talks.

In a small room sat a youngish, athletic, dark-suited Russian I had never seen. This guy could pass himself off anywhere as perfect KGB.

"Hello, Ahmstairr, Svelkov. KGB."

I waited.

He offered me a cigarette and left the pack between us on the table. It seemed peculiar, after all these months, to share a light-up with an authority.

"Ahmstairr, what your friend Benack trying to do?"

I told him Pete didn't tell me his private thoughts, that we were not close friends. I wanted to disconnect myself from Pete and his behavior. Then I told Svelkov about the prisoners' dissatisfactions, as though he didn't know.

"But you get good food."

I explained the difficulty of living almost exclusively on kasha. I hastened to add that I knew kasha was nutritious and appreciated by Russians, but hard for the rest of us to get used to.

"Who you think really provokes this revolution, Ahmstairr?"

"Benack is not the only one. There are others."

"Do they ever have political meetings? Do they have contact with outside?"

I told them I had no such knowledge, and doubted it.

"Benack. He ever mention CIA to you?"

I guess I tried not to roll my eyes. "Never."

"Never before your arrest, before you came here?"

I hated that absurd subject. I'd hated it with Aleshkoi. There was no way I could satisfy him that it was a useless direction. Furthermore, it offered me no way to turn the conversation in directions that would serve me. Finally *he* turned it around:

"Very good you stay out of *bund*." I was struck by that German word. "If you try to calm down men, calm down Benack, Lean, the Englishmen, we will consider all when comes time to consider early release for you." He leaned back, relaxing the tone of his face. "You like to read, Ahmstairr?"

"Yes."

"What writers you like to read?"

"I really only know American writers."

"Yes, American writers. Who you like?"

I had to say somebody. "Ernest Hemingway."

"Ah yes, Hemingway. In university, I read many American writers. In Russian, of course. Hemingway very interesting, very strong."

A couple of weeks later I was called to headquarters again. This time Svelkov slid two items across the table: his pack of cigarettes and a paperback copy of *For Whom the Bell Tolls*.

"About struggle of antifascists in Spain," he explained.

The conversation didn't go deeper than the previous time, but the friendliness grew easier.

Next meeting he brought me *The Old Man and the Sea*, and two books by Theodore Dreiser. I hoped he wouldn't ask me about

149

Dreiser, because I'd never read him, but during the ensuing days I fell in love with his writing. I learned from Svelkov that every Soviet citizen knows of Dreiser, that every student reads him. Another American I'd scarcely heard of, Jack London, is a Western god in the Soviet Union. London railed wordily against American capitalism, but he told good, dark, moody stories, too.

This time Svelkov led me in new directions.

"In America, in university where you *pedagog*, true many students drug addicts?"

Students are rarely addicts, I told him. I gave him the most accurate description I could of the prevalence and use of drugs in schools, and among youth in general.

"True you buy drugs on streetcorner?"

I told him that that had been asked in my trial, and how mistaken the assumption was, for the most part. Again I tried to give him an accurate description of the realities of drug distribution. As I talked, I thought of my last week in New York, just before going to Amsterdam. Visiting a friend in a swanky high-rise apartment on Manhattan's Upper East Side, I had said to myself that there was at least one apartment in every building—maybe one on every floor—that had at least a few specks of cocaine stashed away.

On second thought, I now said to myself, maybe there's not a seller on every corner, but there are consumers on every block. Is that so different? I said nothing of this to Svelkov.

He appeared absorbed, yet frustrated that I was not confirming the pictures in his mind. He changed the subject again.

"Your confinement in Soviet Union, how you compare with confinement in United States? You get fair treatment in Soviet Union?"

"I told you that the prison diet has cost me my health, but that's because it's unfamiliar. We are treated as well as Soviet prisoners, so in that sense it is fair. I realize my crime was serious, so the punishment is serious."

"Where you prefer confinement, in United States or Soviet Union?"

What was he getting at? What was the right answer to help my case? "I would rather it be in the Soviet Union, if there's not much more time to go. In America, I'd be in a jail cell. Camp is better. But if I have to stay here for my full eight years, I'd rather do it in the United States. The food is more familiar, and they give more, and my family and friends could visit me." Then I was sure to add: "But don't get me wrong. For people born and brought up in the Soviet Union, used to your food, this system is much better."

I was satisfied that my impromptu reply was positive enough, yet critical enough to make me credible.

But he was already somewhere else. "In your camp you have many Chinese. Of Chinese, how many spies?"

That knocked me off balance. "Why ask me? You arrested them."

"You must know even one."

"I always heard that when someone is arrested for spying, you put him somewhere else, in a prison."

"*Da, da*—yes, yes. But no, no, not mean that. Many Chinese in camp here for contraband, for illegal border crossing. Do they pass letters to outside?"

"I—" I threw up my hands.

"They ask many questions about Soviet Union?"

"How would I know? They live by themselves. They talk Chinese to each other, so they don't learn Russian. Anyhow, what do most of *us* know about the Soviet Union?"

At subsequent meetings, Svelkov never let go of the subject. He never seemed satisfied that I wasn't holding something back about the Chinese.

The Chinese were the only foreigners to live in their own barracks, so hung up were the Russians about their traditional enemies. The Russians walled them off—from themselves, from us—then wanted to know about their every move, every thought, and had no way of finding out. I distantly befriended a Chinese here or there who'd learned a little Russian, and got a general picture of who that isolated group was.

Actually they were two groups, in the main. One was of educated

151

Chinese; at least five were doctors who practiced acupuncture. They had listened with eagerness to Radio Moscow's daily shortwave assaults against the Cultural Revolution. In Chinese, they had heard of the great accomplishments of the Soviet Union, the birthplace of Leninism. But they had misconstrued those broadcasts as an invitation, abandoning their practices and their homes, and heading for the better land. At the first town they hit after slipping across a poorly guarded place along the border, they were manacled and charged with illegal crossing and "civilian espionage," a lenient charge that entitled the bearer to incarceration in a labor camp instead of a prison. No matter how they enticed these runaways, it seems the Russians couldn't imagine any Chinese crossing into the Soviet Union, except to spy.

The other group was of the extremely poor from the northernmost villages of China, near the border. They too were drawn by the rumors and broadcasts of a better life, which the Soviets apparently never intended as an invitation, but simply as a boast.

The Chinese are the one exception to the Soviet policy of getting rid of foreign prisoners at the first convenient opportunity. Those hated and feared Chinese, always assumed to be spies, never got out. That is what I consistently heard from old-time, well-traveled prisoners. After their sentences—sometimes three years for illegal crossing, sometimes ten if espionage was added—they were sent to a remote region of the northern reaches of Mongolia called Chutag. The place was too remote to escape from. Anyone trying would die in the snowy mountains. A doctor named Li, who had been there and back, told me that the only dependable supply of food was something called *salo*, a kind of uncooked pig fat, highly salted and very chewy. It's a staple all across the Soviet Union, and was occasionally given to us at 5–1 as a special nutritious treat. I could never eat it. Conserves of fish, even the putrid kind we got at the *magazin*, were a rarity in Chutag. He never saw bread, except small quantities of the black, rocklike stuff.

So the Chinese in Chutag, educated and poor alike, stole or destroyed property or assaulted each other—just to get back to the better Soviet life of prison camp. Many of them succeeded, two, three, four times. In that sense they were recidivists, hardened repeaters.

During most of my sentence, when we had about a hundred foreign prisoners, about forty of them were Chinese. Always they were the largest group in camp.

In one way, the rest of us benefited. The Chinese doctors set up a clandestine practice in acupuncture. In the workshop they secretly made needles. When they practiced, say, in a barracks, either theirs or ours, prisoners would form outposts to watch out for guards. Because the practice was Chinese, a guard detecting it might come down on it hard.

But they probably wouldn't interfere with Li. Word spread of his achievements. He fixed my sciatica, and performed greater miracles on other prisoners. A guard smuggled his wife into an acupuncture treatment by Li, which cured her of a limp. Guards began coming from other camps, sometimes bringing family members. Li never lacked for cigarettes or morsels of attractive food. For my treatments I gave him a pair of nail clippers that the consul got for me from the embassy commissary for ninety-eight cents. It bought Dr. Li's undying devotion.

Li's good works did nothing to diminish the certainty of guards that Mao Tse-tung had dictated a plan for the yellow race to take over the world. Guards assured us repeatedly that the Chinese were just waiting till they got strong enough to overrun the Soviet Union. In the ordinary speech of Russians, Chinese come out not as political rivals, but as devils. I almost never heard Chinese called merely by their Russian name, *Kitaets*. Always they were *Kitaets khitrye*— cunning Chinese. Actually, that was spoken as one word, *kitaets-khitrye*, like damnyankee or dirtynigger or jewbastard.

Other constant one-word epithets on the lips of guards as well as Russian or foreign prisoners were cunningarmenians, fascistbaltics (a one-stop putdown for all Lithuanians, Latvians, Estonians, and Finns), smartassgeorgians (or smartasscircassians, or anyone else from the Caucasus region of the south), and, most frequently of all, filthysouthcentralasians (which, incidentally, was a fairly accurate characterization).

Except for the Chinese, who lived separately, the most numerous national groups in camp were the Azerbaijanis and North Koreans. The Azerbaijanis were Soviet residents, but had no citizenship. Actually they were Iranians who had crossed into Soviet Azerbaijan after the Second World War. The Soviets never sent them back, but also had never given them citizenship. So they're stateless, and their lawbreakers go to the camp for foreigners. These people are very direct. If a man, for example, caught his wife in bed with another man, he wouldn't rant and rave, nor would he apply for a divorce. He would arrange his own, murdering both offenders on the spot. Local custom required it, under the threat of dishonor for the rest of his life. That's probably why we had so many Azerbaijanis.

Our high number of North Koreans was explained by a far different source of violence. The Soviet government contracted with the Korean government to send labor crews, mostly to Khabarovsk, on the mountainous, frigid border of Manchuria. Foods, if shipments got there at all, were canned and preserved. Civilian Soviets refused to go there to work, cutting trees, doing military construction. But Koreans, even poorer than the border Chinese, jumped at the chance for two- and three-year contracts. In the roughhouse world of these labor crews, drinking is almost a necessity for survival. Then someone stabs, someone steals, and he's sent to Mordovia.

The Koreans loathed Americans. Two things we constantly heard from them: "You bombed our houses." "You killed my mother (or my father)." They'd say it in Russian. The Koreans picked fights with Westerners, pulled homemade knives, stole. Practically everybody complained to his consul, and eventually the Koreans were moved out of 5–1 and sent to a camp of their own.

One unusual Korean, named Yong Zan Ho, was a friend of mine. He envied the prosperity of South Korea, and couldn't ask me enough questions about the West. He picked up Russian quite well, and even insisted on learning some English from me, constantly writing down words and asking for definitions. He was an excellent worker, doubling and tripling his *norma*, and kept me supplied with extra food. Our friendship and talks had to be kept more or less secret from his fellow Koreans.

I can't think of Yong without thinking of the war—an actual war—that broke out between the Koreans and Azerbaijanis. I guess it was inevitable that the two largest groups would go at each other for domination of the camp, yet when it happened it astounded me.

I was talking with Yong on a hot Sunday afternoon, when suddenly a commotion broke out in front of the next barracks, maybe a hundred feet away. It seemed to be between a Korean and an elderly Azerbaijani. Within seconds, three were fighting three, then thirty were leaping on thirty, roaring, clubbing, climbing all over each other, slamming guys to the ground, kicking them in the face.

Yong was gone—darting into the crowd to join his countrymen. I saw brooms, sticks, clubs, and knives. Almost all Koreans and Azerbaijanis had knives, made in the machine shops and smuggled into the barracks. Often at the end of a day, at the *tsekh*, guards frisked and searched us, but rarely found anything. If they did—the isolator for the offender.

The battle lasted at least a half hour. Instead of breaking up the fight, the guards fled to headquarters. An alarm horn seared the air, hailing off-duty guards from town. After enough guards had gathered, a formation of them separated the warriors and ended the fight.

At the *sanchast'* I treated twenty-seven casualties. One Korean's belly was slashed open, but nobody died. And nobody won. Military commissions came to investigate. The KGB came. A prosecutor came. Finally the official hubbub died down. But we had something to talk about for weeks.

One nationality was held in special contempt, although we had none of them as prisoners in 5–1. They were the Mordovians. Any time Lieutenant Ramashin—a true and typical Mordovian—strolled by, someone was sure to mutter, as though no one else had ever heard it, "Tsar Nicholas told best truth about Mordovians. Twenty Mordovians equal one Russian dog." If any prisoner, foreigner or Russian, made the faintest verbal slap at Mordovia, even about its weather, someone was sure to ask, "You know what Tsar Nicholas said about Mordovians?"

Svelkov's curiosity about the Chinese was something I could do nothing to satisfy. One day, after one of his futile attempts to pump me about them, he sprang a surprising question.

"How you like, Ahmstairr, to stay in Soviet Union?"

"How can I possibly like it? I'm in a prison camp."

"No, no. I mean after sentence."

Twice before, a question like that was put to me, and I didn't know what to make of it either time. In the hospital camp, a dentist once asked me if I'd like to stay after my sentence. I thought he was just making conversation, a sort of comparative study in international living. Then he said he knew people he could talk to about it. I felt certain he was KGB, or had been asked by the KGB to ask me. A short time later a psychiatrist at Butyrka Prison in Moscow asked the same question, but was far more pushy about it—as though he was uncomfortable with the line of questioning, but had to ask me. "You can stay, you can stay," he said impatiently. "Don't worry, you get good money. Don't worry about crime you committed. Foreigner can commit crime, is all right, you not Soviet citizen when you committed crime."

And now Svelkov.

"In another year, I'll have completed my half-sentence. I'll be eligible for clemency. I miss my home."

Would he repeat the promises I'd heard so often about amnesties, about foreigners not staying long? Not quite. But what he did say caught my attention.

"I cannot give promise, but I think if you decide to stay in Soviet Union, then no need to hold you in camp. Perhaps sentence finish quickly."

I said I'd think about it, but knew I wouldn't, not seriously. If I'd known at that time, however, that there was no early release ahead of me, I might have been seriously tempted. At least I wouldn't have been hungry every day. I could have found girl friends and

156

taken them to bed. Freedom is freedom, even if it's in the Soviet Union. Sure, I'd miss the comfort and familiarity of America, but that might be a fair price for getting out of six more years of confinement.

Next time Svelkov brought it up, I stalled by saying that I'd have trouble adjusting to so different a language.

He waved that away. "Language, you learn. New place, you learn. We not send you to far place. You live in important city, with culture, with books, with intellectuals like yourself."

I couldn't imagine they'd let me live in Moscow or Leningrad; they wouldn't want me to mingle with Westerners, except for their purposes. They wouldn't want me to be able to call an American consul, maybe arrange a rendezvous, and get smuggled into the embassy for political asylum. They'd probably keep me in a city closed to Western visitors, like Gorki or Rybinsk

"If you want to stay in Soviet Union," he said at still another meeting, "we find you nice apartment, perhaps you teach English, you get nice *stipendiia*."

"How much, do you think?"

He lifted his eyebrows and lowered his lids in the characteristic Russian way of shrugging off an imponderable. "Maybe hundred fifty, two hundred rubles in month."

That would be about double the wage of a Russian worker, probably the salary of a legit college professor.

"You have plenty of people to teach English."

"You are born American. Very useful to have people sound born American."

Of course. That must be a need of theirs. But for what? Did they want me for a Tokyo Rose? For shortwave news broadcasts to America? Or just to be a translator? Maybe I could get the Gorki franchise for Berlitz.

Svelkov's seductiveness on this subject fascinated me and, at the same time, scared me. It could lead me into an awful trap.

As matters turned out, that line of conversation didn't lead anywhere.

12

TOURING AMERICA

My little pair of ulcers, one peptic, one duodenal, as well as other ailments, caused me to spend roughly half my time in the hospital camp, fraternizing with Russians. Hospital life for me, however, was not the experience of deprivation it was for most others. Whenever I returned to camp, the guard checking me in would look confounded.

"Ahmstairr," one of those Mordovians finally spluttered on one of my arrivals home, "from where you get all this? Everybody else goes to hospital carrying big bag and comes back with nothing. You go with nothing and you come back rich. What you do there?"

His question was rhetorical, of course. He didn't expect I'd blurt out voluntarily whatever my sweet racket was, and I think I imagined some of the things he probably imagined. But none of his imaginings could have approached the reality.

Yes, I'd fallen into a racket, all right, that made me both rich and slightly ashamed. You might say it was a form of show business.

I was putting on travelogues. About America.

On the very first evening of my first hospital visit I began to realize my potential as a tourist attraction, but even more as a circus freak. Any foreigner from Camp 5–1 amused hospital inmates. A foreigner broke the monotony. If nothing else, he was someone to jeer at and mimic and taunt.

But an American? Here, in a prison camp? Most of them had never seen an American. They couldn't believe the miracle of their luck. These guys didn't know what to do with me, make of me, ask me. Finally one little guy with big boils on his chin cracked the ice of speechless curiosity:

"Tell me, how many murders in one day in New York?"

I guessed as best I could: "Four or five."

Some of those toughs thumped their asses down on their mattresses, dumbfounded. Others slapped their palms to their cheeks, pivoting their heads from side to side, emitting the tragic whimpers heard from grandmothers in babushkas.

"Is true Constitution of America says anybody can carry gun in pants?"

"Is true you can buy gun in any store?"

Sort of true, I indicated, trying to clarify the fine points of the guaranteed right to bear arms, within the limits of my command of Russian.

"How much costs kilo margarine in America?"

"How much costs car in America?"

"Is true in America worker owns car?"

Yes, sometimes two.

They couldn't believe, but tentatively they let themselves believe, because it sounded so unbelievable.

"How much worker get in America?"

"Oh, maybe two hundred fifty rubles a week." This was 1976. "Different work, different pay."

"A-mer-i-ca," one tough intoned reverently. "Two hundred fifty."

"What work you do in America?"

"*Pedagog.* I teach languages."

I figured I'd better tell them that, even though I hadn't taught in several years, because that's what I'd told Aleshkoi and testified at the trial.

"*Pedagog*," one said with surprised awe. "In university."

I sort of nodded, not saying yes or no. Why trouble them by explaining the indefinable position in academia of Berlitz?

"If you are *pedagog*, why you carry contraband for drug gang?"

Aleshkoi had asked me exactly the same question and wouldn't get off it. So had the puzzled guards in my labor camp. A professor of languages has a high and well-rewarded status in the Soviet Union. While those others remained suspicious that I was a CIA agent, these prisoners had no trouble understanding my reply:

"I could always use more money."

Many of the guys around me were there for the simple act of trying to get more money, through the only channel that could promise any. The most severely—and, it seemed, the most frequently—punished crimes in the Soviet Union are not crimes against persons, not violence, but economic crimes against the state. That fact helped explain to me the fascination of these guys with America. Prisoners I met who committed economic crimes were the types who tended to be rebellious and antiestablishment. They were the ones who felt most oppressed and deprived by their system, the ones who had a taste for an occasional schnapps or French cognac, for puffing an American cigarette. There was no way they could get those luxuries by moonlighting as a cab driver or store clerk or starting a spare-time mail-order business. The only way was to do something shady.

The favorite means was *valiuta*: trading privately in foreign currencies, particularly American dollars, which is illegal and severely punishable.

Russians seek to buy dollars with Soviet rubles for two main reasons. First, in Moscow and other cities open to tourists, at airports, at resorts, special goods not for sale to ordinary Soviet citizens can be purchased by tourists with dollars: rare caviars, unusual textiles, objects of art and craftsmanship. The special locations where these items are for sale are nicknamed *valiuta* stores. The reason for these stores is that the Soviet government is always in desperate need of dollars (or the equivalent in other Western currencies) for foreign

160

trade. Russians, of course, take a certain risk in buying at the *valiuta* stores, since they supposedly have no source of dollars. But they buy at them anyway.

The second reason Russians want dollars is that many of them do go abroad, as exchange scholars, as members of trade delegations, on artistic tours. Their allowance of dollars to spend overseas barely pays for their rooms and meals. But if, before leaving, they can buy extra dollars with rubles, they can then buy Western clothes, transistor radios, records, whatever. In Moscow, the value of the ruble is artificially pegged at about one dollar. In the money markets of the West, however, a dollar costs about four rubles. Thus, there is tremendous advantage in buying extra dollars before leaving Moscow. The only way to do so, of course, is from a black-market dealer in currency.

One night, conversation in one of my seminars about America took a new direction—and so did my fortunes. A muscular guy, tattooed to the armpits, said, "Ahmstairr, tell about *publichnye doma.*"

Whorehouses (I was struck that these toughs used the euphemism "public houses") do not exist in the Soviet Union. That's absolutely official, because prostitution is against the law. But unhoused prostitutes roam in every sizable city, especially Moscow, available to every social class. I heard about it from all kinds of Russians, from underworld incorrigibles to educated *valiuta* manipulators.

In the dining rooms of any tourist hotel, in the streets, on park benches, hookers hook. Of course, under socialism their private enterprise works differently. For one thing, prices are lower than in leading Western capitals, simply because hardly anyone has enough to pay high ones. In fact, a money payment is not always expected. A hooker in a hotel dining room will often just sit at the table of a male stranger—when no tables are vacant, that's more or less an acceptable practice—and start an acquaintanceship that can lead to an invitation for dinner with wine and a few turns around the dance floor. In exchange for a high old time, the woman is expected to agree to a trip upstairs.

Prostitution is sometimes a full-time occupation, but that involves major risks for both parties. Every Soviet citizen must carry an internal passport, which must always be up to date as to the citizen's place of employment. A woman can arrange a life of leisure by getting a highly placed foreman or factory manager to inscribe and stamp her passport. She puts out, he stamps. It's a sweet arrangement, until they're caught and sent away for parasitism, a serious crime against the state.

Without fail these guys would ask, "True that prostitution legal in America?"

I told them it was in certain places, like Las Vegas, a great center of gambling out west. I didn't see any point in splitting hairs about Sherry's Ranch actually being in another county of Nevada that they'd never heard of, or in emphasizing that it's the only county in all of America that licenses whorehouses.

They wanted to know how a man picks his girl of the evening, how old the girls are, at what age an American girl—not a prostitute—begins to fuck. (In different seminars I answered with different ages. No matter what age I said, the audience responded with open-mouthed astonishment.)

After the first of these travelogues, a tattooed tough asked, "Ahmstairr, *kurit' nado?* You need smokes?"

He tossed something toward me. What landed on my bed was not a cigarette, but a whole unopened pack. Russian Marlboros, the name licensed by the American manufacturer, but actually made in Moscow from a harsh Soviet mixture. It was an impressive—and expensive—gift, costing about a ruble and a half.

Next night he came by with a friend, also tattooed, from another ward. The friend, with a gooey smile, asked, "Ahmstairr, *chai* and *konfeta?* Tea and a sweet?"

I knew what he wanted. The sweet would be one of those sourballs. But what the hell, it was sugar, and that was food. I nodded and waited a few seconds till he began asking about America. And Nevada. And the legal whorehouse. And what they'll do for how much.

Later I learned through a couple of prisoners that the KGB had inquired about my "political lectures" on American life. But the investigators apparently decided that I was no threat to the stability of socialism. As long as the lectures covered whorehouses and drugs and murders and gunplay, I was feeding their notion of American capitalist decadence.

In a way, the seminars fascinated me as much as they fascinated my audience. I never got over how their faces froze in wonderment beneath a thin film of sweat, and afterward, their unfailing ability to come up with a payoff. Maybe just a tin of that horrid fish conserve, but sometimes a tin of real fish, sometimes preserved beef, which I hadn't tasted since my arrest. Sometimes, incredibly, a chunk of halvah.

The riches thrilled me. And a strange sorrow rose from my belly every time. They wanted me to tell them about America's prostitutes, and I would. And every time I did it, I got the feeling I was working at Sherry's Ranch. The customers just had to dangle the price, and I'd put out.

But I listened to my ulcers. They said loud and clear, "You want food? Play to the guys with tattoos."

I soon learned to spice up the show to give the tattooed more of what they wanted.

For a while, but not for too long, I wondered how some of these tattooed guys had so much that they could give it away for entertainment, while the other prisoners were as hungry as I'd been. Soon I realized I'd become jester to the prison's ruling class. They ruled not only the society of prisoners, but to a great extent their guards as well.

In the Soviet Union, they are called *blatnye*.

THE LAND OF BLATNYE

Neither English nor any of the European languages I've learned has a word that means the same as *blatnoi*.

Blatnoi is the name of a peculiarly Soviet lifestyle of super-machismo. It streaks, like the grain found in granite, throughout the lower-class layers of the classless Soviet society.

Blatnoi is tough. But not John Wayne or Arnold Schwarzenegger tough. It's more like Mr. T or Hell's Angels tough. Compared to the *blatnye*, however, Mr. T is suave and Hell's Angels are organized and disciplined.

When he's not incarcerated, a *blatnoi* usually works at something outdoors and menial, whether on a farm or in a city. He gets along on relatively low wages and cheap vodka. His status, the only wealth he's likely to know, comes mostly from bullying his wife, his kids, his co-workers, his dog, the boys at the tavern.

In a prison camp, however, a *blatnoi* flourishes. He's not only the richest but the most respected guy in town. Those he bullies include the guards. From experience, guards know that if a *blatnoi* owns an illicit knife, and he usually does, he'll stab when he's frustrated. Guards also know that, without haggling, he'll pay for a

164

privilege he wants. That means if anything is smugglable into camp—
tins of good fish or meat, coffee or tea, halvah, and maybe even
chocolate—the *blatnoi* is the guy least likely to be prevented from
smuggling it.

One evening I entered the bathroom of my hospital ward and a
burly Russian, standing in front of the door at the first stall, barred
my way. I'd seen this guy around. In my travelogue audiences, he
sat silent and gruff. He was the only man I'd ever seen with tattooed
toes.

"Not now, come back," he growled. Then he called after me,
gentler, as to a friend. "Here, stay, American. You watch. You
enjoy."

"No, thanks, I'll be back."

"Come, American, you watch. You enjoy."

I took a look, and saw what I knew I'd see. One of my most
faithful *blatnoi* travelogue patrons, his back turned to us, was standing in the stall with his pants down. On his left buttock he wore a
startling tattoo, a crude profile of Lenin; on his right one, a portrait
of Stalin. In front of him a smaller man I couldn't identify, also
with his pants down, stooped compliantly, whimpering childishly
and rhythmically, palms pressing into the wall.

After a few moments of wheezy grunting and floppy hip-
pumping, the *blatnoi* in the stall sweatily got his rocks off.

It was now the lookout's turn, but with a gentlemanliness that
gave me the creeps he asked, "You want try, American?"

"No, no, thanks."

"You try. You enjoy. I wait." He giggled.

"No, not my glass of *chai*."

He patted my shoulder understandingly, furnishing my cue to
get the hell out of there.

Another time, late at night, I lay awake in the dark in a ward
of surgical patients. A *blatnoi* hobbled in on crutches, stopped at a
bed opposite mine, and banged the frame with his crutch.

"*Chto, poidëm.* Hey, you, let's go."

165

The sleeper moaned a protest, like a child not wanting to get up for school, begging to stay with a dream.

"*Ëb tvoiu mat'*, let's go!"

Somehow lifting himself to face his inescapable duty, the sleeper plodded ahead of his oppressor to the bathroom.

Scarcely fifteen minutes after the wretch had returned to bed, another intruder roused him gruffly and ordered him up. Later, still another. I watched the procession for half the night, and the next night, until I was transferred back to my camp.

This was new. In my own camp for foreigners, I'd never seen enforced pederasty. For one thing, the elite KGB, in charge of foreigners, wouldn't permit it. Besides, in Camp 5–1 we didn't have *blatnye*, a purely Soviet phenomenon, although we had other kinds of equally tough toughs. Anyhow, our numbers, usually about a hundred foreign inmates, were too small to produce an active community of pederasts. A hospital camp accommodated about five hundred, enough to turn up about twenty abusers to enforce a system against two, maybe three victims.

Always the victimizers were *blatnye*.

I say "victimizers" and "victims" because prison pederasty is not homosexuality in any sense of mutual love or enjoyment or, for that matter, genuine consent. The *blatnye* distinguishes as a category the *natural'nyi* pederast, as though respecting the turf of a homosexual by choice. That fellow, left to his own lovers, is not to be raped.

Also, there are occasional pederasts who present themselves for pay, who are held in at least as much contempt by their patrons as the victim or enslaved pederast, who is far more common. The enslaved pederast submits simply as an alternative to having all his bones broken.

In American and most Western prisons, the male rape victim is usually young, lean, and blond. The Soviet *blatnoi* couldn't care less about the prettiness of his sex object. The victim could be the Hunchback of Notre Dame. All that's wanted of him is an aperture.

A sentence to pederasty is a punishment meted out for specific cause: violating the prisoner's code. The two most common violations are stealing from a prisoner's *tumbochka* and failing to pay up after losing at cards. (Cards, and therefore cardplaying, are illegal. The men make cards out of used X-ray film, available in a lively black market from prisoners holding certain hospital jobs.)

The pederast victim is doomed to his enforced servitude for the remainder of his labor camp sentence, even if it's a full fifteen years. But that is not his only punishment. As an object of disgust, he may not eat in the mess hall in the presence of other prisoners. He must wash his metal eating bowl in the bathroom and keep it in his *tumbochka* so it will never come in contact with the bowls of others. In the food service line, the pederast must stand last. If the food runs out, which it often does, he gets none. The server must watch out, too. When he spoons out to the pederast, he must take care that his ladle does not touch the untouchable's bowl. If it does, the server is mandatorily punished with a severe beating, a civic responsibility usually shouldered by the *blatnye*.

The code of treatment of pederasts is observed with full knowledge and approval of the guards, who share the victimizers' contempt for the victims.

The laws banning tattoos in the Soviet Union are about as fuzzy as those on growing marijuana in Amsterdam. The tattoo artist violates the law, but the wearer of a tattoo does not.

While the tattoo is the badge of the *blatnoi*, it is sported by aspiring fringe elements of the lower classes. At one of my four visits a year with the American consul, always witnessed by a militia officer, we were joined by a Soviet lieutenant colonel. It was summer, and the officer rolled up his shirtsleeves. His forearm was emblazoned with an ineradicable tattoo. Somewhere, before he rose from his vulgar origins, he had harbored a dream of growing up *blatnoi*.

Among the lowest and most defiant *blatnoi* types, I've seen guys with tattooed eyelids. The right eyelid would say IA RAB, and the left K P S S. Most of the time, of course, the message is invisible because the eyes are open. But when the guy demurely flutters his

167

eyes closed, what it says, left to right, in abbreviated form, is "I am slave [of] Communist Party Soviet Union."

The dedicated anti-Communist who's holding his breath waiting for the overthrow of Soviet tyranny would be making a mistake to count this rebel among world-class political dissidents. What this *blatnoi* with the defiant lampshades is trying to say, to his government or to anyone else who crowds him, is not a message of revolution, but more simply, "Fuck you."

I once got up the nerve to ask one of those eyelids guys how he stood the pain of the tattoo needle. The guy blinked a time or two, and confided, "I don't remember. Vodka."

A guard spotting a case of politicized eyelids is obliged to send their owner to the hospital's resident tattooer (more accurately, the un-tattooer). Un-tattooing the poor guy's eyelids is more painful than the original tattooing, and is done without benefit of vodka.

You can also spot a *blatnoi* by the way he coughs. *Blatnye* prisoners tend to be recidivists, and the years of poor food and exposure to damp cold in labor-camp barracks gives them *tuberkulëz*. Next to ulcers, tuberculosis is the most widespread disease in hospital camp. I don't recall ever seeing a TB patient who wasn't *blatnoi*.

To me, the most disconcerting mark of a *blatnoi* was a mouthful of steel teeth. Civilian dentists in the Soviet Union offer the option of inexpensive steel instead of gold for false teeth, but few people try to save money that way. Sometimes a prisoner reveals a rivet here or there when he smiles. But when you see a mouth that's *all* steel, you know it belongs to an old-time prison repeater, therefore a *blatnoi*. Prison dentists rarely use anything but steel.

There's still another, and most unforgettable, way to identify a *blatnoi*. He wears *sharik*, or beads. What he wears, actually, are not beads, but small metal ball bearings, and he doesn't wear them around his neck. They encircle the head of his penis. In an illegal operation, for which a black market thrives, a doctor cuts four or five slits around the circumference of the *blatnoi*'s foreskin. When the light bleeding stops, the doctor inserts the ball bearings into the slits and bandages the wounded member until it heals, leaving the metal beads permanently implanted. The *blatnoi* believes a studded penis makes him sexually irresistible. His wife would have to be nuts to leave him, and he can count thereafter on driving any girlfriend into volcanic heaves of ecstasy.

While *sharik* usually identifies a *blatnoi*, it is not a sure-fire test. For example, Volodia, my cellmate at Lefortovo, with great pride displayed his beaded dick to me, and was the first to tell me of its powers. Now Volodia, convicted of *valiuta*, was far from *blatnoi*. White-collar criminals are never *blatnoi*, and the *blatnye* do not practice white-collar crime.

Weird and kinky as they may seem, *blatnoi* types kept surprising me. In Camp 5–1, where of course we had no Russians, the nearest thing we had to *blatnoi* types were Greeks, about fifteen of them. These were Soviet Greeks, born in the Soviet Union of Greek parents who had fled their native land after the Germans occupied it. They are considered stateless: *bez grazhdanstva*, which literally means "without citizenship." When these young flagless Greeks committed crimes, they were usually thrown for long sentences among us foreigners.

One night, through word and gesture, these supermacho Greeks questioned me about drinking in America; then one of them asked about drugs. Actually he mimicked shooting himself in the arm, sniffing powder off his knuckles, and pretended a dizzy, floating head. He asked if I'd done any of that.

Clearly, I had to reply as a tough if I was to hold their respect. I answered, *"Da."*

Their faces wrenched with disgust and disapproval. A couple of them mimed retching. For weeks I sensed their distaste. I became the Ugly American, an untouchable. Finally the contempt wore off.

I could never get clear as to where these toughs drew their lines.

"Ahmstairr," a feverishly curious *blatnoi* asked during one of my early travelogues, "is true American girls take cock to mouth?"

What did they want this time, the prim answer or the true one? Many do, I said.

Shock. That grandmotherly headshaking of incredulity.

169

"Men take *pizda*, cunt, to mouth?"
Many do.
Uch, uch. Unbelievable.

After observing *blatnoi* abuse of pederasts, I wondered what served a comparable purpose for the foreign toughs who lorded their way around 5–1. One day I found out, near the *tsekh*, our camp factory.

Every day at noon, what passed for lunch was brought to the *tsekh* from the barracks zone, where the kitchen was. The food was hauled in a rickety wagon, which, in turn, was dragged by a decrepit mare. People who served the food had to unload it, set it up, and serve it. The men ate, then the servers cleaned up and reloaded the wagon. All this was accomplished in a half-hour break. During that half hour the old gray mare was humanely permitted to stroll free with her empty wagon in a pasture behind the *tsekh*, out of sight of the munching crowd.

One day, I can't remember why, I strolled back there myself. The question that had floated idly through my mind was suddenly answered.

Several Greeks, two Bulgarians, and a Mongolian were taking turns fucking the horse.

The wagon had a small, low platform for the driver's feet. These guys mounted that little platform, opened their pants, each revealing a surprising erection, and inserted it into—actually, I wasn't sure then, and still am not today, as to just what a female horse has where.

The next day my surprise was transformed to curiosity. I strolled again in that direction, just far enough to get a peek without being seen.

The very same cast of characters was fucking the horse.

Every day the scene was repeated. Neither their appetites nor their erections ever diminished.

Guards knew about it. I could tell by the way they made a point of never strolling or looking in that direction. One day the commandant of the camp walked by that pasture toward the *tsekh* in

170

midday. He cut an angle to the right, then back toward the left, so he could come our way without seeing what he obviously knew was there to be seen.

I mentioned earlier that only a small percentage of the prisoners, the hard-core *blatnye* and the toughest of the foreign toughs, indulged in these exotica. Most prisoners were, in most ways, fairly normal guys. Many had wives and kids; many others had girlfriends. The Soviet labor-camp system permits family visits of three days several times a year—actually, conjugal visits—for all except the most hardened criminals condemned to the *osobye* regime. The *strogii* regime, a more severe one than mine, permitted two visits a year. Mine, *usilennyi*, allowed three. The softest regime, *obschii*, permitted four a year.

The local Hilton and the honeymoon suites for these visits were two rooms (with two single beds each) in the *vakhta*, the barracks of the militia who guard the periphery of the camp and who transport prisoners to other points. They are the VV, the Vnutrennaia Voiska, Soviet internal troops. The small building also houses the controls for the camp's entire electrical system, including the juice for the barbed wire fences.

While offering no bath or shower, a room has a hot plate and visiting relatives are permitted to bring food.

Children may come, but when only one room is available the whole family must share it. The parents must turn the kids loose outside and hope they stay outside while father and mother try to make up for their lost private time. The doors have no locks.

To arrange permission for a visit by a girlfriend, an unmarried prisoner simply has to state that he and the woman cohabited as civilians.

Some unmarried prisoners opt for an even better deal than that. A lot of men acquire pen pals—friends or sisters of other guys' girlfriends and wives. They exchange photos and become, over a period of time, what one might call devoted. Sometimes a woman embarks for camp not only to visit, but to marry a prisoner—before they have ever met. It can be a very good deal for both parties. He gets the visits, the food, and the sex. She gets an allotment of half his prison earnings, an amount that will not be paid to him until his release. The usual salary when I was there was seventy rubles a month. Half of that was deducted by the MVD for the prisoner's upkeep, leaving thirty-five rubles for his future—or to be sent to his wife. If he has a short sentence, a single man is not that interested in denying himself for so small a kitty. If he's in for ten or fifteen years, he doesn't give a damn about his long-term future. He wants his loving here and now. So by marrying, even sight unseen, both parties come out big winners.

14

ISOLATOR AND
PSYCHO-ISOLATOR

If people had been telling me the truth, I should have been out of Mordovia, out of the Soviet Union, in a year, no later than October of 1977. Everyone had said it without doubt: the American embassy people, the KGB, my cellmate in Lefortovo, the MVD officer Ramashin, all the other guards, practically every foreign prisoner I'd ever met in Camp 5–1, and every Russian prisoner at the hospital. So certain were their predictions, I took them as promises.

But here it was the beginning of January 1979, and no sign of a *pomilovka*, that precious piece of paper telling my keepers to let me go and send me home. Every time I met with the American consul, I asked about clemency, amnesty. The consular officers kept changing, but their helpless shrugs remained the same. All they could do, they said, was to insure that treatment of me conformed to international covenants.

At one such visit the consul said that my aunt in New York could write to ask for clemency under Article Such-and-Such. I asked the consul to notify her how to do it. They did. She wrote. Weeks later, she got a reply from the Soviet government: No. Reason:

the seriousness of my offense, and not enough time had yet been served.

The real reason was not my crime or my time served or anything to do with me. The reason was a rising heap of quarrels between my President, Jimmy Carter, and their Chairman, Leonid Brezhnev. Crowning the heap was the Soviets' invasion of Afghanistan and, in retaliation, President Carter's announced boycott of the 1980 Olympics in Moscow. Those events, which in the past would not have interested me beyond the headlines, controlled my life.

If only the United States would arrest a Soviet spy or two, perhaps I could be traded for him or her, or them. But would Washington give up a juicy Soviet spy for a slightly used contrabandist? I didn't know. I just knew that everyone had promised I'd get out, and I was still there.

I had written to President Gerald Ford, appealing to him to do whatever he could to get me out. I had received no answer. Then, at the suggestion of the consul, I wrote a letter to President Carter. I waited and hoped.

If I had known for sure that I'd have to serve every day of my eight-year term, maybe somehow I'd have braced myself to survive it. If I had known my *pomilovka* would arrive at some specific date, my keepers could have put me through any kind of ordeal, even torture, and I'd have survived until then. But this uncertainty was driving me crazy. Sometimes I wished I had never heard all those delicious promises of amnesty, of clemency, of the Russian policy of not wanting foreign prisoners to hang around.

When I say it was driving me crazy, I mean that literally, in a way. When I'm really cornered, I feel a powerful drive to act insane as a way of making people give me what I want. When I was a little kid and my parents were separated, I found that acting outrageously made my mother throw up her hands. She'd turn me over to my grandfather, who'd comfort me and want to give me the world. After my parents got back together and drove me crazier than ever, hanging out that window got their attention as I'd never had it before, got their sympathy, even got my father to drop everything and drive me to a hospital where that shrink with the soothing voice listened to me for hours on end.

I had to do something crazy to get out of that camp. I don't think I planned it in the sense of thinking it through. It was a compulsion that came more from my bones than my brain.

Before daybreak on a cold January morning in 1979, I leaped out of bed, shouting at the top of my lungs, and ran out of the barracks towards the *shtab*, the guards' headquarters. Except for head count, we practically never saw guards around the barracks. If you were going to rouse them with craziness, you had to give them curb service.

"I saw him! I saw him! He had a knife! I saw him!"

"What, what? Who you saw?" It was Ramashin, on night duty, coat and shirt opened, hair askew, clearly roused out of sleep.

"At my window, knocking on my window. He had a knife in his teeth!"

"Who? Who?"

"I don't know. Kennett. It looked like Kennett."

I don't know why Kennett, the young English smuggler in his twenties, came to my tongue, except that I hated Kennett. Kennett had helped stir that protest over having to work on Christmas day. Because I had refused to take part, Kennett began turning everyone he could against me.

Instantly I realized the guards could check out Kennett right now, find him in his bed fast asleep, probably snoring with his Beatles accent. That was okay. I'd look all the crazier.

Sure enough, Ramashin roused another sleepy guard to go check on Kennett. When he returned, Ramashin stared at me, puzzled, suspicious, trying to make sense of this. He kept asking, and I kept insisting I had seen some guy at my window with a knife in his teeth.

The commandant of the camp ordered me to the camp isolator for fifteen days, the maximum sentence. The only prisoners who stayed longer were those they really wanted to break. A prisoner

175

considered too dangerous to have contact with the others—perhaps someone who seriously assaulted or killed another inmate—might spend his whole sentence in the isolator. A fifteen-day prisoner got one bowl of soup and one piece of bread every two days. Those on long-term isolation were fed every day so they wouldn't starve.

The isolator looked like a one-story barracks, except its windows were barred. On either side of a corridor was a row of metal doors, each one sealing an isolation room. Inside each of those doors was a barred door. The outside wall admitted a vague light through a small one-way window. The prisoner couldn't see out, but someone outside could see in. A tiny, eerie, mesh-covered electric bulb dangled from the high ceiling. The room was bare. No chair, no bed, no floor mattress, nothing. Nothing, that is, except a squat, tarnished milk can with a hinged lid. The lid was a nice touch, but didn't do much good, for a sickening stench overwhelmed the room, hitting me like a collision with a wall.

Talking from one room to another, besides being futile, was absolutely forbidden. The total quiet, the absolute nothingness, filled my ears, filled the room, enveloped the stench, stretched minutes into hours that had no beginning or end, days into years that had no number or measure. The silence made my throat go dry. I'd reach for a *makhorka* cigarette, and of course had none. On arrival, the *zavkhoz*, a sort of trusty in charge of the building and the prisoners in it, had stripped me of my clothes, of anything I had. He took my shoes, my socks, giving me just a loose top and loose pants of coarse cotton to wear in the freezing room. A heating pipe about an inch in diameter ran through the room, but the heat was turned off much of the time. When addressed by a guard, a prisoner usually had to clutch the sides of his pants to hold them up. They were never the right size, and belts were forbidden, of course, as potential suicide instruments.

In the silence, any sound filled all space, all awareness. It gripped and consumed all the senses. Through the blindness of the solid door I heard a soft, slow, rhythmic creeping, a wheezy, scraping snore that terrified me. I put my ear to the door to make it out,

176

fighting my urge to shrink back. Then it moved away. Next day I heard it again. Then the next day. Each day more mysterious and fearful. On the fourth day the sliding slat in my door was open when the weird wheezing came again.

It was the *zavkhoz*, mopping the floor.

Each day did have two exciting social events: the morning and evening head count by the commandant. A guard escorting him slid open the door slat, and sometimes opened the door. They stood back to avoid the cloud of stench.

"Aha, a live one!" the commandant muttered every day, every visit, at every door. Then he asked, *"Pretenzii est'?* Any complaints?" Not an idle question, but avoidance of trouble with consuls of foreign governments.

Regardless of what the prisoner said, the commandant replied, "All right." Nobody could accuse him of not hearing out the prisoner's complaint.

Actually, there was one other big event: the commotion in the corridor at about ten o'clock at night, when a guard came to open the door of each long-termer, so the prisoner could go a few feet down the hall to the *sklad*, the storeroom, to fetch a thin mattress. The guard then reached high on the wall of the prisoner's room, turned a lock, and pulled down a Soviet version of a Murphy bed.

We short-termers had no bed at all, and were not permitted to lie down on the cold, clammy floor until ten o'clock. That made ten o'clock a big event. Even though the floor offered no rest, at least something changed.

Some prisoners passed part of the day doing calisthenics. I walked, pacing back and forth, to the degree I could in a room about five feet long and four and one-half feet wide, about a pace and a half each way, back and forth, diagonally, this way, that way. That was all I did. That was all I *could* do.

In a few minutes I always returned to what I'd been doing much of the day: sitting huddled against the wall that was warmest, the corridor side.

Pretty soon, all the sensations became one: the silence, the cold,

177

the dozing on a stony floor, the fitfulness, the wakefulness, the aches and pains of being too long in one position, the endlessness of time, the timelessness. Soon I stopped thinking. I slid along on pure time and emotion.

Then my emotions began living a life of their own. My mind raced, lifting me into a pleasureless high, through a mosaic of flashbacks of when I was free. First I reentered the freedom of life in the camp, among those crude men that I now no longer disliked. I could move among them, talk to them, or walk away. I was a free person among them. I craved their company again.

Then my high took me out further, millions of light years away, into a past that couldn't have existed because it was too good to be true, but which I now remembered more clearly than memory.

I remembered my mother taking me to the park on a Saturday, Eastside Park in Paterson. I was four years old. I didn't know if I knew then that I was four years old, but now with eerie clarity I knew I was four years old. We walked to a big fountain in the middle of the park, and I tried to climb to the rim of the fountain. She tried to hold me back, but I wanted to mount the rim. Then she changed her mind. She let me climb it and, holding my hand, guided me around its entire circumference. I felt grown and serene, of magical capability. I was overjoyed that she trusted me and I felt her pride in me. I felt loved.

Then her hand became my grandfather's, and he was walking me through Palisades Amusement Park. My other hand clutched a great wad of cotton candy, some of it pasted to my lips like sweet glue. I couldn't understand my grandfather not wanting any, but I felt his gladness for me.

My fantasies slid into food, from one food to another. I savored pizzas with crunchy, chewy crusts, heaped with cheese, with anchovies, without anchovies, with juicy pepperoni. I remembered in Milan discovering a topping of fresh garlic and white clam sauce. My mouth filled with the sensations of the Indonesian restaurants of Amsterdam, cubes of chicken blanketed with curry and scoops of cashews. Then all of it washed down in a cool lava flow of chocolate ice cream.

That cool flow in my gullet seeped through my body and I was twelve years old in a swimming pool in New Jersey, and my brother taunted me to climb the diving board. That diving board was three, maybe four times as high as I was tall. My brother, transformed to a threatening monster, grabbed my elbow and yanked me to the ladder. I climbed up and looked down. *I can't jump. That blue pool is too far down, too small, I'll miss it and splatter and be dead.*

"You're up there, jump!" he yelled at me. "Jump, you pussy. Don't you fuckin' come down that ladder!"

More than I couldn't bear to jump, I couldn't bear to be a pussy to my boxer brother, winner of twenty-one out of twenty-one fights, eighteen knockouts. Even though I would lie pancaked, smashed and bloody, I wouldn't have to face his shaming of me. I leaped off the end of the board, the water crashing in my ears.

I hated that name my brother called me, "pussy." I hated it and hated myself when he called me that. I hated my knowledge of what all girls had, because when I thought of it, I'd see my scared and shameful self, my pussy self. When I got older and craved what girls had, I always wanted to get a girl's clothes off, and when she finally stripped and I saw, unless she was a total turn-on for me, I'd turn off. It made me feel my shame.

Then I learned about aphrodisiacs, pills and powders that friends got me, that made wanting a girl feel hot and breathless and sweaty, sometimes so much so that I'd get embarrassed if she noticed. I loved the high, the feverish wanting, even more than making it.

And now, in this swirling stupor, I remembered when I was fourteen years old in the hospital, the week or two after that crazy kid stabbed me because he thought I was fucking Cindy. Four times a day, every four hours when I was awake, they came with a syringe full of painkiller. I heard one nurse tell another I got morphine and Demerol. Soon after the shot I didn't care whether the pain got killed or not, I just wanted that delicious feeling. I wanted it back

179

sooner than four hours, and I'd yell at the nurse that I hurt, I hurt, but she wouldn't let me have it sooner.

And the aphrodisiacs reminded me of that, although the high wasn't the same. Every time I met a girl I wanted her. I could count on it to make me want her. The only thing better that I knew was that surge through my genitals, all through my body, when I hung out that window, when I got my hands on that briefcase of gems, when I made it past the customs man in Moscow, whenever in some way I got away with something—with what felt each time like raping the rules, raping the law. I could count, absolutely count, on that rising tension of needing to come, and then the orgasmic relief and triumph of making it through. Nothing for me could beat that, not even orgasms with women, because I couldn't count on them happening before I turned off, and when they did happen they rarely satisfied whatever it was I so breathlessly anticipated. But beating the rules—if the danger was great enough, that high had never failed me.

Maybe it would be different if I loved the girl. Twice in my life I've almost loved girls deeply, or at least felt I might love them deeply with time. But both times we broke up before we gave ourselves the chance. I don't clearly know what a person means when he says he loves someone deeply. The woman who can make me feel that way hasn't come my way.

Yet out of the swirl of feelings of my isolation, a face broke through those confusions about love. Again I saw the face of my grandfather. This time he was older, really old, ninety-one, and he lay gray and still. I really deeply loved my grandfather.

I got the call in Houston, where I had a job in a mail-order house. This was in 1972. My brother said I'd better come right away, Grandpa was in a hospital. I raced to the airport and arrived at his hospital room door ten minutes too late. The sheet was already over his head.

A young doctor, an intern or resident, told me I shouldn't be in there, but I wouldn't leave. My brother, who's extremely strong, tried to coax me out, then pinned my arms back to pull me out, but I broke free. At any other time he'd have slugged me, but he and the doctor sensed something and left me alone. I lowered the sheet to my grandfather's wrinkled neck. I squeezed his head in the palms of my hands and kissed him on the lips. A flood of tears just flowed out of me.

I was crying for when I was four years old and my mother had to work and my grandfather drove me to nursery school every day and picked me up afterward to drive me home. The day that now came to me, pure and brilliant as one of those morphine highs, was a day it snowed heavily, and after school I looked for his car, and it wasn't there. But then I saw my grandfather waiting for me on the sidewalk, his hand gripping the rope of my sled. He'd dragged it three miles so he could pull me home through the fresh snow.

My tears were not for him, but for myself. I loved him, and now he had deserted me. It was not that I needed him the way I had when I was little, but I still needed him. My mother had been gone for two years. And even my love for her felt more like forgiving her for never having enough time for me. She would have given me more if she had known how. I remembered feeling, hearing myself say to Grandpa's stilled face, "This is it for me and my life. Now there's nobody left in the world for me." I even remember feeling angry at my grandfather as I stood there. What right did he have to leave me all alone like this? Now who was I going to love?

But he left me with something. I knew I'd loved someone.

After ten days of my fifteen-day sentence in the isolator, the commandant, apparently impressed by my predawn "vision" of knife-biting Kennett, ordered me to the hospital. Not to any ordinary part of the hospital, but to Corpus 12, the psycho-isolator, the one place a nonmedical commander can send a prisoner for "diagnosis." The psycho-isolator is related to the camp isolator in name only. The camp isolator is purely for punishment. The psycho-isolator at the hospital purports to serve some sort of therapeutic, or at least diagnostic, function.

I'd heard about the psycho-isolator, which the Russians pronounce *pseeko izolator*, a name clearly adapted from the West. Actually, most guys spoke of it as the *dur dom*. *Dur* means crazy. It's the nuthouse or loony bin. I didn't know much about what happened there. All I knew at the moment was that you were sent to the psycho-isolator for acting crazy. I had this overpowering urge to make them think of me as nuts. Since no sane means had shortened my prison term, maybe that would. Besides, where would they treat a man with softer kid gloves than in a psychiatric ward?

Ha!

The psycho-isolator was itself somewhat isolated from other wards. It stood next to the morgue, a white wooden barracks like the others. The prisoner in charge, the *zavkhoz*, greeted me with the demand, "Who are you?"

He was dark and wiry and hunched, with the hunted black eyes of a Middle Eastern terrorist. He ordered me to strip, and took my small bag of possessions.

"My cigarettes."

"Cigarettes not allowed."

Poking through my bag, he pulled out a small jar, for which I'd traded dearly.

"That's honey."

"Honey not allowed." He crammed it back in the bag.

Dismayed and confounded, I began removing my clothes.

"*Bystree, bystree!* Faster!"

I'd heard that from guards so much that I paid no attention.

His forearm smashed against my chest and I fell back against the wall.

"*Ia bystree skazal.* I said fast!" Practically pressing his eyes into mine, he hissed, "*Tot dvenadtsatyi korpus.* This is the Twelfth Corpus."

He tossed shoes at me. The left one was too big and loose, the right one too small. As I struggled to get into the tight one, I tried to figure out why he'd taken my shoes and given me these.

Annoyed at my trouble with the shoe, he grabbed me by the skin of my neck, squeezing it tightly in his fist. My skin was all he

182

had to grab. I was totally naked. Again he threw me against the wall and began slugging me in the stomach and chest.

I fought my urge to slug him back. This beating humiliated me and scared me out of my wits. Violence in camp I'd seen, plenty of it, but committed only between equals, prisoner on prisoner. I'd seen guards control their tempers till their faces flushed, but I'd never seen one break the rigid rule against striking a prisoner. This was the first (and only) time I saw someone in authority inflict violence on a prisoner.

In my white gown and mismatched shoes I followed him down a corridor to Box 2, at the end. He slammed the door shut. In one wall, shared with the adjacent cell, nestled a small black stove for coal or wood. The stove was stone cold. The room was icy. This was January near the latitude of Alaska, and I was naked except for a white cotton gown, my body trembling with chills. Eventually a trusty showed up with kindling and a few coal chunks. But his fire didn't last long. Each day he came once or twice, but the fire was out more than it was lit. I knew I couldn't resist a fearsome illness from that clinging, paralyzing cold, and I resigned myself to it.

My second day there was a Saturday, the day for the weekly shower and shave. A trusty unlocked my door and, leaving it half open, told me to get ready.

"What do I do to get ready?"

"Take off clothes!"

I lifted off my cotton gown and stood there, feeling like an idiot.

The *zavkhoz* called, "Ahmstairr!"

I stepped out of my box.

He motioned me to stand at the door. Down the corridor, several men stood naked at their doors. Every half-minute or so he called a name, and one of those men ran to the far end of the hall and disappeared. Finally he called my name. Like the rest, I ran.

"*Bystree, bystree,*" he commanded, smacking me with a fist on the small of my back as I passed him.

I expected to enter a shower room. It was literally a bath room, its tub the old-fashioned style, with curved legs. A prisoner was just

183

climbing out. The *zavkhoz* handed him a razor and waved him on.

"Get in," the *zavkhoz* ordered me. "You have thirty seconds."

Seconds? I wanted to shave first. I always shave before I shower. How was I going to refill this bath *and* bathe, all in thirty seconds? Then the truth became obvious. I was to get down into the same water that the other guy had climbed out of. That *all* those guys had climbed out of. I looked down at the gray, stale water. What I saw couldn't possibly be. Fragments of feces floated in it. Then a saving grace. Next to the bath squatted a small water heater with a shower head on a flexible hose. At least I could rinse myself off. I got a better idea. I'd just step into that filthy water, less than knee-high, and just shower. The moment I flipped on the shower, the *zavkhoz* burst in, raging.

"What are you, crazy? That's not for you, you shit!" He pounded me and I slipped into the filthy, soapy water, splashing it. How was I to know the shower was for trusties only?

In the next room I shaved with no mirror, scraping my face with a heavy razor, the blade locked into it, that thirty prisoners had used before me—without changing, for week after week. It was like scraping my skin off with jagged fingernails. I bled so badly, even the *zavkhoz* got scared, and he called the doctor in charge. The doctor, a preoccupied, nervous young man named Viktor Viktorovich, looked puzzled, took me into another room, and asked how the bleeding had happened.

I flooded him with every detail of my twenty-four hours of horror. He seemed more alarmed at the energy of my outpouring than at the horrors themselves. I sensed a worry over what would happen if I told my crazy story to anyone else. He patched my face, and must have done more after I left. The stove guy never neglected my heat again. The following Saturday, a trusty handed me the shower head. At my turn to shave, the *zavkhoz* put a new blade in the razor.

But by that time I was doubled over and shriveled with dysentery. I didn't know if the previous week's bath had caused it, or living nearly naked in the cold, or both.

On Monday morning, the *zavkhoz* pulled my door open and announced, "Ahmstairr, *étap* today." French for a transfer convoy. The Soviets adore French military terms. So I was to board a convoy train, either back to my own camp or to somewhere else, he didn't know where. I didn't care where. Reamed by the unrelenting dysentery, I just wanted to be out of there.

Even as I tell this, I can't explain why the psycho-isolator was run that way. I'm sure it was intentional, yet I don't think that all I endured was intentional. The intentional part was that the Soviets threw prisoners who acted crazy into that kind of place to separate the real crazies from the malingerers. It was a reliable form of gross diagnosis. Anybody who was putting on an act would rapidly want to get his ass back to labor camp, an instant restoration of mental health. But the behavior of that unforgettable prick, the *zavkhoz*, I'm quite sure, was beyond official policy and was unique. He ran that place as a real loony bin because the psychiatrists in charge didn't care enough to examine what he was doing. That sadistic maniac made the most of his job. Soon after I left, the wretch was transferred to another job where he had no authority over others. I'll never know whether my explosion at Viktor Viktorovich had anything to do with it. In his new job, that maniac's fellow prisoners, who knew his reputation all too well, isolated him, harassed him, hounded him. Before long he killed himself.

The Soviets clearly have two attitudes about prisoner suicides. They dread the self-murder of a foreigner or of a well-known political dissident, and will even knuckle under to the demands of one of those who threatens a hunger strike. Word of such a suicide usually gets out, and the Russians will go to great lengths not to look cruel in the eyes of the world. But ordinary Soviet criminals are another matter. Criminals are aberrant and annoying problems, distractions from the work of building Soviet socialism. The suicide of a common criminal is simply a problem getting rid of itself.

In the case of the psycho-isolator *zavkhoz*, they may have been right.

185

TO BUTYRKA

The first person I saw on the *étap* train was Darrell.

"Where we going?" I mumbled. The days of dysentery, of straining to empty what was long empty, had left me so weak that even saying simple words was another strain.

"The consul."

The last thing I needed was a trip to Moscow in a Stalin-era cattle car.

"Where's Pete?"

"Wouldn't go."

Each of us had now and then refused these four-times-a-year journeys. The strains of the travel-changing and waiting outweighed the pleasure of complaining to the consul.

We always met the consul at Butyrka, one of three large prisons in Moscow. The meetings had to be in Moscow because no foreign consulate officials—in fact, no foreigners except prisoners—were permitted to travel to Mordovia. We prisoners paid a high price for the Soviets' weird obsession with secrecy. But, in a sense, the Soviets pay a higher price. They have to maintain what amounts to a special railroad and a complex system of prisons and guards to move us to the consular officials, instead of them to us.

The train line from Moscow runs through the length of Mordovia all the way to Saransk, the capital and Mordovia's only large city. It goes by, or connects with, every camp in the long archipelago of prison camps. From Camp 5–1 and the village of Leplai we had to ride for about an hour on a squeaky branch line to the larger village of Puotma, on the main line. Does that mean we left Leplai an hour or two earlier to connect with the archipelago train at Puotma? Hell, no. It means we left three days to a week earlier, then lay over in the Puotma transit prison, just for that one-hour connection. Don't ask me why. Tight, efficient scheduling is not a Russian specialty.

For us, that delay was no casual matter. In that transit prison, and on the train to Moscow, we lived like animals in the zoo. I don't mean that as a trite metaphor; I mean it literally. Twice a day a guard came by to ladle out a drink of tepid water. Twice a day, toilet call. There was no mess hall, no scheduled meals. Once each day, each of us got what was called a herring. It was a whole fish, head and all, seven or eight inches long, saturated with salt and dried, preserving it for months, some knowledgeable prisoners said for years. We had to tear it open, clean out its guts, remove its skin, and try to eat what was left. I couldn't, until my hunger got desperate. The reward for overcoming that hurdle was fierce, unquenchable thirst.

On leaving our camp—in fact, on getting beyond the second of three fences of the camp—custody of us passed from our MVD guards to the internal militia, the Vnutrennaia Voiska. Almost all these guards were Soviet Central Asians—Azerbaijani, Tajiks, Kirghiz, Uzbeks, and more. Russians hate them, and they hate Russians. That's why they fit their duties extremely well. Soviets look upon convicts as the worst scum, and want them treated accordingly. If a prisoner in transit attempts escape, his Asian guard won't bat an eye before shooting the runaway. In the southeastern reaches of the

187

Soviet Union, the opposite is practiced. Russians guard Asians. The hatred works just as effectively there.

I doubt that this is a written policy. It certainly violates the letter of the Soviet Constitution. But in my aggregate of two years in the hospital camp I heard of this policy over and over again, matter-of-factly, without variation, from experienced criminals, experienced prisoners who knew about prisons everywhere.

These Asian guards weren't brutal or overtly cruel to us. Just callous and lazy. Not giving a damn about us, they'd find the slightest excuse not to let us out of our rooms or out of the boxcars for our daily walk. They'd neglect and delay toilet call until our yelling and cursing annoyed them so that it was easier to let us out.

I made at least a dozen long-distance journeys during my sentence. Figuring an average of a week each way, I spent almost six months in the transit prison and in prisoner cattle cars. It was the worst of times, yet in one way the most interesting. There was no place like the transit prison for learning about the entire national system of Soviet labor camps and prisons. Just as, in the cocktail lounges of American and European airports, business travelers and tourists talk about little but the hardships of travel delays and lost baggage, so in the transit prisons and trains, prisoners exchange stories about the hardships of their exotic prison travels. Prisoners are rarely encamped in or near their own republic, where they're likely to get soft, neighborly treatment. Someone sentenced in Riga, Latvia, well north of Moscow, is likely to serve his time in, say, Kazakhstan, near the Chinese border. Whoever makes those decisions has an immense range of choices. The Soviet Union spreads across eleven time zones.

Political dissidents usually are kept relatively close to Moscow or in Mordovia, where the KGB can watch them closely and meet with them often, trying to break them down. Sometimes, however, the KGB wants to break up networks of dissidents who have underground communication systems. They've got plenty of geography for separating them. The law enforcers seem especially eager to break up and scatter rings of people who have committed economic crimes against the state.

Except for its outermost regions, where the camp labor is to cut trees in frigid temperatures, Siberia, the symbol of banishment, is not the worst of sentences. Guards are friendlier than in the Russian regions, and they're easier to corrupt because they're more remote from Moscow's supervision. The worst camps are in the Ural Mountains, particularly the region of Perm. The winters are unbearable, the food almost always in short supply.

About five percent of convicts, the most violent criminals, go to prisons instead of labor camps. The labor camp system, based on minimal internal supervision, can't handle a murderer who might be expected to repeat his crime. Also sent to prisons are those convicted of military espionage. Francis Gary Powers, the pilot of the American U-2 shot down during the Eisenhower administration, served his time at Vladimir, the largest and most infamous of Soviet prisons, in the city of Vladimir, about a hundred miles east of Moscow. A number of guys who told me they served time while Powers was there spread stories about Powers having practically an executive suite, with a television set in his cell. I even heard that the Russians supplied him with vodka, a luxurious diet, and women. I never found a prisoner who said he saw any of that, or who even knew someone who saw any of it. I didn't believe a word of those rumors. They just didn't jibe with what I knew first-hand about the Soviets and the way they treated even favored prisoners.

The curious thing is that in the transit prison of Mordovia, sex between men and women prisoners, arranged by guards, was more likely than in any executive cell at Vladimir. First of all, it may surprise Americans and Westerners that there are many labor camps for women. Well-traveled prisoners said with consistency that forty percent or more of labor camp prisoners are women. Many are prostitutes, but many more are employees who have had their hands caught in the government till, or shoplifters and factory pilferers. Women are unloaded at the transit prison by the trainful. We could

189

always tell when their train was coming, because they liked to sing Russian folk songs in groups, sometimes sounding like choirs.

The militia guards were delighted when the transit prison housed both men and women.

One summer night during toilet call, a militia guard asked me furtively, *"Ebat' khochesh?* You want to fuck?"

I looked at him, startled. Was *he* propositioning me?

"I have empty room. I get girl."

A trainload of choristers had arrived the night before, and my *étap* was to leave at dawn tomorrow.

My first thought was of my own stickiness and sweat. My second thought was of hers. This prison stank of years of prisoners being unloaded from cattle cars. In summer it was an oven, in winter an icehouse.

I said no. But an Englishman named Wilson said yes. They negotiated momentarily, and Wilson gave the guard a carton of English cigarettes. The deal seemed riskless enough for the guard. Only one other militiaman was on duty with him, and he was probably selling sex elsewhere. Their commanding officer was no doubt asleep. Since the guard-prisoner relationship in transit prison was temporary, a guard didn't have to worry that a prisoner might have something on him.

I don't know what the girl got out of it. Maybe just a few minutes of recreation before her long trip back to camp. I've heard that sometimes the guard collects from the girl, too. I've also heard that sometimes the guard splits his fee with her.

In twenty minutes or less, Wilson was back, silent and, I suppose, satisfied.

A month later, back at camp, Wilson was sent to the hospital with syphilis.

As bad as that transit prison was, the train was worse. On a long trip, such as to Moscow, it stopped and started, started and stopped, at stations, between stations, the prisoners never knowing why. It was scheduled to make certain stops, where we'd be let out for a walk and a piss. That was supposed to be twice a day. Each of those stopping points quartered a detail of militia armed with submachine guns. The militia men on the train, however, had only pistols, so if a train stopped between stations they couldn't let us out of our slatted compartments, which we called cages. Rather than break that rule, they'd let the prisoners burn to death.

In fact, that's just what happened in 1980. A fire broke out in one of the cars. Smoking was prohibited in these dry-wood cattle cars, but men crouched in corners, cupping their hands around lighted cigarettes, and the movement of the train dispersed the smoke. The guards usually detected it, and would simply call out to stop smoking.

This train carried seventy prisoners, all Russians, crowded three or four to a cage. That's known, because a lot of prisoners saw the train leave. The only other thing that's known is that the fire swept through the train and all seventy prisoners burned to death. The guards were forbidden to open the cages. So they didn't.

I heard nothing of any guard or officer being transferred or demoted as a result. After all, they had done the right thing. They had followed the rule book. The lives did not matter, because the prisoner is the lowest scum of socialist society. His death is no loss.

So there I was, on *étap* to Moscow, retching from the psycho-isolator. I had a small chunk of black bread and a dab of butter folded in a piece of paper. I passed them to Darrell.

He looked at me, confused. "Don't you want it?"

"Can't." I tried not to think of the salt-drenched fish that would soon be distributed.

When we arrived at Butyrka, a doctor or nurse received us as per standard procedure, running a lightbulb over our scalps and body hair, checking for lice. I didn't have to complain that I was ill. The woman saw it instantly, and ordered me into quarantine.

That delayed my consul meeting for two weeks. Good. I'd come to dislike meeting the consul with Darrell or Pete, or, worst of all, both together. Sometimes, when I knew they were going, I declined to go. At one meeting the consul-general himself, Clifford Gross, was the man who met us. I thought that was a nice gesture. Pete apparently didn't. When Gross got up and extended his hand, Pete responded, "Fuck you, I don't want your dirty hand."

Darrell, too, embarrassed me with his surliness. I wasn't terribly pleased that the United States government didn't seem to be doing a thing about getting us out of there. Today, in fact, I hold my government partly responsible for the long terms we served. I think that if Washington had really cared about getting us out, they could have found a way of applying pressure on the Soviets. But why take it out on these consulate people? Clearly we were somewhat better off cultivating their friendliness, and had nothing to gain by losing it. In fact, no matter how disgracefully Darrell and Pete acted toward them, they remained fastidious in getting Pete's messages to his wife and Darrell's to his sister. At one meeting they gave Pete the news that his wife wanted him to know she had had to sell their house in Las Vegas because she couldn't keep up the payments. It was a dream place, with an underground nuclear bomb shelter. For a few seconds I thought Pete was going to break down and cry. But he recovered and became furious and abusive with the consul instead.

At these meetings, the consul provided us with gifts and goodies from the embassy commissary, purchased with money sent by our relatives.

They were also good about keeping us informed of news of that whole wide world out there which we heard little about. Once the consul took the trouble to give us interesting details about some big boxing matches. He must have figured I'd be specially interested because my brother was a fight manager. I remember asking him about "Billygate," the capers of the President's brother. I'd heard about Billy on Radio Moscow, which we heard in our camp barracks. So he told me about Billy peeing on the runway while waiting for a group of Libyans, and some other carryings-on. At another meeting, the consul described the bizarre, unbelievable mass suicides at Jonestown. I had a funny reaction. I was embarrassed that a Russian militia colonel was sitting there listening to that weird story of crazed

192

Americans. At one of those meetings the consul told me that an answer had come to the letter I'd sent to President Carter. It said the White House was looking into my case.

"Is something going to happen?"

The consul shrugged and said nothing. Clearly, that letter was diplomatic double-talk meaning "Forget it."

In March 1980, Pete was released after serving more than two-thirds of his five-year sentence. My eligibility for early release would not come for a year and a half. If the Soviets were to keep me for my full eight years, I'd have to stay till June 27, 1984. Darrell, who could not get early release because of his not-guilty plea, was to get out in 1983. After Pete's release, which came while I was in the hospital, I saw little of Darrell, virtually losing touch with him.

16

PROTSEDURNAIA

In the summer of 1979, after three years of Soviet custody, my ulcers gripped my insides like fingers of fire. I knew they were getting worse, and I desperately needed treatment beyond spoonfuls of baking soda.

My head spun with confusion and conflict. I now had the job of dispensary *fel'dsher*, which, besides putting me in charge of the baking soda, made it fairly easy to get into the hospital. After all, I ran the daily *priëm*, the sick call, as the chief helper to the visiting doctors who made the decisions. I served them well and they liked me. I just had to say the word, and one of them would put me on hospital *étap* pronto.

But how could I go to the hospital, even for a short stay, and also keep the dream job of *fel'dsher*? Once they replaced me, even temporarily, I could kiss the job good-bye.

One afternoon at *priëm*, the internal flames and chest pressure so seized me that I almost passed out. The doctor, not noticing, asked me to get something. I don't think I even heard. He glared at me for ignoring him, but then saw clearly that something was wrong. I was sure I was having a heart attack. He asked me what was wrong, and I told him.

My conflict was resolved. He sent me to the hospital.

Two or three days later, when I was already feeling better, one of the head hospital doctors stopped me on my way to a clinic.

"You Ahmstairr, *Amerikanets*."

"Yes."

"In 5–1, you *fel'dsher*."

"Yes."

He sucked the earpiece of his eyeglasses and assessed my face. "We need new *fel'dsher*."

A thrill shot through me so fiercely I thought it was a new attack of heartburn. The hospital had a number of *fel'dsheri*, but kept losing them as they returned to their camps or finished their sentences. But as a foreigner I didn't dream I might be made one.

"You go to *protsedurnaia*, the procedure room, in surgery and talk to *vrach'*."

Vrach' means "doctor," but only when the word is spoken in the third person, without use of the doctor's name. When the doctor is addressed directly, or a name is attached, then the proper word is *doktor*. It had taken me a while to get used to that.

Damn. If I was to get this break, why did it have to be in surgery? I didn't want to wipe up after operations. I certainly didn't want to lean over bloody bodies *during* operations. But better a tableful of blood than going back to camp. And this time I'd make myself so essential to this *vrach'* that he'd never let them send me back.

The *protsedurnaia* occupied a small building at the end of a path a couple of hundred feet beyond the surgical ward. Behind its door was not an operating room, as I had imagined, but walls lined with neat cabinets of pharmaceuticals and supplies. No wonder it was a separate building. Just as in camp, the room with the drugs was separate, with a locked door. A white-coated nurse answered my ring.

"Is the *vrach'* in?"

195

"Yes."

"Dr. Birkov sent me to see him."

She admitted me, locked the door again, and resumed what she had been doing, counting pills, as though I didn't exist. Finally, without turning from her work, she said, "*Vrach*' not 'him.' *Vrach*' is woman."

"I'm sorry. Where can I find her?" I'd grown accustomed to a predominance of women as doctors. But surgeons, so far as I knew from the hospital camp, were males.

The nurse took her time silently finishing her task, then finally turned and stood, directly in front of me. "I *vrach*'. I Dr. Marenko."

"Oh."

This one, who couldn't yet be thirty, a bone-cutter, a bloody surgeon? Waiting for me to state my business, she looked at me squarely, without expression, through transfixing blue eyes. Her dark brown hair was tailored trimly, almost boyishly, different from most Russian professional women, who prefer Late Barbara Stanwyck or Early Grandmotherly Neglect. She stood straight and proud. Although absolutely expressionless, she was taking me in, too. For the first time in three years I had a tremor in my belly, faintly reminding me of how long it had been.

"Dr. Birkov sent me to see you."

"Already you said that."

"He said you need a *fel'dsher*. In my camp, I am a *fel'dsher*." Her eyes narrowed with puzzlement. "From where your accent?"

"*Ia Amerikanets.*"

Cool, suppressed astonishment. "*Amerikanets.*"

"I am the *fel'dsher* in Camp 5–1, the foreigners' camp."

"How arrive American in Soviet prison camp?"

Oh God, if I tell her—with all these drugs in her room, she'll throw me out of here before I have a chance. "A customs violation at Sheremet'evo. I failed to declare all that was in my suitcase."

"How you read instructions? How you read labels? We must give exactly, or we kill people."

"I am *pedagog* of languages. I've learned Russian quite well. I'm very careful about reading labels. In my *sanchast'* I haven't killed anyone yet. I promise you I won't kill anyone here."

She frowned with impatience, rejection. "Today I busy. You come tomorrow. I show you everything tomorrow."

That night I didn't sleep, out of sheer excitement and anticipation.

During our first morning I learned that Dr. Marinka Marinkievna Marenka was not a surgeon, but had recently received her medical degree to become what corresponds most closely in the West to a pharmacist.

Every morning we had to furnish the surgeons with their medicines and supplies for the operating room, and fill a sheaf of prescriptions. By ten or ten-thirty that rush was over. The rest of the day was a breeze, checking up on inventory, filling standing orders for the next day; and I'd have to keep the place spotless. All was peaceful and predictable except for an occasional emergency customer who might interrupt us for minor first aid, which, for some reason, was a duty that fell to us.

One late morning, the quietest time of our day, she hummed as she filled a rack of syringes.

"You know who that?"

"Who?"

"Duke Ellingtone. That is 'Sateen Dohl.' "

To check it out, I had to hum it myself. Son of a gun.

"You know this?" Her tune was unmistakable, but gargled. She vibrated the back of her palate as though clearing her throat.

"That's 'Blueberry Hill.' " I laughed. "Louis Armstrong."

"I have much jazz. I have records." She fell silent. Then: "Do you love persecution of black people?"

"Of course not."

"You go sometimes to Garlem?"

The Russian language has no *h* sound. All American poverty, all persecution of blacks, all slums, and much of capitalist oppression is concentrated in the one black ghetto Russians hear about, Garlem.

"Sure, but not too often."

197

"True, American can walk in store and buy gun, like baby doll, like chewing gum?"

That one again. "Well, in a way, yes."

"Oompossible to believe. Policeman not stop you?"

"No. It's legal."

"Oompossible to understand. Patient from foreigners' camp, Englishman, told me one prisoner can get two sentences at one time. True?"

"Sometimes."

"He said prisoner can get sentence of ninety-nine years. That true?"

"Yes."

"But if he old enough for prison, he cannot live ninety-nine years."

"That's to make sure he never gets out."

"But if he gets two sentences of ninety-nine years, who else not get out? His brother?"

"It's just a formality. In case one sentence is canceled by a judge, the other sentence keeps him in jail."

"But if judge wants prisoner to stay in jail with one sentence, why he cancel other one?"

"Legal formalities."

"Oompossible to understand. In Soviet Union we more respect people. Prisoner gets, most, fifteen years. Punished enough. What is good to keep prisoner all his life? No sentence in Soviet Union for all life."

I didn't know how to say it without sounding critical. "Many here get death."

"Of course."

"We don't give many criminals death."

"But person who commits crime against all people has no right to live. Deserves death."

"We give death only for murder. Someone takes a life, he gives his life."

198

"But you have many, many murders. You take so many lives?"

"Only the worst ones get death." I had no taste for going into the differences between having a slick, high-priced lawyer and a reluctant public defender, between upper-class murder of a spouse by impersonal contract and lower-class, point-blank shooting of a subway cop.

"We don't have so much murder. Murder terrible, but murder hurts only one. Crime against state hurts everybody. Yet for hurting one, you give firing squad."

"We don't use firing squads. Except in one state, a state with not many people, called Utah."

"Then how you give death?"

"Sometimes with gas."

"Gas? Why gas?"

"It's gentler, more humane."

"Criminal murders someone, and you worry to be humane?"

"Sometimes we put him in an electric chair. A huge electric shock from his head to his ankles kills him."

She blanched. "Yes, I know. Electric shock through whole body! Oompossible to understand."

Next day she asked how much her work would pay in the United States.

I explained that the answer would be complicated. In a hospital her work might be done by a nurse, or a specialist that we call a pharmacist.

"How much a nurse gets?"

It's hard, I said, to translate ruble value into dollar value, because some things in America cost much more, some things much less. A nurse, however, earns enough to have her own small apartment. Then I remembered that rents are low in the Soviet Union because housing is subsidized, so that wouldn't shed much light. I said that a nurse could have more clothes, probably better clothes, than a young woman working in a factory, yet she wouldn't have really expensive clothes. She could eat in a nice restaurant maybe once a

199

week even if her boyfriend didn't treat her, buy theater tickets once or twice a month, have a television, a stereo, books and records, a car, and take a vacation once a year.

"Car? Nurse has car?"

"Oh yes."

"All nurses have cars?"

"Maybe not all. If a nurse lives near her hospital in a big city that has buses and taxicabs, she might save the cost of a car and put it away toward a *dacha*, a country house."

"Nurse buys *dacha*?"

"If she doesn't buy a car. But if she buys a *dacha*, she'll need a car. So she may go partners with another nurse to buy the *dacha*."

She scrutinized me. She couldn't believe. She wanted to believe.

"How much pharmacist get? As much as nurse?"

"More."

"More than nurse with car? How much more?"

"That depends. If he works in a hospital, enough to get a bigger car than the nurse's, a bigger apartment, maybe better furniture. But if he opens his own pharmacy shop, and if he is a good businessman, he might get double or triple what a nurse gets."

"Why you pay him more in shop than in hospital?"

"In a shop, nobody pays him. He makes profit. He buys for one price, sells for a higher price. The more he sells, the more he makes."

"Your pharmacists steal money from sick people?"

"They don't steal."

"You said they buy for one price, they sell for higher price. That is crime. We send our functionaries to jail for that."

But your price-doubling prison guards do it, I wanted to say. I let it go. "Profit is how he gets paid. It's perfectly legal."

"Then pharmacist makes more than doctor."

"No, the doctor makes more, much more."

"How can doctor get more than capitalist pharmacist?"

"Because doctors charge high prices."

"Who takes care of poor black people? They die?"

"This is hard to explain, but hardly anybody pays doctors anymore. Everybody puts money for doctors into a big fund called Blue Cross. Blue Cross pays for hospitals and doctors. When poor people have no Blue Cross, the government pays. But doctors take care of everybody."

"So, like us, socialism."

"Well, doctors don't call it that. Americans don't believe in socialism, especially doctors."

"But if doctors have socialism to take care of poor in Garlem, why they get so much?"

"Actually"—I didn't know if I should say this—"until we had Blue Cross, and until the government paid doctors for poor people, not many doctors got so much. They didn't have three cars and a boat."

"Boat? For what doctor needs boat?"

"For weekends."

"Doctor has boat for pleasure?"

"Many do."

"Oompossible. Not all doctors live near sea."

"No. Inland, many have airplanes."

She waved her hand derisively at my kidding, and turned her back on me, giggling.

I laughed too. Then I leaned close to her, closer than a prisoner dares lean to a prison doctor, and whispered, "But it's true."

Next day, in late morning, our time of day, she opened her briefcase and took out something to show me. It was a fat, ripe, red tomato.

"From your garden? You grew it?"

"Yes."

"Beautiful," I said, handing it back. "You should be a farmer."

"Eat. I bring for you."

Why would she take such a risk, bringing a prisoner this gift? Was she actually saying I could sink my teeth into it, let its sweet seedy juice run down my mouth and gullet? The wealth of it!

With a knife, she cut it into luscious quarters.

"Eat," she repeated. Her eyes darted toward the door and back. No one was likely to come. But if someone did—

I placed two of the tomato quarters in front of her.

"I have other one." She cut her own tomato into quarters.

My excitement transcended the gift of her food. By taking me into her garden, she had taken me into her home, into her private life. I wanted more, but knew I mustn't ask.

"You must have your own house." There, that wasn't asking.

"Yes, small house." A wan smile.

"Not in Leplai."

"No, Puotma."

"You must take care of it all alone?" I bit my tongue for asking.

"Yes, hard. No time." She laughed. "Every New Year I hang *ded moroz* high on chimney. You know *ded moroz?*"

"No."

"*Ded moroz.* He fat happy man, gray hair, brings presents to good children at New Year. I have no children, but I hang anyway, for village children. Last winter I so busy, I leave *ded moroz* hanging. In July, too late to take down, so I put on him bathing suit. Someday, you go through Puotma, you look for chimney with *ded moroz* in bathing suit. My house."

Next day—what intuition could have informed her of the most private, secret me?—next day, unbelievably, she unwrapped two hard-boiled eggs, one for each of us.

Almost every day, something. Fresh bread. Sourballs, but not the moldy kind sold at the *magazin.* These were bright, fruit-shaped, crunchy, with soft, fruit-flavored insides, even more thrilling than pure sugar.

Then she brought apples. And halvah. And every day she made tea. She boiled it in a small kettle on the hot plate we had for sterilizing instruments. Not tea from Soviet Georgia, which is bitter, but Indian tea or Ceylon tea, rich tea of real orange-red color. Russians don't put sugar in their tea. They hold a cube of sugar between their upper and lower front teeth and let the tea run through.

202

It's a tricky technique, and my attempts to master it gave her daily amusement.

One late morning she asked about my family. I told her about my mother, the slightest bit about my father, a great deal about my grandfather, and that they were all dead. The only one remaining was my brother. She wanted to know what work he did, whether he was married, and so forth. I explained that he owned a shop in Philadelphia that sold blue jeans, glossed over his experience as a fighter and fight manager, and said he was divorced.

"Easy to get divorce in America?"

"Fairly easy."

"I, too, divorced."

My curiosity flared, but I asked nothing.

She volunteered that after two years her marriage had sunk in a flow of vodka. He was an assistant factory manager in the city where she had studied medicine.

At the end of that day, I was working near the door as she was leaving. Before clicking it locked, she seemed to linger for an extra moment, looking at me. Her eyes rounded in a kind of sad resignation, as though to say, "What can't be, can't be." Then she erased her expression and briskly left.

After one of those morning conversations, a particularly warm one that I hated to end, she gently ended it by asking where a certain medicine bottle was. I took it down from the shelf and, as I put it in front of her, touched her on the shoulder ever so lightly. So lightly that it could have been an accidental brush.

It's hard to explain this, but what I was doing was inconceivable. A prisoner, under no circumstances, under *no* circumstances whatsoever, touches a guard, an officer, any nonprisoner in authority.

Well, I shouldn't say under *no* circumstances. Once, and only once, I did, in a sense, transgress that rule. I had to. It was the middle of the night back in camp, and I'd had to make my way through the woods to the camp outhouse, where, in the darkness, I squatted. By this time I was used to squatting, Soviet-style. Unlike American outhouses, Soviet outhouses—in fact, all Soviet toilets

203

in every prison I've been in, and most public toilets everywhere, I've been told—have no seats, nothing at all above floor level. There's just a hole cut in the floor. The user plants a foot on either side of it, crouches low, and performs. As I squatted, the door thrashed open, admitting a ray of moonlight and a powerful gust of vodka breath, and in clattered Lieutenant Ramashin, on night duty again. Why would he inspect this, of all places? He greeted me cheerfully by name, and, with an egalitarian camaraderie that made me extremely nervous, dropped his pants and squatted over the hole beside mine. Upon finishing, he reached drunkenly behind him in the darkness to tear a piece from the collected pages of *Pravda*, and his foot slipped. His leg plunged into the hole, Ramashin's body collapsing on me as he sounded an alarm: "Ahmstairr! Ahmstairr!"

That was the moment of my loss of respectful distance. I actually touched him, touched an officer. My pants still down, I grabbed Ramashin's arm with my left hand, throwing my right hand under his opposite armpit, and lifted him out of his purgatory.

I awaited my punishment.

"Thank you, Ahmstairr. Good boy, Ahmstairr."

But my punishment came. The fragrance of his leather boot catapulted me out of that shack, dragging Ramashin with me.

"*Fel'dsher!* Take me to *fel'dsher!*"

Ramashin leaned clumsily on me as we hobbled to the *sanchast'*. I rang the bell and stopped breathing until Walter Haefelin sleepily opened the door a crack.

"Ankle twisted," Ramashin wheezed to Haefelin. "Take off boot."

Haefelin looked to me, as though his gaze would make me do it, as though I were Little Willie, his manservant. I looked away. Haefelin reached to pull off the boot, then withdrew his dainty hands. They just hung there as he tried to reason through this problem. Finally he filled his nighttime pail with water and invited Ramashin to stumble outside, where Haefelin washed the boot down before gingerly yanking it off.

So, at laying a hand on authorities I was not entirely a virgin.

My breathing began to quicken. I didn't want Marinka to hear

204

it, yet I did. Had she noticed the touch of my fingers? How could she not have noticed? Did her eyes wince, flicker in the slightest? I mustn't look directly at her. But my eyes, my ears, the air, gave me no message. She must have noticed. But she didn't stiffen. It must have been all right.

If it was all right, it must have secretly stimulated her the way that daring, crazy flick of a touch had stimulated me.

The next day or so, nothing. We talked as usual. The warmth, the closeness hung in the air. Let it hang there. Let it do its work. I was too scared to make the next move.

But in a couple of days came a moment when a move was imperative. When it was right. I don't remember what was happening that moment, and I don't know how I knew, but I knew. I touched her not on one shoulder, but on both, and squeezed my hands around them. She looked straight at me, offering no resistance. Her willingness flushed her face. I drew her close to me, pressing my mouth against the side of her neck. She accepted it, sucking her breath in. Yes, it was all right. I washed kisses all over her face.

My whole body pounded with eagerness, with terror. I couldn't tell one from the other. I was terrified that she would turn on me and terrified that someone would knock on the door, that I'd have to run to open it, trying to look composed, that it would be the commandant of the hospital: "Aha, Ahmstairr! Discovered! Back to camp! Back to *tsekh*, new investigation, new trial, ten more years!"

What was my heart pounding about? The woman or the danger?

This goddammed government-issue underwear. These fucking oversized, loose, Russian cabbage-farmer boxer shorts. What was I to do with this thing, with this indignity of my excitement? I hadn't whomped up such a hard-on since Amsterdam. Concealing it from her was hopeless. Should I move my belly away? Should I press it to her? Should I make a joke? Should I say something loving? How can she be excited by my excitement when my head is shaved bald?

She must be remembering now, remembering who I am, remembering who she is. I'm a prisoner, I'm permitted a bath only once a week, I starve on kasha and my belly flames with heartburn. I pander to the *blatnye*, taking candy for tales of painted whores and cocksuckers. I sleep among those pederast abusers. To these Russian guards, her countrymen, I am shit. They call us that to our faces. She is remembering all that now. I cringe at her contempt for me, feel the rise of her shame at herself.

No, it can't be. Her palm is stroking my thigh. She slides it up and down slowly, ever so slowly, hungrily.

Then she—no, she wouldn't do that.

She seizes me.

It's all over. She knows my hardness, grips it. I know her hunger, savoring it.

The wall between us explodes.

Her hands are all over me, mine all over her. I've got to get us down. No, not that cold floor. The wall? I don't know her well enough for standing up. God, must it be that excuse for a treatment table, that narrow wooden bench in the middle of the floor? I *cannot* do it on that.

I hoisted myself on the table, just to sit on it. She swung my feet to the table top, then hoisted herself up, sitting heavily across my knees. The awkwardness got fierce, and the pulsing fiercer.

"Off, off," she grunted.

Off what? Off the table? Off the clothes? What?

She dismounted, tapped my belt, a command, then hoisted her skirt, stripped herself beneath it, and remounted the table, reaching for me.

This was really happening. I climbed on her and she squeezed my waist between her knees. I slid her skirt up beneath her. There she is, there she really is, the precious woman of her, and she is giving it to me, and I am now for real going to plunge this swollen giant of a thing into her.

"Gerahld," she sighed, almost a cry, "Gerahld." She'd taken to calling me Gerald, and I loved it. "Door, door. You remembered to lock?"

I couldn't remember. Of course it was locked. It was always

locked. Could I have slipped this time? Could the commandant just *walk in?*

A trembling, an overwhelming terror, enveloped me ecstatically at that instant. Oh no God, no, no, there it goes. The hot fluid in my groin slipped over the edge and I couldn't hold it back. Oh God, too late, too late to call it back. Hoping she wouldn't know, I plunged myself into her anyway, hoping she wouldn't be angry at me.

So sorry, Marinka. I moved and ground and wiggled the best I could, even though the sweet after-keening in my belly begged me to lie still.

And then she erupted, with a heave, a wailing gasp, a burst of sweat. Not much, but she came, oh thank God. That little puff of sweat confirmed for me it was real. I remembered that much from my once-life. Now she'll be glad for this. Now she won't hate me, won't hate herself for fucking a prisoner.

I hoped she had no idea—no, there was no possible way she could have any idea—that the moment of my involuntary, helpless surrender was fired not so much by her as by her erotic question, the Spanish fly of the unlocked door, of the indecent exposure to the threat of the commandant.

I lay there, safe in my secret, and wondered. Had she come— for me, for something that was really me? Had she allowed me to be for her more than I had allowed her to be for me? I wouldn't ask, couldn't ask. But I wished I knew.

"Gerahld," she whispered after a while.

Sure, she wanted me to get off her, get dressed, get safe again.

"Gerahld, I wish—I wish I could go to America. For moment, I felt I in America."

In the days that followed, we had to pretend, even toward each other, that the wall that had separated our worlds was still there. We worked exactly as we had worked before. I remained deferential, the respectful foreign prisoner, she the benevolent boss. I didn't hint at making a move on her, at presuming that I had some standing permission.

207

At first I didn't recognize her move. She handed me the key to the "special" cabinet that held addictive painkillers and the like, the only one my keys wouldn't open.

"Bring alcohol," she said.

When I reached the bottle toward her, she was putting out our tea glasses. The pot was not on. It wasn't time yet.

Pouring a finger's depth into each glass, she said, "Taste bad. But good."

Alcohol for sterilizing is kept potable in the Soviet Union. Drinking it is discouraged by poisoning only its flavor, although I'm sure many medical technicians, and perhaps nurses and doctors, have cultivated a tolerance for the flavor of turpentine.

We sipped, and she asked, "Door locked?"

Those became the signals thereafter, one or the other, the alcohol or the door, or both. The signal was always hers, never mine.

We grew less awkward, but no less apprehensive, no less aware of the terrible consequences to both of us if we were ever caught.

She began to talk more of her long, secretive, perilous affair with America.

I'd never have known it from her earlier questions, her comparisons and taunts, but she'd yearned, as far back as she could remember, to see America. More serious than that. To live in America, become an American. With scarcely any clear vision of what American life was about, except from shortwave broadcasts and a few jazz records, she gave herself to this yearning. From Russian prisoners I'd heard about that puzzling longing, how widespread it was among the Soviet young. Maybe the travel restrictions that kept them locked inside the Iron Curtain made them feel imprisoned, and they created America as their symbol of all they were missing on the outside.

Marinka's longing was more than a dream. She had already acted. And she ventured, for all its risk, to tell me about it. In considerable numbers, Jews were being permitted for the first time to emigrate from the Soviet Union, most going to Israel, but some to the United States. They could take their spouses, Jewish or not.

She knew a Jewish man, somewhere in a city she didn't name to me, who expected to get out. He had promised to marry her and take her with him.

"Will he really do it?"

"I don't know."

"Do you love him?"

"He nice man. Love him? I love to live somewhere new. I love him let me see America."

"Would that be worth a marriage without love?"

She shrugged, not saying her answer.

"Would he expect you to stay married to him?"

"He understands why I want to marry him. He will let me go."

My life with Marinka required reorganizing some of my business arrangements. For all the smuggling of gifts and cash from the outside, the most active commerce was in bartering the benefits of desirable jobs.

I began to get chummy with the *blatnoi* creep who ran the shower room. I knew him to be a liar as well as a pederast brute. But business was business. He knew I'd just become a *fel'dsher*. I lightly laid on him one day that he ought to let me know if there was anything he needed.

He scrutinized me intently. "You get me mustard plasters?"

"I could try."

Back at camp I'd learned that a craving for mustard plasters had nothing to do with sore spots. Guys would scrape the mustard off the cloth, boiling the paper to remove every last speck, and make a paste to spread on their food.

So, through the benefits of free trade, every morning thereafter I was able to shower, sweetening myself for my new life with Marinka.

Until one morning the unthinkable—but the inevitable—happened. The *zavkhoz* called to me as I was smoothing my bed.

"Ahmstairr! *Étap* today."

After three months of a sort of heaven, it was all over.

17

PUOTMA

I would like to tell now of the meticulous planning that led to my escape, of the patience and endurance I had to call upon to dig a tunnel through Mordovian frozen earth with a stolen wooden tongue depressor.

But it didn't happen that way. I bolted Camp 5–1 with no planning at all, with scarcely a serious advance thought about it, on a night in August 1979, a night when all the camp lights went out.

The camp lights had gone out before, fairly often, usually during electrical storms, and the fact is, I'd thought about escaping every time they did. But the thoughts never made sense. I'd had a fantasy, naturally, about digging a tunnel under the three fences that surrounded us, but what prisoner hasn't? When my fantasy went far enough to lead me out of there, I'd next imagine making my way around the streets of Moscow, without figuring out how I'd get there. All I knew of Moscow was what I'd seen on the day of my bust, riding with my KGB escorts in that van from Sheremet'evo airport to Lefortovo. But that didn't limit my imagination. In this daydream of escape I imagined wandering around downtown, eventually spotting American tourists. American tourists are unmistakable in a crowd of Russians, prisoners had convinced me. You can tell them by the cut of their clothes. I'd search for an American who looked something like me, and I'd stop him on the street. I'd speak to him in English—in American—and he'd be glad to hear my voice, my accent, in Moscow, where not many Americans float around.

I'd say, "Listen, friend, this is a matter of life and death, an important matter of the national interest of the United States. I am a fugitive from a Soviet labor camp. Don't ask me how I got there, because I'm not at liberty to discuss it. The important thing is that I've escaped. Now I've got to get out of the Soviet Union and I need your help. I've selected you because you look like me.

"I need your passport. Now listen to me. There's no risk at all. All you have to do is take a taxi to the American embassy and report that you've lost it. They'll issue you a new one on the spot. At no risk, no sacrifice, you'll have saved my life and done an important service for our country."

How could he not give it to me? Of course, first he'd ask why I didn't get in that taxi and go to the embassy myself. My answer would be ready. Outside the gate is a pair of Russian guards. I'd never get past them. They've memorized my looks. They're just waiting till I make a stupid move like that, just waiting to pounce. That's the one place I cannot go.

Well, then, says my tourist friend, if I look enough like you so that my passport can be yours, why wouldn't they pounce on me?

You don't look *that* much like me, I'd say. Anyhow, you'd just have to keep insisting on who you really are, tell the guard to come inside with you. Show him your driver's license, your Hertz discount card, let him or the Americn consul call your hotel. You'll have no problem establishing who you are, because you *are* you.

I always knew that scene was pure daydream. Even if I could dig my way out of this place, how would I get to Moscow? How would I live once I got there?

The more I thought about it, in fact, the more I realized this prison was escape-proof. For a foreigner, at least. True, the fences around it were flimsy compared to those around American prisons.

211

But that didn't matter. The larger prison outside—this closed country and its closed life—were far more effective as a high-security system than was the camp itself.

Again I went through those thoughts on that August night when the lights went out.

The camp had gone dark at about ten o'clock—ironically, "lights out" time. Usually the power returned in a few minutes, seldom more than an hour. On very rare occasions the lights remained out for a day or two. But even then I'd hear the hum of an emergency generator pumping juice into the barbed wire that surrounded the camp. No matter what, the barbed wire had to be fed.

As I lay awake running those fantasy scenes once again, knowing they led nowhere, unconsciously I waited for the generator to remind me of how trapped I was. I must have been at the edge of sleep when a thunderclap shocked me awake. "Don't sleep," it seemed to roar. "Don't sleep now, you fool. Tonight's the night. When will you have a better chance?"

I listened for the generator. Silence.

When will I have a better chance? Chance, hell. Do I really have any choice about it? This is 1979. My sentence runs till 1984. I'm thirty-six years old. Am I to wait until I'm past forty, letting them take all my best years and leaving me with the crumbs of my decline? Their last denial of clemency sent a perfectly clear message. They have no intention of letting me out of here until the last hour of my sentence. They made a show of us at the trial, and they're going to make a show of me all the rest of the way.

They've promised and promised. The KGB promised we'd be out of here in a year. All those prisoners promised us that foreigners get out soon, without exception. Ramashin and his whole crowd of MVD guards promised us. All those consuls and vice-consuls with their solemn blue suits and funeral ties promised us. But the high councils of the Soviet government, maybe the Supreme Soviet itself, the only ones who can make the promise good, have clearly decided to hold me as an object lesson. And it wouldn't surprise me a bit to learn that the United States government itself has entered into some secret agreement to keep me locked away. The United States was spending millions trying to block the mass international transfer of dope. I could be *their* object lesson, too, at no extra expense or trouble. All they had to do—and perhaps had already done, I began to think—was to get word to the Soviets: Keep that motherfucker. Let him sit out his full sentence. You won't hear a peep of protest out of us.

Why is that generator still off?

Did the surge of current that blew the lights burn out the generator? As long as that emergency generator stays off, the barbed wire is dead, as harmless as a back scratcher.

I lifted myself from my bed enough to peer out the window.

Fog. A potato-soup fog. A couple of hours ago I'd seen the moon. Now there was none. Just thickness. If the lights were on, I doubted that I could see as far as the *shtab*. If the emergency supply of juice for the fence was off, probably even that ear-piercing alarm was dead. If somebody tried it *tonight*, how in the world could they ever—?

If somebody tried it, which way would he head? Where would he go?

As soon as I thought of the question, I had the answer. I knew where I'd go.

My thoughts began to race frantically. They were no longer thoughts, but surges of wild hope, of high risk, of impending peril.

At about one in the morning, lights still out, generator still silent, I got out of bed, into my clothes, out of those barracks, and tiptoed through the fog, quiet as a hunter, toward that fence.

Should I test the fence by flicking a finger across one of the wires? Would that split second of contact kill? Would it so startle me that I'd yell, even gasp? If I had a piece of metal— No, that wouldn't do. I looked around in the dark fog, practically groping, and found a piece of wood about a foot long. How do I do this? I stood it up a couple of inches from the wire, leaning the stick toward it, then let it go. Damn it, the stick fell without touching the wire. I did it again and again, until it fell right, making contact between the wire and the ground. No spark. No puff of smoke, not a hint of a current. I felt the stick. It was cold.

Now I flicked my finger across the wire. Nothing. I reached for a higher wire, did it again. Nothing.

Nothing to stop me.

At the height of my waist, I stretched two wires, spreading them away from one another. They gave. The piano tuner must not have been around lately to tighten them.

I spread them again, this time squeezing myself through the fence. The barbs scratched my clothes without touching me. About seven feet before me stood another, identical fence. I got through that exactly the same way.

Lucky this was summer. In winter, guards on skis circled the space between the two barbed-wire fences at least once a day to inspect for footprints and pack down the snow. Any escapee would leave a road map of where he'd crossed and where he'd gone.

Beyond the two barbed-wire fences stood the seven-foot-high fence of pointed planks, three more strands of barbed wire along its top. I couldn't stop to play Benjamin Franklin here, testing for electricity. I mustn't break the momentum of getting over. In one thrust, I leaped up, grabbing at that fence top, and hurled my body between those wires as though they weren't there. As long as they carried no charge, the hell with the scratching.

I landed with a thud, but then stood still as a statue. I was sure I didn't gasp or grunt.

Nobody heard. My God, I did it. I am outside that fence. Outside that prison camp. Free. An exposed, dangerous, thrilling kind of free. To have me again, now they have to find me.

Nobody heard. I was certain now.

Uh-oh. Wrong.

From beyond the clearing that separated the camp from the village of Leplai, from one of the dwellings, lifted the accusing bark of a dog.

Shut up!

The dog barked again, this time twisting it with a weird howl.

214

Some kind of dog language, the evil bastard, rousing the others. Sure enough, from another house another bark, then another. Leplai, invisible in the black darkness, was alive with dogs.

They'll awaken every guard, and in moments I'll be surrounded with flashlights and shot dead. Dead. This is it, the end of my life. Because of that one fucking dog.

Maybe I should have been grateful for their yowling. I had imagined running through Leplai, to the railroad track on the other side of town. That would have been a mistake. All I needed was one insomniac peering out one window in that dark village, and I'd be a dead man. I cut around town, hoping I wouldn't fall into a swamp or a ravine or smash into a tree or even break a twig. Good old Mordovian earth. Flat, no surprises, frozen hard, even in midsummer.

At the far edge of the village I still moved quietly. Silence was more important than speed. The dogs were quiet now. I had a few hours to get some distance from this place. I had to make my way around—far around—that little railroad station. Maybe a night watchman lurked there.

Puotma, where our little branch line met the main line, was maybe twenty miles down the track. If I walked fast, at a four-mile-an-hour clip, I could make it in five hours. Six o'clock. Too late. I had to do it in four, four and a half at the most, just had to, to arrive in darkness. No, even five-thirty was too late. Somebody would be up making coffee. I had to make it in four.

The fog began to thin just as I no longer needed it for cover. The faint gleam of the tracks began to show. I could run well off to their side, at the edge of the woods, yet use the tracks for a road map. Every few minutes I slowed to listen for sounds of a search party. I had to stop my breath so I could hear, making me all the more breathless, making it harder to resume my pace. My right shoe pinched the base of my big toe, raising a blister, which flared to a flame. No time for that. Let it burn. I pretended it was a bonfire and I was cold, and the fire warmed me. It worked. I don't know if it was a state of mind, or adrenaline, or relief or hope or what, but I had never felt stronger or healthier. I had to get to Puotma and I *would* get there.

Time was a single moment, just a single long-stretched moment.

I don't know how I sensed that Puotma was there, just ahead of me, but I knew it. On every one of those *étaps* to see the consul, maybe a dozen of them, I had had to ride the train to Puotma, to the transit prison. But I had not been aware of any landmarks. If I had been, I couldn't have seen them in the darkness. But I knew the village was there. And there it was.

The house I wanted was two houses from the track, on the right, at the near edge of town. At the first houses on the right, I slowed. Against the dark sky I tried to make out the chimneys. Merciful God, the first subtle shadings of dawn reached out to help me. There hung that silly, dear, glorious *ded moroz*, giver of gifts to good children at the beginning of their new year. Until that moment I guess I had never believed in Santa Claus.

I lifted my hand to rap my knuckle on the door. No. She wouldn't hear it. I mustn't bang. I picked up a stone and, to the right of her door, tapped lightly but sharply at her window. I tapped again.

The curtain yanked open.

And there was the face of Marinka. Wrenched from sleep, she looked puzzled. When she saw it was me, her eyes widened and froze.

Her face disappeared and the door opened. She let me in and closed it instantly.

"*Gospodi.* God forbid. What have you done?"

I didn't have to tell her. She knew what I'd done. I couldn't speak. I don't know whether I lacked the strength, or the breath, or merely the words. I just lifted my hands and spread them to say, Yes, I know it's bad, I'm sorry.

"You know you can't stay here."

I nodded.

But I wasn't going anywhere.

And she wasn't sending me anywhere. She motioned me away

216

from the door, away from the window, to a small table in the middle of her tiny kitchen. She lit her stove without turning on the light, and put on a pot of tea.

As my breath came back, I told her of the night's events.

Her eyes absorbed every word, but she said nothing. I saw in her eyes resentment, anger, confusion at this unexpected thing happening to her. She asked me questions and I searched her voice. No, her anger was not at me.

"Come," she ordered, leading me to a closet at the end of a tiny hall. She pulled out some clothes. Men's clothes.

"He never took these."

I got out of my prison things and tried on her ex-husband for size. Good fit. Everything was going right.

She stuffed the prison clothes into a bag, absentmindedly searching around for a place to hide them. She shoved the bag into the closet. That reminded her of something. She took a bottle from her kitchen and stepped out her front door. After looking up and down the street, seeing no one, she splashed her front steps, the walkway in front of her house, up the street and down, and out to the middle as far as she seemed willing to venture, maybe twenty-five feet.

When she reentered, I smelled kerosene.

"They will come with dogs," she muttered. After what seemed a long time, she asked, "Where you go now?"

I shrugged. I had no words. I had no plan. I had nothing I could say.

Another long time. Then she made a decision. I could see it in a faint twitch of resolution. "Today I make telephone call."

"To whom?"

"To somebody."

"Where?"

"Where you make call? From telephone, you make call."

"What telephone?"

"In Puotma we have telephone. You think we don't have telephone? In post office. Nobody hear me. Nobody know who I call."

"Please, it's my—I have to know who you're calling."

"Not just yours, mine too. I asked you to come here? Now is my life, too."

"Tonight, when it's dark, I'll leave. I'm sorry, I had no choice. Tonight I'll go."

"Go, go, you cannot go like that. No place to go. They find you, they don't ask, they shoot. Please, no more talking until I make telephone call."

"To *whom?*"

"Later we talk. Now you sleep."

She disappeared into a room off the rear of the hall, opposite a small sitting room. I followed her to its door. It seemed to be her everything-else room: a sewing table, unpacked boxes, a laundry bag, pictures both hung and unhung, skis, and winter clothes lying across a daybed. She dumped the clothes on the sewing table, pulled down the cover, and commanded:

"Sleep."

While I stood there, empty of reaction, she went back to the kitchen and returned, handing me another cup of tea and two pills.

"No, I mustn't."

"You must."

"I'll rest. But I have to keep my head clear."

She pulled the window curtain closed, surely for security rather than to shut out the light.

"What time does your train go?"

"No work today."

"How come?"

"I arranged day off. Many things I must do. You picked fine day to make visit."

I closed my eyes. I was still running. My body craved rest, but my mind made sleep impossible. Each time a sound jarred me from a half-doze, I was surprised that sleep was not impossible. The possibility of it scared me. I had to stay alert.

After a while—I don't know how long—I heard her front door close.

218

"Marinka?" I murmured.

No answer. She was gone. What do I do if there's a knock on the door? Come on, now. You do nothing. Nobody knows she hasn't gone to work. It's normal that nobody answers. Get some sleep, jerk.

The sound of the front door startled me out of—out of what, where? My God, I remember where I am, why I'm here, how I got here. Who is it? Whose quiet steps are those?

Marinka's face was looking down at me.

"What time is it?"

"You slept."

"How long have you been gone?"

"Not long."

The sunlight said nine, ten o'clock.

"Are they—? What's happening?"

"Militia everywhere. They look. They ask people in store. Women shake heads, uch, uch, terrible. They think you hide under house in Leplai, maybe still running to Saransk."

She could be biting her knuckles. Instead, she seemed amused.

"So it was a bad time to try to make your call."

"I made call."

"You still won't tell me where."

"I get tea."

She returned with a tiny tray in one hand, dragging a chair by the other. She sat down and arranged the tea. She knew she was driving me crazy.

I'd wait her out, damn it. I wasn't going to ask her again.

Finally the silence cracked her. "I called Moscow."

"Moscow? Who in Moscow?"

"I know man in Moscow. I cannot tell you much. What I do not tell you, Gerahld, don't ask me. I know man in Moscow. Really, I don't know man. I have number of telephone. He is member of group—you understand word, underground group?"

"Of course."

"Group helps political, what you call, political—"

219

"Yes, yes." I didn't know how to say in Russian that I knew about dissidents.

"They, I don't know, they arrange internal visas, they make passports for people who must leave Soviet Union."

Unbelievable. "How do you know them?"

"I asked you, Gerahld, don't ask me."

Okay, I wouldn't ask. I just stared, incredulous.

"All right, I tell you little bit. I know only little bit. You remember I tell you of my friend, Jewish friend. He devotes whole life to get out. If he cannot get out as Jew, he will get out illegally, as dissident. Through underground. That's what he swears. For me, too bad if he doesn't get out as Jew. Only as Jew can he marry me and take me with him. Still—" She formed a careful thought. "Still, if he must go illegally, if one day he just disappear and I hear no more, he wants me not to worry. I call certain number in Moscow, and someone will help me know if he is all right, if he left safely. Maybe, maybe possible, someday, he said, maybe they also help me—"

"So you called your friend about me." I didn't like that. "Are you sure we can trust him?"

"No, not friend. I told you, I called number in Moscow."

I was losing my grip on this. Part of me lay still mired in that exhausted sleep. I had to shake that off and grab hold of this unbelievable, thrilling gift. The excitement of it threw me back to that moment in Amsterdam when Mr. Lee dangled the names Singapore, Kuala Lumpur, seducing me into images of James Bond, Humphrey Bogart. Now more seduction: an underground would spirit me to freedom! But beneath that thrill I fluttered nervously with the echo of David and the fat man. Everything went wrong when I entrusted my life to others who were so sure of what they were doing that they forgot about me.

I don't know this man from Moscow. I don't know Marinka's Jewish friend. I hardly know Marinka. Am I to entrust my life, everything, to that gray mystery of a man in Moscow and his underground?

"What can he do?"

"He come."

"He's *coming?* Here?"

"Yes."

"How?"

"On train. How else he come?"

"When?"

"Tomorrow. Too late for train today."

"Who are these people? What do they do? How do they work?"

"I told you, Gerahld, I don't know. I only know—even what I know, I must not know. Don't ask me what I don't know."

Well, she was clearly telling me one thing. I didn't have to leave. I didn't have to figure out my next move. Nothing to figure until that character got here.

Soon Marinka left again for her errands, for whatever it was she had stayed home to do. I fell into tense slumber again. When I bolted awake and looked into her kitchen, I saw she had returned. A canvas sack of groceries sat atop her table. Marinka was out in her sunny garden, stooping, picking tomatoes. She saw me and came in.

"You lost already in big city of Saransk. Majority at store absolutely sure."

"What do the others say?"

"Minority faction says you already dead in woods. Dogs found you, bit you into pieces. Authorities ashamed, so they say nothing."

She began putting together a dinner, full of delicacies, full of affection, full of memories of those late morning hours at the *prot-sedurnaia*. But no spoken word of affection or memory. Scarcely a word about anything. I'd reach for a vegetable, for a utensil, for a chance to help her. I'd put them down again, my head blank with distraction. Peeling a potato was too much to manage.

We ate, almost silent. The meal was wonderful, but I don't remember a thing about it, even whether I enjoyed it. After we cleared the dishes, she broke the silence, asking this detail or that, filling in blanks about my flight. But nothing about tomorrow, about plans, about the future. Nothing about America. Nothing about ourselves.

There was nothing to do but go to bed, she in her room, I in mine.

Sleep came, fed by the security that I was dead in the woods, eaten by dogs, if not lost in Mordovia's capital city of Saransk.

18

MOSCOW

Marinka was still at work when I heard the train rattle into Puotma. To this day I don't know how he identified the house. Would she have risked directing him on the phone? Would he, a stranger, at a time like this, have asked around for her by name? But there he was, rapping at the door.

I didn't hesitate to open it. No way could he be KGB. He was in his fifties, with gray eyes that were at once alert and sad. Soviet men, I had noticed, grew old in one of two ways: either with the belly-out authority of Brezhnev and Premier Khrushchev, or hunching their shoulders into a stoop. This man hunched with humility. His suit of brownish black had not seen a steam presser for weeks, if ever. His shoes, as scuffed as a farmer's, were narrow and thin-soled. A city man.

Before either of us said a word, his eyes impersonally searched for acknowledgment that this was the right place. I put out my hand. He took it and said, almost in a whisper, "Call me Dmitri."

Now I knew what his name wasn't.

"Amster," I responded.

Inside, he scrutinized me and said with the gravity of a political pronouncement, "Hmm, *Amerikanets.*"

"Yes."

He nodded almost imperceptibly, absorbing the importance of it. Then:

"So."

I waited. No, he wasn't about to start talking. That was his cue for me to start.

I narrated the previous morning's escape. I told him of my continuous expectation of an early release that never came, and my readiness to take practically any risk rather than face another five years in labor camp.

He nodded still, with solemn comradely understanding. Then the inevitable:

"What their charge against you?"

I hadn't thought through how to handle this with him. "Contraband."

He solemnly digested that too. His next question—about what I had carried—would turn him against me. I waited for it.

"I must take your picture," he said, reaching into a worn briefcase. From it he withdrew a thick book and opened it. The edges of its pages framed a cavity from which he removed a case for opera glasses. Out of that he drew a small camera.

Picture? What the fuck for? Who is this guy?

"Picture? Why?"

"Your visa. You must go on train from here to Moscow. How you travel without visa?"

"To Moscow? When?"

"I go back on seven o'clock train tonight. Tomorrow we fix papers. Next day I come on morning train, we go on seven o'clock train."

"Then what?"

"Then we do best we can."

"Best you can to do what?"

224

He shrugged with that fatalistic Russian pursing of the lips. "We try to find passport."

"Find it? Where?"

He fluttered his palm to say, Down, boy. "Not jump too far ahead. First, Moscow. Tomorrow, world."

"But can't you tell me? What do you mean, find a passport?"

The shrug and the grimace again. "How find? In street, we look for American tourist. We take time until we find tourist who look like you. You young. Maybe we find tourist younger than you, but look like you, maybe student. He needs travel money. If he sell passport to us, he can go to embassy, say he lost passport, and get new one. We try. We try one way, try another way."

My plan, my daydream, almost exactly! I was born to this intrigue business. I was beginning to have confidence in Dmitri.

Marinka arrived, greeting him with a tense mixture of cordiality and distance. Clearly they hadn't met. As they conversed, she lowered her voice and began to speed the pace of her Russian, the way natives do to bar foreigners from understanding. He speeded his accordingly. For a short while they talked about me, then about her friend and her. Then something about marriage, spoken very fast. I made a show of not listening.

That evening, after he left, and the next evening, Marinka tautly went about her chores, saying little, almost as though I weren't there. When I said something or asked a question, she answered distractedly, like a mother responding to a child when her mind is somewhere else. At one point, I took another stab at the forbidden question:

"Why is Dmitri—?"

Her eyes whipped at me with reprimand. Of course. I shouldn't use his name, not even privately, here.

"Why are they taking this risk?"

"Must ask? You make need for risk. They take risk."

"But they don't know me."

She said nothing. But the puzzle of it wouldn't let me go.

"Are they doing this for me? Or for you?"

She shot me another shriveling glance, but said nothing.

I kept wondering about it that night, and all the next day while Marinka was at work. Fragments of her rapid conversation with Dmitri replayed in my mind, like a tape slowed down for me to understand. Just as she had told me, her plan to marry her Jewish friend, while apparently stemming from real friendship, was a ruse for legally getting her out of the country. But I knew that Marinka had talked to Dmitri of marriage not only in connection with her friend, but also in connection with me. Only one explanation made sense. While she planned to marry her friend to ride out of the country on his back, so to speak, she told Dmitri her real reason for wanting to get out was to get to America—and marry me.

Wonderful Marinka! That made getting me out a matter of importance to them, linking me with their previous commitment to get her out. But why they were undertaking such a complex risk to get her out—to that I still had no clue, nor was I ever to have one.

The only other explanation that made some sense was that helping an American fugitive get home somehow dovetailed with their commitment to help anti-Soviet dissidents escape to America.

The day after next, at the same time, I listened for the chug of the train arriving from Moscow, and soon saw Dmitri arrive at the door.

From his briefcase this time, with the detached pride of a professional showing graduation pictures for approval, Dmitri handed me my internal visa. There was my face, staring dumbstruck in the unique way that is reserved for passports and driving licenses. Then he handed me a sheet of paper, also with my photo, a permit to travel into and out of Mordovia.

"Your name," he informed me, his finger running along the typing on the printed white card, "is Vladimir Alexandrovich Susnov. Your occupation, disabled."

Dmitri peered at me for a sign that I acknowledged his cleverness. I was puzzled and must have looked it.

"Visa must show where you work. Problem, yes? You speak like foreigner. Where you work if people hear you speak like foreigner?"

From his coat pocket he withdrew a gray armband and pinned it around my sleeve.

"This means disabled, first-class. Here, card say 'Disabled, first-class.' Not required, work. Not required, work stamp. You know how you disabled?"

I looked at him blankly.

He squeezed his lips shut with thumb and forefinger, like a clothespin. "You mute. You cannot speak. You hear, yes. Speak, no. So nobody hears accent. No accent, nobody gives you attention."

"Beautiful," I said.

Instead of beaming, he turned stern.

"You *must not* talk. Not move lips. Understand?"

"I understand."

"You don't understand. Without experience, you cannot understand. We practice."

Dmitri asked me questions, surprised me by suddenly calling my name. Once he yelled, "What you doing?" I almost answered, "Nothing," but caught myself in time. He drilled me in expressing myself with facial and hand gestures, never uttering so much as a grunt. We practiced this drudgery until Marinka came home. It reminded me of the way I had made Pete and Darrell practice with those overweight suitcases.

This time Marinka scarcely conversed with either of us. We ate mightily for our long train ride—potato soup, kolbasa and kasha, fresh bread, a shot of vodka (like Dmitri, I slugged it down at one gulp), and tea. Despite the meal, my stomach fluttered.

"Is there some back way I can get to the station without being seen?" I asked Marinka.

She started, clearly not having thought about it.

"No, no," Dmitri said with quiet assurance. He *had* thought about it. "We walk together. Nobody looking for two men together."

It was time to go.

227

Marinka and Dmitri shook hands, exchanging some unexpressed comradeship.

Marinka faced me. I started to reach for her hand. It wasn't there. She looked up at me. I embraced her. I was too tense, too apprehensive of the coming minutes and hours, to feel anything. I did not feel her trying to draw anything from the embrace. There was something formal about it. Maybe it was a show for Dmitri.

Would I ever see her again? How could I? How could I not?

Moscow's surburban villages began sliding by the train window at dawn. They were replays of Puotma and Leplai, but more densely packed, shacks crouching behind irregular hedges and gardens. Then came tall, pale yellow façades of vast apartment blocks. My misshapen awareness, distorted by fitful sleep and strained wakefulness, brought back the unreality of these city sights from that van ride three years earlier to Lefortovo. Only this time, the escort controlling me was not KGB but Dmitri.

Just as I had then, I wondered now: Where am I going? What's ahead of me?

I wanted to ask Dmitri questions. I wanted to ask him for assurance. I simply wanted some talk for companionship. But I had to sit silent, gagged by that gray band on my arm. It not only marked me as a cripple, it was making me one. A couple of times during the night when it was obviously safe, I poised my lips to say something, ask something. Dmitri's foot rapped smartly against mine. He took this mute business seriously. Even when nobody, *nobody*, could see.

Outside the station we boarded a bus, then changed to another. Early birds in work clothes, in neckties and dresses, glanced at my armband, at me, with low-key, sleepy indifference.

We got off in a district of newish apartment buildings and, after walking several blocks, entered one. Dmitri pressed a button for the elevator. None came. A woman, descending the adjacent stairs, grumbled without even looking at us:

"Every day different. Today, stuck at three. Yesterday, five."

We started up the stairs. Dmitri muttered, "We shoot Sputnik. Why we can't fix elevator?"

I ached just to grunt a response, but that floppy, repressive hand of his motioned me silent. On the sixth floor he unlocked a door, admitting us to a sunny apartment with dead-white walls and a smell of ever-damp plaster. Its few sticks of furniture—a table, straight chairs, second-hand lamps, a gramophone sitting atop a bookcase that held few books—were more scattered than arranged. A smaller room, just as sunny, was furnished only by a mattress on the floor, no linen or blankets. Clearly, nobody regularly lived here.

This would become my home, I didn't know for how long.

From this point on I will say practically nothing else about the apartment and my stay there. For two reasons. First, I want to avoid even the slightest risk of dropping a clue as to the location of that safe house, not so much to protect it as to protect the people who brought me there. The weird thing is that I myself have no idea where in Moscow it was located, or, for that matter, whose safe house it was. I learned nothing about the organization that hosted me, and wouldn't tell what I had learned, if there were anything to tell. The second reason is that during my stay there the predominant thing that happened was nothing. Each day seemed exactly like every other.

Every third day or so, Dmitri brought me food, plenty of it, and newspapers, magazines, books. My skill at reading Russian vastly improved, even while I feared losing my ability to speak it. Once, he came with another man. The stranger lurked wordlessly near the door, looking out the window as though hiding his face from me. Another time he came with four people: that same stranger, two other men, and a woman. A committee of underground dissidents conspiring in the heart of Moscow. In *my* living room. The very idea of it awed me. Dmitri introduced me to them, but not them to me.

"You please take nap," Dmitri told me, nodding toward the bedroom.

I left them, closing the door. They turned on the radio, loud.

To talk, they must have sat there practically in a football huddle, lip-reading each other.

When Dmitri came alone I hungered for talk, for hearing words, saying words, any words. He gave me that hand-flopping motion to relax, cool it. It was like snuffing out my life. A few times he let himself in at two or three in the morning, plopped on the hard couch fully clothed, and left soon after dawn, never explaining why he'd come. The apartment had a telephone. Dmitri never used it. He told me the minute we first arrived that I was never under any circumstances to answer it.

Almost every day, sometimes two or three times a day, it rang, and it would keep ringing forever.

One day I asked, "Why does it ring?"

"People want somebody else."

"How can you tell?"

"I know nobody calls us. We give nobody number."

"How can so many people have the wrong number?"

"Maybe not many people. Maybe all same person."

"You'd think that after so many tries he'd look up the right number."

That puzzled Dmitri as much as the ringing puzzled me. By the time we untwined our puzzlements, I'd learned that Moscow had no phone directory. None. Nor could you call directory assistance. If people wanted you to have their number, they'd give it to you. If they didn't give it to you, clearly you had no business having it. The same applied to stores, offices, government bureaus, even hotels. Dmitri didn't seem to think this system strange.

I recall only one visit when Dmitri talked more than he had to, even seeming to enjoy it. There was something I had wondered about, I told him, since I had first met him in Puotma. I took out my internal visa and asked how he had gotten that purple rubber stamp to straddle both the card and my photo. "Do you have your own rubber stamp?"

He looked hurt. "Our stamp? This stamp official."

"How?" I knew I was breaking the rules to ask, but I couldn't resist.

I had touched a subject of his pride. He didn't give me the squelching gesture, but took my card.

"Look. If we had stamp, what good to stamp new picture? Old card has already old stamp. New stamp on new picture not fit old stamp on old card. See, here, look. Same stamp."

"You mean this is a genuine old card? You didn't print it yourself?"

That same hurt look. "How print? This card official."

"You mean there is a real Vladimir Alexandrovich Susnov?"

"No more. He was mute, but now finished, dead."

I stared at him.

He laughed. "No, no. We don't do that. He died, plain, by himself. We hear someone dies, we make arrangements"—a vague hand motion—"we get his old visa card."

"But his card must have been stamped—right across his picture."

"Aha! Almost you understand!"

No, I didn't.

He teased me with a haughty silence, then relented.

"You know when egg cooks long in water? Egg cooks hard, *da?*"

"Of course." Why was this guy twisting my leg? Marinka must have told him of my perverted craving for hard-boileds. Now he was sticking it to me.

"Okay, cook egg very hard. Take off cover, egg hard but still soft like, mmm, rubber, *da?* Now take old card, put on table like this. Take spoon with two drops vodka. Two drops most. Better than vodka, hospital alcohol. Drop alcohol on egg. Now take egg, roll on card like this, very careful, roll over stamp, very straight, very careful. What happens? Stamp no more on card. Stamp on egg. Comes perfect. Now lift old picture from card, paste new picture. Now roll egg on card with new picture, very straight, very careful. Look. New visa. Stamped perfect, just like official."

His eagerness to explain that fascinating technique left me with a faint suspicion that he'd read about it in a detective novel. But I

231

couldn't fault his explanation, and besides, who cared? That conversation was like a party. I lived on it for days. He never talked that much again.

To fill the time, I exercised. I ate. I washed my clothes in the sink. I washed them again, before they needed it. I reread the newspapers. I ventured out for a walk every two or three days. To avoid becoming a familiar sight in the neighborhood, I went out at different times of day and walked different routes. But how different could I make them? I never dared venture more than two or three blocks away. I relished going to the busy street where that bus had let us off so I could look in restaurant and shop windows, but as soon as I stopped to look I'd get scared and steer away. The walks didn't relax me. While I craved seeing people, my fear of being seen by them made my heart pound so hard that when I returned I had trouble making it up the six flights. (At least half the time the elevator was stuck, remaining so for days.)

September brought the first snow. November pinched my nose and fingers with frostbite. But not my ears. Dmitri had dropped off a worn fur *shliapka* with earflaps. December brought a gift that lasted into February. Its crackling cold seemed to freeze the eyes of passing strangers, making them walk with heads down, buried in their earmuffed *shliapki*. I buried my face in mine. Nobody looked at anybody. I felt safer. Sometimes I ventured out on two successive days, feeling especially protected if the snow was falling.

Each day of isolation and uncertainty brought me closer to craziness than anything in the prison camp. Each time Dmitri showed up with a sack of food, I'd instantly ask, "Anything new?"

He knew there was only one kind of news I was interested in. "Nothing new," he'd say.

After a while I'd just greet him with a questioning look, and he'd shrug.

One day, after his shrug I blurted out, "What's going to happen?"

"I don't know. We only can wait."

"Is somebody trying? All this time, not even one passport?"

"Passports we have, we can get. But none right. Picture not look

232

like you. Or information not right, too short, too tall. I don't know."

"How much more time do you need?"

"We don't know, we don't know. What more can we tell you?"

The discouraged tone alarmed me. The new collective "we" made it sound worse.

"I'll go crazy. I can't stay here. What the hell am I supposed to do? Turn myself in? Go back?"

He said nothing, but looked glumly out the window. What did that mean?

"You've been thinking of that."

"We try think of everything."

"How can I go back? Impossible to go back."

He wouldn't look at me. "I know, I know."

"They'd kill me. I may as well go have a good time in Moscow and jump under a bus."

"They cannot kill you."

"Why can't they kill me? Why can't they give me another fifteen years? That's worse. Be quicker and easier with the bus."

"For what they give you fifteen?"

"Man, I escaped, I flew."

Now he turned to me. "You must telephone American embassy."

"What the hell are you talking about?"

"Very important you call embassy."

"What the hell for?"

"They must know you flew. Must know you live."

"You think they don't know by now? What good does that do?"

"They don't know."

"Of course they know. I haven't shown up for a consul meeting in seven, eight months. I'm supposed to see them four times a year. You think they haven't asked?"

"Oompossible they know. You think American consul get call from KGB, from somebody in Kremlin? You think somebody say, 'Apology, apology. American cannot come to meeting today. He flew over fence of labor camp and make fool of Soviet Union'? That what you think, yes? You think—"

I stopped listening. Ho-lee Russian Easter! I'd thought of every-thing, *everything* to do with my plight, but I hadn't thought of that obvious, central, controlling fact. They could hunt me. They could catch me. They could re-try and re-sentence me. They could torture me to tell how I did it, to tell who helped me, to try to get me to name names. They could isolate me till I died. But they couldn't send me back to camp. To any camp. To any prison where I could meet other prisoners. They couldn't tell the consul, who could then tell reporters from the outside world. They couldn't let anyone know I had flown their coop.

They're Russians. Russians don't let anything out that's an em-barrassment.

In fact, they couldn't do anything with me, except— There was no possible way they could hide the embarrassment that I was to them—as long as I still existed.

As long as I still existed. *Hey, I've got to get in touch with the American embassy.*

"But what would I tell them?"

"That you live."

"Could they give me political asylum?"

"Oompossible."

"I'm their citizen."

"First, how you get into embassy for asylum? Guard outside stop you, ask for passport. Second, how can they keep you? You are Soviet prisoner. Legal prisoner. Guilty. Americans cannot steal you."

True. Trying to seek refuge in the embassy was as bad as sur-rendering to the KGB.

What choices did I have?

Three. I could think of three, no more.

One, I could try to skip the country, somehow slip through the border. Didn't thousands of refugees do it in World War II? Oom-possible. Hundreds of miles to the border, no way to eat, no way to sleep, without attracting attention. Suppose I survived to the border, even slipped across, then what? Then Poland or Romania. And then what? Then East Germany or Czechoslovakia or Hungary.

When Stalin built Eastern Europe into a buffer zone with an Iron Curtain, he sure fenced me in. Oompossible.

Two, I could stay here, living like a caged lion for God knows how long, waiting for a passport until my brains curdled. But could I? Dmitri was all but telling me my lease was up. They had tried, really tried, but they couldn't get me out of Russia. So they had to get me out of *here*. They had to. I was becoming—I already was—a mortal danger to them.

Three, I could give myself up to the Soviets. *Dear Chairman Brezhnev: Sorry for error, please cancel successful escape.* Oompossible? That option was insane. Preposterous. Yet—yet of the three choices, it was the only one that was beginning to make some sense.

Right now, I'm trapped, with no apparent escape. If I go back, *they're* trapped. What do they do with me? They *can't* send me back to Mordovia. Are they going to send me where I can give new travelogues—on my winter vacation? "Forget America, fellows. Let me tell you about my high life in Moscow." Send me to Vladimir, like Gary Powers? Vladimir has prisoners, too, who transfer around, feeding the grapevine. In a year, less than a year, every prisoner from here to Vladivostok will know about the American who made suckers of the vaunted Soviet militia.

Only two things they can do. One, having arranged it, they can announce my unfortunate death, accidental, from an overdose of kasha deprivation, and just stonewall American demands for an investigation. Or, two, they can pledge me to silence and get me out of their hair, just ship me the hell home, rid themselves of this insufferable, oompossible pain in the ass.

I checked it through again. It came out the same. Those were the two, the *only* two, choices they had. Kill me or ship me out.

Ladies and gentlemen, the game is Double or Nothing.

By God, I think I'll play.

"You think I ought to surrender and go back, don't you?"

Dmitri squeezed his forehead with long, tremulous fingers, unable to say anything to me.

"Okay. I will."

235

"You must call embassy. From telephone on street."

"Okay. I will. I'll need some money. I'll need their number."

He took a slip of paper out of his pocket and put it on the table. So he'd been carrying it, waiting for this conversation. Next to it he put some coins, enough for a baker's dozen of local calls.

"Today. I'll call today. After you leave. I need to think about just what to say."

Suddenly he turned to me, seizing my trousers belt with two hands, stooping slightly, like a supplicant. His eyes were filling with tears. His voice trembled, just like my mother's when she pleaded with my father to lay off.

"You don't know what will happen to you. *Pozhaluista*, please, please, you must remember every moment, this place not exist, we not exist. Wipe from mind everything you remember, so you say nothing to give incrimination to us. If you make any mistake to lead them to house, to me, then every one of us, whole organization, *pizdets*, *pizdets*, end, finished."

"Of course."

"Embassy can protect you. Tell embassy, main demand, main condition if you go back, KGB not squeeze you for information. Must promise not squeeze you. Then embassy can protect you."

"Suppose they promise. Can we trust a promise?"

Dmitri hunched his shoulders with dread. "If they not keep, then *pizdets*, the worst, the end."

That word, which I'd heard often in camp, derives from *pizda*. It means cunt. Strange that at this moment I should wonder about its etymology and what cultural message it bore.

After he left, when there was nothing to do but go out to a street telephone and get the job done, my throat went dry and my hands began to tremble. I stared at them shaking. I laid them on the table, palms up, which steadied them. Now only the fingers quivered. I tried to swallow and couldn't. I gulped two glasses of water. What the hell was the matter with me? I thought I had this all figured out, that everything was okay, that I had them over a barrel.

Walking, walking fast in the cold February air would fix me. I

236

went out and headed toward a phone booth I'd seen near the bus stop. Halfway there, a hot flush shot up from my gut. How the hell could a mute talk on a telephone?

Chrissakes, Jerry, calm down. How does anybody around here know I'm a mute? The armband just says I'm disabled. For all they know, I could have a paralyzed sphincter. But still, that bus stop is a bad spot, too many people. There's another phone booth the other way on a quiet street.

I headed there.

19

LEFORTOVO

In that icy booth, unable to tell the shivers from the trembles, I struggled to insert a coin and handle the slip of paper with the number. The quiet of this street felt like a spotlight on me. I wished I'd gone to the busy one. Somebody was watching me. I could practically hear his eyes focusing. I told the operator the number I wanted. Do they automatically trace calls placed by foreign accents?

"Embassy."

The voice startled me. Is this the right one? Did she say United States? What language should I talk in?

"Dennis Reece, please."

"Moment, please," she said. Accent, Russian. They let Russians work there?

"Look, I can't wait—" She was gone.

"Consul office."

"Dennis Reece, please."

"Who calls, please?"

"Look, I don't have time, please put him on."

"Who calls, please?"

"I can't tell you now. This is urgent. Is he there?"

"Hold, please."

Damn, damn it. I mustn't stay on this phone more than one minute. I can't allow time for a trace. I can't give myself time to slip and say too much. For Chrissakes, woman, Dennis, the whole pack of you, if—

"Can someone else help you?"

"Tell him this is an *emergency*. If he's there, make him pick up. If he's not—"

"Hold, please."

"Hello. Who is this, please?"

"Dennis? Mr. Reece?"

"Who is this, please?"

That was him. At our meetings at Butyrka, his distant, foggy monotone always seemed the voice of a middle-aged professor coming out of the face of a thin Midwesterner not yet thirty. I wished my favorite vice-consul, Larry Napper, hadn't been transferred.

"This is Gerald Amster."

Silence.

"I—"

"Where are you?"

"In Moscow."

"Moscow? Have you been released?"

His calm scratched at me.

"No. I escaped."

Again a pause. "You're kidding."

"No, it's the truth, I—"

"Say, would you hold on a second?"

I practically felt his hand covering the mouthpiece, saying something to somebody. Asking someone to pick up another phone? Turning on a recorder?

"What did you say? You're in Moscow?"

"Yeah, I escaped."

"We heard you were sick. They said that was why you haven't come to—"

"Look, I've got to get off. Can't talk now."

"Well, what will you—?"

"Can't give you any details now. I'll reach you again, don't know when. Hey, tell that girl not to ask who's calling. I don't want to say my name again."

"They never informed us. Mr. Amster, are you all right?"

"I'm okay. I'm okay. Think of options for me."

"Think of what?"

"Options. Things I can do."

"When will you call?"

"Said I don't know."

"Don't do anything rash. Consider carefully before you act."

"Don't worry. G'bye."

My whole body quaked. People watching me from doorways were closing in. From the corner, something lunged toward me. I whirled. Come on, it's a kid on a bike. Immediately behind him wheeled a half-dozen more. Fucking Russian kids, why do they always move in packs? I ached to flee home, to race down that street. Don't, damn it. Walk. Stand straight and calm and walk. You don't have to feel calm, but you damn well better look calm.

So what did all that get me?

I reviewed the call line by line, and decided it had got me plenty. First and above all, they—my countrymen, my protectors—now knew that I had escaped, that I was in Moscow, and that I was okay. Second, I had learned that six months after my disappearance the Soviets had still not told my embassy. Extremely important. That said the Russians were chafing with embarrassment, and gave me a strong hint that I was holding the commanding cards. My calculations may not have been so dumb after all. Third, I had started Reece thinking about options. I didn't know where it would lead, but at least he wasn't wishing a plague on me. "Are you all right? Don't do anything rash." I needed his help, and he sounded like he just might give it.

Didn't know when I'd call again, hell. Maybe I'd meant it when I said it. But I knew I had to get my next step started, and I'd go nuts waiting. Late next morning—a Tuesday—I was out. This time

240

to the phone on the busy street, actually drawn by the danger of it, just like the old days. Got there and felt as though I was standing naked atop the Kremlin wall, all of Moscow gaping. Couldn't stand it. Got the hell away and found another phone on a side street.

"Dennis Reece, quick, it's urgent."

Click, click, no questions. Good boy.

"Hello."

"This is me."

"Who?"

"Me. The fish that got away."

"Yes."

"Have they said anything yet?"

"Well, no. As a matter of fact, I've placed an inquiry. It may take a little time."

"How long?"

"Can't say. But what do you plan to do?"

"What do you think I can do?"

"This is very unusual. You're legally theirs, you know. We can't change that."

"Except I'm not theirs now."

"The awkward thing is, we have no official information."

"Look, I can't talk long. How about telling them I'll consider going back? But they've got to guarantee two—no, three things. One, no punishment, no harm of any kind, for taking off. Two, consideration for early release, as though this didn't happen. Third, no interrogation, no pressure. Anything I don't want to tell them, they drop it."

"If they agree to those three, you would what? Turn yourself in?"

"Maybe." Good tone, Jerry, show your power. But do I dare admit I ache for advice? "How do you think that'll go down?"

"Let me take a reading on that at the Foreign Ministry. When will you call again?"

"At the what?"

"The Foreign Ministry."

"How they going to tell you? This is KGB. Even the MVD can't decide on this. I know this is KGB."

"Yes, but we've got to approach through the Foreign Ministry. They can take it anywhere they see fit."

"I'll call you when I can."

I didn't want to risk being seen every day at a phone. Anyhow, I knew Reece's feeler through the Foreign Ministry would take a little time. This would have to go to KGB. Might have to go to the top man at KGB, Andropov. After all, I wasn't just a prisoner, not just someone who had embarrassed them by leaping their fence. Hell, Russians had done that. But someone had to decide whether to permit public embarrassment by, of all people, an American, and that took someone high. We were playing Superpower. In this game, every play, every trading chip, counts. They had me cornered and I had them cornered, both at the same time. Thinking about it made my head swirl. And gave me diarrhea.

After three days, I couldn't wait any longer. On Friday I called again.

"Yes, they have verified what you said."

"What do they want to do?"

"I must tell you that this is not an official matter in the embassy. Let's put it—I'm the only one here who knows about this."

"But you said they verified it."

"Yes, but officially I have asked them nothing, and they've said nothing."

"But what did they say?"

"Well, actually, they've said nothing. As yet. They have your conditions, your request. Let's not say 'they.' My personal contact has them. They need time to study it."

"Study it? What's that mean?"

"It may be just a very short time. But this is unusual."

"How much time?"

"Maybe just a few days, maybe less. But they did say one thing, and this is very important. You must not say anything to anyone

242

about—about how you got to where you are. They want absolute silence. Does anyone now know?"

They want absolute silence. I'm winning!

"Nobody. I'll call you when I can."

I waited through the weekend, through Monday and Tuesday. I could wait. I was winning. On Wednesday I called.

"Yes, I've heard. If you give yourself up promptly, I have their assurance you will not be harmed. It will not affect consideration of your early release. They will not press you for information. This is all unofficial, you understand."

All three. *Everything.* They're on their knees. On their knees to *me.*

"What's that mean, unofficial?"

"Unofficial. Our government didn't ask. Theirs didn't answer. It's just between me and my contact."

"Suppose they renege?"

How can they renege? They can't renege. Reece knows I'm alive. They know Reece knows. No matter what else happens, if I go back, they have to let me see him every three months. If I tell him to notify my aunt to tell AP and UPI that I escaped, that I surrendered with their promise, that they broke their promise, Reece has got to send word to my aunt. If any reporter then asked Reece about it, he couldn't lie and say it didn't happen. He might say, "No comment." Then the papers would know.

The Russians know all that. They have already thought it all through. There's no way they can renege.

"All I can say is, that is what they told me. Now, they have two conditions as well. They will hold to their side of the bargain only if you hold to these conditions. First, that you go back into custody promptly. Second, and this seems to be their key interest, that you stay absolutely silent about your experience, including—and they seem to emphasize this—including to people within the system, prisoners and guards alike."

Music. They're sweating as much as I am.

"Will they keep their word?"

"All I can do is tell you what I asked them and what they told me."

"But my life's on the line. I have to know—"

"I can only say that it's been our experience that when they make unofficial indications like this one, they tend to keep them."

"If I did it, what would they want me to do?"

"Do you know where *Energeticheskaia*, Energy Street, is?"

"No."

"Do you know your way around Moscow?"

Damn it, I didn't want to talk about Moscow, about locations, about what I knew or didn't know. Any such talk risks hints. Even avoiding hints risks hints.

"No."

"Do you have any money?"

"How much?"

"For a bus or a taxi."

Jeez, I didn't want to answer that on the telephone—with them listening.

"I can manage."

"You want to find your way to an Energy Street bus, to Lefortovo. You're familiar with Lefortovo?"

It's Old Home Week. "I know the place. When?"

"I'd make it very soon."

"Today?"

Pause. "I'm sure they'll be ready. When you get there, you are to mention the name of Colonel Belenkov, KGB, whose office will give them instructions. Colonel Belenkov."

They're swallowing my terms. The more they worry about my silence, the more they have to get rid of me quick. They're practically committing themselves to early release of me at my time of eligibility, five years, four months of my sentence, about a year from now.

If I'm winning, how come I feel that at any moment a squad of snoops lurking in doorways is going to pounce on me and tear me to pieces? Why this compulsion to run, not walk?

Thank God, Dmitri was in the apartment, even though I hated for him to see me so out of breath, so shaky. I wanted him to have confidence in me, especially as I recited the back-and-forth of the phone conversation.

He grimaced, his face asking, Is it worth anything? Can you trust their word?

"Look, I have no choice. I can't live like this anymore. You can't take this risk anymore."

That suffering look seized him again. "They will squeeze you to tell. You must forget. You must instruct your mind, you never saw me, never saw my friends, never saw this place. Promise or no promise, they will squeeze you."

"I've got no choice but to trust them. And what choice have you got but to trust me?"

Even as I said it I wondered what I'd do if they stuck hot forks up my ass and demanded to know where I'd spent my winter. Short of that, however, I knew I was covered, Dmitri was covered. If the Russians kept their promise, I'd just give them broad, reasonably credible answers, and they wouldn't press me severely for more. If they broke their promise, they'd shaft me to the limit. So there'd be no profit in telling them a thing.

All the cards were mine. Why was my heart pumping like a jackhammer? Why couldn't I make my hands stop shaking?

I told Dmitri I'd need some rubles, and he gave me a fistful.

At four in the afternoon, the beginning of twilight, my taxi drew up to the iron gate of Lefortovo.

"Da, da, Ahmstairr," said the puzzled guard in the kiosk to the left of the gate. He remembered me after three years. I didn't remember him, but their uniforms make them all look alike.

"Tell them to call Colonel Belenkov to say I'm here."

He phoned inside. Then he waved the taxi away and I waited.

An officer of the day appeared and led me through the two

double-key doors. He instructed a guard to take my bag, fetch my regular-issue blanket, sheet, and tin cup, and carry them to what would be my cell. Colonel Belenkov must have given him one hell of an instruction. I was a guest with a room reservation, a guard serving as my bellboy! The officer led me directly to Little Lubyanka, the investigational section. In a small room I stripped, bent over, and passed inspection, the officer seeming to apologize for its routine necessity, very polite. He asked if I'd eaten. I said no. He brought me to a room with a small table, an interrogation room. By God, this was the same room in which I'd spent all those weeks, day after day, leading up to my trial. In minutes, a meal came on a tray. Kasha again, but good kasha. With butter on it. And slabs of cheese and kolbasa. And a bowl of cold borscht with a dab of sour cream. Guard's food.

At about 7:00 P.M., a voice behind me broke into my after-dinner reading of *Pravda*.

"*Zdravstvuite*, hello, Ahmstairr."

Aleshkoi. It was like seeing an old friend, a face out of my high school yearbook. So he'd abandoned his dear wife at the dinner table to welcome me. Aleshkoi's look of greeting wasn't a smile; it wasn't a reprimand. I can only call it a curious leer. Yes, he was glad to see me, but disappointed in a friend doing what I had done. I think he admired that I'd brought it off, but detested me for it.

"Must get interpreter. Alex not here anymore, promoted."

"I don't think we need an interpreter."

"Ah-haaaaah," he sang in mock esteem. "You become true Soviet man."

"I've had a first-rate education."

His face turned official. "I think you already know—" He pressed his lips together and swallowed as though something sour had come up. "You don't need say what you don't want. If you want tell me details, I listen. But you not required."

"Right."

"You need cigarettes?"

"I always need cigarettes."

246

He slid half a pack of filters across to me, opening a fresh pack for himself.

"How you got out?"

"Well, there had been a big rainstorm, and the lights went out. All the electricity in camp, even the fence."

"What time?"

"The lights went out about ten."

"What time you go?"

"Sometime after midnight."

"What time, exact?"

"Look, I didn't check the clock in the railroad station and write it in my diary. Maybe one o'clock, maybe two. I don't know. It was dark."

"What time, exact you can?"

What's he harping on that for? To help pin the blame on someone at camp? To figure out where I headed before daybreak? Fuck him. That's his problem.

"I told you it was dark. That's the best I can do. Let's move on."

Aleshkoi swallowed his surprise gracefully.

"What clothes you wore?"

"What clothes could I wear? My prisoner clothes. And the little black *shliapka* on my head that they give trusties."

"Where you run?"

"To Puotma, to the train station. I knew what time the morning train to Moscow came. I stayed out of sight, then got on the train."

"How you got on train?"

"I walked on."

"When woman ask for ticket, for visa, what you show her?"

Before the conductor appeared, Dmitri had told me how to handle showing my visa to *her*, so I guessed that conductors were always women.

"Nobody asked."

"Oompossible."

"Nobody asked."

"What you do if somebody asked?"

247

"I didn't have time to think about it."

"But what you do *if* somebody asked?"

"I tell you nobody did. I was lucky. Look, I am true Soviet man, so I don't believe in God, right? But sometimes I think God believes in me."

"How you get on train in prisoner clothes?"

"I didn't."

"Ahmstairr. Please, Ahmstairr. You said you wore prisoner clothes. You don't want answer, don't answer. But don't talk foolish."

"Look, the town is full of clothes hanging on lines, because nobody in Puotma has discovered drying machines, right? The clothes were all frozen stiff, so I risked catching a terrific cold in the balls. But I dressed well."

"Ahmstairr. Don't expect me believe that."

"You asked me. I'm telling you."

His eyes drooped, frustrated, resigned. "Tomorrow we talk more."

"Can I have a partner in my cell?"

"For what you want partner?"

"I hate being alone."

"Oompossible."

"Why?"

"Ahmstairr, I not give you formal answer. I tell you simple. Important part of agreement, your part, is you talk to nobody, correct? You made promise, and you must keep promise, you never tell anybody your story of escape. You know why? Because your story oompossible. Absolutely not possible you get on train. Not possible you go by self to Moscow. Tomorrow, day after tomorrow, I listen to your story all you want. *I* listen. But you tell oompossible story to nobody else, absolutely. This our understanding, yes?"

"Right. We understand each other completely."

"So. No cellmate, silence easier."

In my little room that night I was surprised to find that the loneliness was delicious. For the first time in six months, I didn't have to stay half awake, listening for every sound on the stairs, every groan and rattle of the elevator, wondering who it was, whether it might be somebody coming to get me. For six months I'd lived the life of Anne Frank, practically writing her diary. This first night at Lefortovo I could throw the book away. I didn't know how long I'd be at Lefortovo, and didn't worry much about it.

There was one thing I was now sure of. Aleshkoi had all but told me I'd never see Mordovia again. If they wouldn't let me have one cellmate, they sure as hell wouldn't throw me back among a campful.

What faintly worried me was not the coming weeks, but the next morning. How should I handle Aleshkoi when he started asking about who had given me shelter? Would he stand for my stonewalling? If he got one whiff of Marinka or Dmitri, good-bye agreement. One tiny hint of an underground conspiracy and he'd check with his bosses. Come hell or high water, they'd go after it.

"Where you stayed in Moscow?"

Good start for the morning. If he was proceeding chronologically, as he mainly did before the trial, we'd already made it past Marinka.

"I slept in the basements of apartment houses. Right near the water boiler. It was warm."

"Oompossible nobody helped you. Who helped?"

Why was I letting him drag me through this? I didn't have to tell him a thing. But if I didn't, I'd be telling him there was important stuff I didn't want to tell him. And then they'd be forced to break the agreement and pursue it. I just had to keep it simple and be more or less credible.

"I lived like an American, okay? In America, when you're unemployed you get a hat and go out into the streets and beg people for food and money. Okay? So that's what I did."

"Oompossible. Against socialist law. Police arrest you in five minutes."

"Actually, I realized that the first day. The apartment house I stayed in most was near a restaurant. I studied what times they threw out their garbage and I lived off that."

"You want me believe you lived six months on restaurant garbage?"

249

"Why not? It was better than I'd had for three years."

"What name of restaurant?"

"I have no idea."

"Where was restaurant?"

"I have no idea. I don't know Moscow. I don't know where the Kremlin is. I've never seen the American embassy."

"You never read name of street on sign?"

"What for? I wasn't going anywhere."

"You make great difficulty, Ahmstairr."

"How?"

"I ask simple questions. You give me crazy answers, answers of sick man. But not sick. These are answers of conspirator. I only want close file. You want open suspicion. Why you make difficulty?"

I put on my crisis face while I raced through a calculation.

"Okay. All right, I'll tell you about her. But I'm telling you right now, I'm not going to tell you her name or anything like that. I'm in love with her and I'm not going to sacrifice her."

Aleshkoi waited with a double look. Partly it said, Let's have it, and partly, I'll believe it when it checks out.

"The morning I got off the train, right there in the railroad station, I met this girl. She'd just gotten back from vacation in Yalta. She recognized me as an American. Do you know that your women are crazy about Americans?"

"Yes. Continue."

"I told her I was a tourist, but couldn't go back to the United States because I was wanted by the police for organizing a demonstration in front of the United Nations in support of Fidel Castro. I'd spent all my money here so I couldn't go anywhere else and I'd overstayed my visa, so I couldn't stay here either. My life was in a terrible mess. She pitied me, bought me breakfast, and we talked and talked, and you know how one thing leads to another, and between lunch and dinner she took me home."

Aleshkoi was nodding, so engrossed, so sympathetic, I thought he might break into tears.

250

"You have become true Soviet man, Ahmstairr. You inspire my heart. So now you demonstrate at United Nations for Fidel."

"I didn't say I did it. I said I told her I did it. I mean, after all, I wanted her friendship. I needed her help. Should I tell her I escaped from Mordovia? Should I tell her I'm an enemy of Soviet socialist society, and I want her to take me in? I mean, I just wanted to make it a patriotic act for her to help me. Besides, I've had a lot of political discussions in the camp, especially in the hospital, where I met a lot of Soviet citizens. I have a new understanding of Soviet life. My ears weren't closed the whole time, you know."

"Tell me more about girl."

"I told you, I won't sacrifice her. She means too much to me."

"I don't want name. Tell me of romance. Tell me what she give you to eat, what books she like, what she say about school. Tell me what you see with her on television."

Leaning to peek at my cards, he's showing his. He doesn't want to know who she is, at least for now. He wants to know *if* she is. If I convince him she does exist, then he can forget it. She's not important, and my story can be more or less accepted as more or less acceptable. But if she doesn't exist, then they have something to worry about. Then they know somebody unknown harbored me, and that unknown somebody might be important.

"I'm not going to say another word about her."

"I promise, Ahmstairr, we not interested in that girl. If you tell me details to make me believe story, nobody bother her. I give you absolute agreement."

"We already have our agreement. I don't want to talk about her anymore."

After a few more sessions, Aleshkoi gave up, never getting close to what he had to know to make sense of our absurd sparring. The foundation of my story was that I had traveled to Moscow without papers. He knew that that was virtually impossible, and therefore that I must be lying through my pores. But the existence of Marinka, or anyone at the other end of the railroad, never occurred to him.

251

And the existence of false papers never occurred to him. So he was stuck with my ludicrous alibis.

Aleshkoi's surrender came in the form of a wonderful revelation.

"Ahmstairr," he said, leaning back and narrowing his eyes, like an artist appraising an unusual work, "you are sick man."

"Why do you say that?"

"What you did is deed of sick man. Story you tell is story of even more sick man. I tell you truth, Ahmstairr, I like you, but I cannot understand you. This no longer normal case for KGB."

I struggled to stem the tingles that rose in me like a flood tide. Solemn, Jerry, look solemn.

He waited for my question, but I didn't ask. Finally he answered it.

"You are case for Serbsky."

20

SERBSKY

Serbsky is a psychiatric hospital and research center in Moscow. It is more than that. Serbsky is the Kremlin of the Soviet psychiatric world.

Back at the Mordovia hospital camp, I once had a talk about Soviet psychiatry with my friend the psychiatrist Viktor Viktorovich. I had read, of course, that the Soviets often send refuseniks, political protesters, to psychiatric hospitals as crazies. I wondered, as many Westerners do, how the Soviets get respected shrinks to do political dirty work and call it science. Do they do it under threat? Are they that hungry for advancement? How do they rationalize it to themselves?

Viktor Viktorovich, no zealot for the system but no rebel either, didn't quite know what I was talking about.

"When you say we call them crazy, what you mean crazy?"

"What do *they* mean when they call these refuseniks crazy?"

"Who says they crazy? Under observation means not they called crazy. Means observation."

"But you don't go into a psychiatric hospital for observation to see if you have a broken leg or the clap. You're observed to find

253

out if you're mentally ill or not mentally ill, crazy or not crazy. So the accusation is there, and meanwhile you're locked up."

Victor shook his head, at a loss as to how to straighten me out. "What means mentally ill? Means person cannot deal with reality of world. When person creates different reality, makes great trouble for other people. Other people make great trouble for him. Person who not fit reality suffers, creates still more distorted reality, becomes still more sick. But if person comes to see the true reality, person feels better, loses illness. Mental illness not stand still, like blindness in eyes. Gets better, gets worse, depending on how he sees reality."

"But you're still saying that if someone doesn't agree with the government, if he doesn't go with the official reality, he's nuts."

"Ahmstairr, please, I understand your bourgeois idea of many realities. You have reality for rich, reality for poor, reality for black people, reality for colonialists, many realities. We have one reality. Socialist reality. We try be one society. Takes time. But that is main idea of socialist reality. One society, one class, one aim. One reality."

"But you didn't answer my question. What I'm asking is how do they get psychiatrists to make medical diagnoses based on official government policy? Don't doctors feel any sense of scientific independence?"

"What you mean, scientific independence? We are socialist society. Medicine is tool of socialist society. Psychiatry is tool of socialist society. Government is tool of socialist society. Not different reality. One reality."

"But, Viktor Viktorovich, in America if a Republican President tells a Republican psychiatrist to declare a Democrat crazy because he's a Democrat, or even declare a Communist crazy because he's a Communist, the psychiatrist will tell the President to stick it. He's a medicine man and the President is a politician. Sure, the President's the head of the whole government, but he can't tell a psychiatrist, he can't even tell a truckdriver, what to do. How can your psychiatrists sit still when the KGB, a police force, tells you what to do?"

Viktor looked pained at my total misconception. "KGB never,

254

never tells psychiatrist what to do, how to make diagnosis. Make terrible insult. KGB, tool of society, investigates Soviet citizen who performs crazy act. Maybe citizen puts match to bomb. Maybe prints illegal pamphlet for counterrevolution, for restoration of suffering under tsar. KGB diagnoses *act*, not person. Guilt of person, not mentality of person. Psychiatrists diagnose person. Maybe person not crazy. Maybe person deliberate criminal. Maybe person, after clear thought, decides, yes, I want counterrevolution. So psychiatrists diagnose person not crazy, and recommend to judge send person to labor camp. In socialist society, one socialist reality, psychiatrists not need KGB instructions. Understand better now?"

I didn't tell him I didn't understand. I didn't tell him I did.

For my transfer to Soviet psychiatric reality, Lefortovo shipped me to Butyrka Prison, the familiar fortress in Moscow that had always been our hotel for consular meetings. This was the first part of the two-part transfer. But the second part didn't happen. A week went by, then two. I sat in absolute isolation, not only from Soviet prisoners but from foreigners as well. Was this punishment? Or was it simply insurance that I wouldn't spread the crazy, oompossible tale of my escape? Finally, after three weeks, the commandant himself, a short, fat, arrogant brute named Birokov, whom I'd learned to hate freshly every time I hit Butyrka, told me one morning to be ready for the train later that day. Train? Serbsky is in Moscow. Why a train?

"Where you go, you go on train."

"Where am I going?"

"You go where you go."

"I'm supposed to go to Serbsky."

"Where you go, you go on train."

They were going to ship me secretly to the frigid outer reaches of the north and let me die, then make up a story for the consul. I just knew it.

"The KGB told me I'm going to Serbsky. I want you to notify Lieutenant Aleshkoi. I'm not going anywhere till he says so."

I knew that demand had no more weight than demanding a note of approval from my mother. But it hit a mark with Birokov, and he relented.

"You go to Rybinsk."

"Where's Rybinsk?"

"Not far."

During the outdoor exercise hour, which I took in a walled-in space of the prison roof, I heard prisoners over the wall, in the main space.

"Hey," I called, "what kind of place is Rybinsk?"

I had to yell the question again before an answer came.

"Nuthouse."

"A hospital?"

"They call it hospital."

"Bad?"

An evaluative pause. "Not bad. Maybe good. If they say you crazy and send you home, good."

"Is that what they do there?"

"Sometimes. If you make good crazy."

They boarded me that afternoon, without explanation, not on a train but a truck, for a journey of four or five hours on a potholed road. Up front rode two armed guards. The rear, where I sat alone, lacked windows, which would not have been bad except that the truck also lacked shock absorbers. So I hardly sat. Nor could I stand. Mostly I slid on its narrow bench and bounced and heaved. The setting sun pierced through cracks in the truck walls, which told me we were traveling northeast.

When we arrived in freezing darkness, an elderly woman in a white coat walked out to the truck, alone. The driver handed her my dossier, stating my name and age and that I was an American. Alone, unguarded, she walked with me to one of a cluster of low, red brick buildings. It felt strange to walk with a frail woman, no guns protecting her.

They put me in a private room, even though most other prisoner-patients lived in eight-bed dorms.

The trouble with psychiatric observation is that you don't know what's happening. Doctors keep appearing: your own doctor, doctors you never previously saw. They come singly and in packs. and they ask questions. Important questions, such as "How you feel today?" You don't want to say fine. If you're fine, why are you here? You don't want to say terrible. Are you trying to get something out of this? So I'd say, "Okay." At least that confirms I'm American, therefore special, and probably crazy.

The doctors move on, asking the next guy, "How you feel today?" Nurses come around with medication. They don't tell you what illness it's supposed to treat, or how it's supposed to change you. You just take it, and it does its work, so the next day the doctors can come and ask, "How you feel today?"

I began asking how long I was to be there. Nobody knew. Was I there for possible release? Nobody knew. What were they observing? Nobody would say. What disorder did they think I had? Nobody would answer.

So whatever my trouble was, it got worse. My hands trembled even when I didn't want to impress the doctors. Sweaty dreams about returning to Mordovia came more frequently and became sweatier. The uncertainties of life in their nuthouse were driving me nuttier.

As they would in other prisons, they put me to work—in a kind of *tsekh*. In this case the *tsekh*, a pleasant place, was the hospital mess hall, between meals. The city of Rybinsk is famous for a lens factory, and we did many of the factory's fringe tasks. My job was to glue boxes for packing lenses. I had to do it all alone in a little room, although after several weeks they let me work in the main room, away from other prisoners. The work was repetitive, but satisfying. Those little boxes came cut flat. I folded one flap and raised another flap, and dabbed a spot of glue, and it was a box. I folded and glued boxes for hours on end. The outcome was absolutely dependable, the simple motions always resulting in a box, and I loved it.

Nobody rushed us. But we got paid, and in the *magazin* we

bought items I had never seen in camp: biscuits, cookies, pickled beets, jars of good green peas, and bonbons.

Soon they let me live in a dorm room. (I never heard their stated justification for isolating me.) But after two weeks they banished me to a single room again, saying I'd been giving after-supper political lectures on America. Guys had been asking me questions, the same old questions. What could I do?

At Rybinsk I was a celebrity, more so than I'd been anywhere else. Aside from being American, I was the first foreigner ever sent to Rybinsk. Rather than titillating me, that made me feel threatened. One guy kept opening the door of my room to demand in full voice—he didn't care who heard—that I let the West know he was being held as a political dissident. Another kept coming more secretively—which was worse—to ask me to send an American woman to the Soviet Union as a tourist, so he could marry her and get out. One guy brought me onions as a gift, then handed me a postcard to mail to a relative when I got home. A second guy always followed, wanting to know what the first guy was there for. Then he'd say, "Don't trust him, spies for KGB. But listen, Ahmstairr, my grandmother has icons from sixteenth century. You get them out, keep half money. We both make thousands rubles."

I'd fake them along to some degree, not knowing who was crazy enough to harm me if I didn't, but vaguely enough so that if they were KGB plants I was clearly faking. But I always felt uneasy that one of those crazies could louse up everything for me.

My celebrity status had its payoffs. On the evening of my first day there, a nurse brought me a small feast of roast chicken and fresh apples, and I wondered why she had risked it. For months she'd been smuggling home-cooked food to her lover, a prisoner diagnosed as a schizophrenic, who was finishing a ten-year sentence. Just before his release he began badgering me for my American address, because there were some "very important" things I could do for him "without risk." So that finally explained the chicken and apples. He must have told his girl, "Take care of the American." As soon as he got out, she quit her job and they married.

258

While I was always nervous about the KGB watching me, I had no evidence that they were doing so. At no time at Rybinsk was I ever questioned by anyone from the KGB. I never had any hint that anyone there knew I'd escaped, or had made any deal to come back. The only shred of evidence of special instructions concerning me was my private room. So far as I could tell, the doctors at Rybinsk were merely requested by the KGB to observe me for a possible release under Article 362, the article of the Russian legal code that permits a prisoner to be released from his sentence upon the recommendation of a medical commission.

Everybody seemed to play the game smoothly, except for one prick of a male psychiatrist, whom I didn't see often. Every time I did, he'd waggle his hands and yell, *"Simuliant, simuliant!"* That's what they call a symptom faker. I don't think the others thought I was faking, but in the end Rybinsk ducked out of making a judgment about me, passing the buck to higher authority.

Twice a year a psychiatrist from Serbsky comes to Rybinsk to pass judgment on special cases—difficult diagnoses, experimental treatments, borderline Article 362s, whatever. After almost two months at Rybinsk, I was brought before him. About twenty Rybinsk doctors sat in the room like students before a master, while this elder, a kindly man, asked:

"How do you sleep? What do you dream about? What kind of family life did you have? What kind of work did you do in United States? Did you commit crime you were convicted of? Why did you commit it? How did you like life in your camp?"

If Serbsky had more authority than these people to get rid of me, that was where I wanted to be. So I was elated when the visiting psychiatrist decided that Serbsky was where I needed to go.

As nuthouses go, Serbsky is a class operation. A few of its special wards house movie stars and party functionaries and interesting cases that get written about in learned journals. Yet most of its patients, segregated from the nice people, are clients of the Serbsky Institute of Forensic Psychiatry. A few were convicts, like me; most were

259

being held for pretrial observation. These detainees, too, were special. As often as not, they were dissidents, refuseniks. Not the kind of lowlife dissidents who tattoo their eyelids, but the kind who write books and run departments of universities. Even the lowlifes among Serbsky inmates were special. We had one guy, a handsome, blond twenty-two-year-old, who exploded a bomb in the Moscow subway. Most were prisoners of the ordinary police, but one room, mine, was for KGB prisoners. One of my two roommates was the former chief medical officer at the Soviet spaceflight center in Kazakhstan. He had tried to run through the gate of the American embassy with his wife and two young daughters, in search of political asylum. Actually, he made it, but his wife and daughters were caught by the Soviet guards posted outside. So he gave himself up. His wife, a neurosurgeon, was committed to a different psychiatric hospital for a short time, and their children were sent to an orphanage.

Serbsky is run by the Ministry of Health, not the MVD. So Serbsky's food was for people, not prisoners, which came as a shock to me after four years. They fed us eggs, milk, fresh bread. Bars on its windows reminded me I was in a prison, but the hospital had waxed parquet floors and, believe it or not, sheets and pillowcases in pastel colors. A daily parade of doctors made me feel pampered: a neurologist, a neuropathologist, a psychiatrist, a psychologist, a hygienist, a physiotherapist, I forget all the brands. My fingers and toes had broken out with sores, so they bathed me in two sulfur whirlpools for my hands, a pail for my feet, twenty minutes a day.

Serbsky rules permitted a five-kilo package—eleven pounds— every week. I wrote to the embassy requesting everything from oranges to salami, including chocolates, to be bought out of the fund my aunt had sent. I got almost everything I asked for.

The most comforting part about Serbsky was the person directly in charge of my care—my original Soviet shrink, Margarita Felixievna Dzerzhinskaia.

After two weeks I could tell they were getting ready for a "diagnosis." What interested me was not the diagnosis but its consequences. So far as I could see, there were three possible consequences.

First, they could send me back to a labor camp, either in Mordovia or worse. Considering the KGB's fear that I'd talk, I didn't think that was really an option. Second, they could decide I was crazy, permitting them to banish me to one of their mental institutions for criminals, such as the notorious hellhole, Kazan. They would no longer have to worry about my telling of the escape, because anyone repeating it would have heard it in a crazy house. Third, they could give me Article 362, release for medical reasons.

I could tell they were getting ready to "diagnose" me because doctors stopped walking in and out of my room, and instead panels of them interviewed me in formal sessions. The most impressive of these was chaired by Dr. Georgi Morozov, head of the Serbsky Institute of Forensic Psychiatry. Nobody at any of these interviews mentioned my escape. I would have believed that nobody there had the faintest knowledge of it, except for two clues. Margarita Daughter of Felix once tipped her hand, I thought, when she questioned me about how I took to prison life. I told her of my stress after the camp strike, then slipped into saying, "But, of course, the last six months have been different."

"Yes, yes," she quickly responded, nervously glossing past it.

Dr. Morozov, addressing me in broken English, asked me a question with a tone of significance that I couldn't figure out at the time.

"How good your memory?"

I didn't know what to say. Would a good memory serve me best? Or a bad one? Would claiming a bad memory make me look like a liar with a good memory? What the hell was he looking for?

He pressed, in English, presumably not understood by the others. "You have trouble with memory? You forget many happening?"

Until the plumbing of my memory—an excellent one—for the telling of this story, I never understood what he must have been getting at.

Even after those interviews began, one young male psychiatrist kept visiting me in my room, always finding moments when I was alone. He had—surprise, surprise—an intense curiosity about America.

261

As though to pay me off, he'd trade gossip about nurses, even patients and doctors. He seemed so unguarded that I didn't trust him until he responded unguardedly to a perfectly natural question.

"What do you think they're going to do with me?"

"With your diagnosis, hard to say."

"What is my diagnosis?"

"Basic diagnosis, schizophrenia. Means nothing. In Soviet psychiatry, schizophrenia has three hundred eighteen classifications."

"Which one am I?"

He looked troubled, not as though afraid of talking too much, but of not making himself clearly understood.

"Not ordinary classification of schizophrenia, but special kind. They mark you recidivistic reactive psychosis."

I must have looked blank.

"I think in American medicine you not find such diagnosis. You know what means psychosis, yes?"

"More or less."

"Reactive means psychosis go away, sometimes come back. Recidivistic means, how you say—"

"A recidivist is a guy who returns to prison."

"Correct. In diagnosis, means psychosis react when person return to jail. We use word only in penal institutions. Not usual medical word."

His frankness encouraged me to dig on. "So what does this mean? I mean, for me?"

"What means? Means brilliant diagnosis to protect themselves. When you go home, your diagnosis give headaches to American psychiatrists. Serbsky now sensitive about that. In 1977 world meeting, when Morozov go there, psychiatrists from America, from everywhere, tear hair, scream at Soviet psychiatry. So, you go home, American psychiatrists examine you, find you not with psychosis. Of course, not with psychosis. Recidivistic reactive psychosis means psychosis come back when you go back to prison. In America you not in prison, no evidence psychosis. Who can criticize?"

"You said when I go home. You think I'm going home?"

262

"I think, from diagnosis, they prepare that you go home. But diagnosis says nothing, so how I know something from nothing?"

A couple of days later, early in the morning, a nurse I had befriended came into my room and puttered at little tasks that obviously didn't need doing.

"If you tell anyone I told you, I have big trouble."

"Told me what?"

She waltzed very close to me to fluff a pillow that didn't need fluffing, and whispered.

"You leave today."

"Three-sixty-two?"

Her eyes brightened radiantly.

Later in the morning, Margarita Daughter of Felix came with the head nurse of the ward. Before reading from an official piece of paper, her eyes twinkled.

"Ahmstairr, the commission has recommended that you be relieved from serving punishment, because of illness—"

Home! This was it!

After reading the endless words of Article 362, she admonished me, "This only recommendation to court. Cannot promise court accept recommendation, but most times court accept. We not know how long court take. But you leave today."

If I had had champagne, I'd have popped it open. If I hadn't remembered I was a prisoner, I'd have kissed her.

If I'd known what was ahead of me, that this was a misleading beginning to a long, tortuous ending, I'd have dropped my head into my hands.

21

RETURN TO SHEREMET'EVO

The day of my release from Serbsky was April 4, 1980, exactly one month after I had checked in. All that stood between me and freedom was a hearing before the Moscow City Court, which had tried and sentenced me.

At Butyrka Prison, one palm-sweating day followed another without a word. On April 18, I was notified that Dennis Reece, the vice-consul, was coming to see me. Maybe that would bring news. It didn't. He brought the embassy doctor with him, and we had a long meeting in the inhibiting presence of an MVD major. Reece said nothing about the escape, of course, nor did I. I told Reece I'd been issued an Article 362 recommending my release. He didn't believe me, I could tell. I don't think he saw the difference between my brand of hell-raising and the pointless mischief of Pete and Darrell.

"The court has to approve it," I added, "but they always do. It's just a formality. Maybe a few days."

Reece looked both befuddled and tentatively impressed. He was the only man in the Western world who knew first-hand of my nervy demands of the Soviet government and that the Soviets had been forced to agree to them. I think he was now startled at my claim that I'd pulled off the big play.

"There's another thing," I added. "A three-sixty-two means being sent somewhere for psychiatric treatment, and some Soviet relative has to take responsibility. My three-sixty-two says I'm to get my treatment in the States. My Soviet relative is the embassy. You. My Uncle Sam."

Reece eyed the major for some kind of confirmation. The major just gazed back.

A few days later, Reece sent the following letter to my aunt in the States:

EMBASSY OF THE
UNITED STATES OF AMERICA
Moscow, USSR

April 22, 1980

Dear Mrs. _____ :

On April 18, the Embassy's physician, Dr. Nydell, and I met your nephew, Gerald Amster, for about seventy minutes at Butyrka Prison in Moscow.

Jerry's appearance was improved from earlier Consular Officer meetings. He had gained weight and his color was better. Jerry said he had been released from Serbsky Institute in Moscow two weeks previously. He praised the care he had received at Serbsky, which included ultraviolet treatment, hydro-salt therapy, and various tranquilizers. He had eaten very well there and had been given doses of Vitamin A. In addition, he had been treated by a dentist.

Jerry related that he suffers, especially in the morning, from a tremor. The tremor was readily apparent during the first part of the meeting, but seemed to disappear as Jerry gradually relaxed. Jerry told us that he helps get rid of his excess energy by performing voluntary janitorial duties, such as waxing and scrubbing the floor, and by walking during his daily two-hour exercise period outdoors.

According to Jerry, a medical commission has recommended that he be released from further punishment under Article 362 of the Code of Criminal Procedure of the Russian Soviet Federated Socialist Republic. The Article reads as follows:

Relief from serving punishment because of illness. In the event that, while serving punishment, a person condemned to deprivation of freedom has contracted a chronic mental or other grave illness preventing serving the punishment, the court shall have the right, upon the proposal of the administration of a correctional labor institution based on the conclusion of a doctors' commission, to render a ruling to relieve him from further serving the punishment.

When relieving from further serving of punishment a convicted person who has contracted a chronic mental illness, the court shall have the right to apply compulsory measures of a medical character or to transfer him to the care of agencies of public health.

When deciding the question of relieving from further serving of punishment persons who have contracted a grave illness other than persons who have contracted a mental illness, the court shall take into account the gravity of the crime committed, the personality of the convicted person, and other circumstances.

Jerry added that because he is a foreigner, he would be allowed to return home for treatment. His statement was not contradicted by the Major of the Ministry of Internal Affairs who monitored the meeting.

Your nephew also stated that he would like to be admitted to the Columbian [sic] Presbyterian Medical Center in Manhattan for continued treatment, should he be released soon. Jerry requested that you make some preliminary inquiries to see if he could be admitted there, or if that was not possible, somewhere else, after his release.

Jerry told me that he had received the several letters from you which I had forwarded to him. He also received the parcel I delivered to him at Serbsky Institute on March 26.

According to your nephew he has been at Butyrka Prison for two weeks awaiting developments in the early-release process. His mailing address is Uchrezhdeniye IZ-48/2, Moscow. You may send him letters directly to that address through the international mail, or if you prefer, we can continue to forward him your letters through the Soviet mail.

Although we are hopeful that Jerry will be soon released, there are several important points to bear in mind. First, the decision of the medical commission must be reviewed by a court. Although Jerry believes that the court's approval is basically pro forma, there is, of course, no guarantee that the court's decision will be favorable. Secondly, it is impossible to say at this time when the court's decision will be made; it is possible that the court will not review the commission's recommendation for several months. As soon as we have any news on this matter we will let you know.

Enclosed is a letter which Jerry gave us during the meeting. If we may be of further information or assistance, please feel free to contact us.

Sincerely,
T. Dennis Reece
American Vice-Consul

At the end of April, Colonel Birokov, the short, fat, sadistic assistant warden at Butyrka, called me while I was exercising on the roof. This was the guy who had enjoyed not telling me where I was going the night I was shipped to Rybinsk. He was my angel of death. Every time I came to Butyrka—at least a dozen times—just seeing him meant some kind of trouble. In the caged-in guards' walk overlooking the exercise area on the roof, he'd stand back as though to hide while he watched. But nobody ever missed him. Every prisoner had radar for his presence. Nights in Butyrka, I'd lie awake and plan ways of returning to Moscow after my release so I could trap this guy and pull his fingers off, one by one. I had never had thoughts like that about anybody, but I hated this man so.

I waited for his bad news as he climbed out of his cage and approached me.

"Tomorrow morning you go."

"Where?"

"Where you come from."

Good news out of Birokov? I couldn't believe it. "Home? You mean tomorrow is court?"

"Not court. You go where you come from."

"To America? Tomorrow?"

"Where you come *here* from you go."

How was I to keep from smashing him? "Will you please tell me what you mean?"

"Moscow City Court cannot make your release. When they sentence you to Mordovia, you change to rule of Republic of Mordovia. Must go to Mordovian court."

"How can they do that?"

"Tomorrow you *étap* to Mordovia."

"I won't leave here, I won't go." I was screaming at this guy. Watch it, Jerry. No, don't watch it. As long as I don't beat his face in, he can't do a thing to me for yelling. I knew he didn't make this decision, and couldn't unmake it, but I hated him. "What do you mean, the Moscow Court can't decide? If they can decide to sentence me, they can decide to release me."

Birokov leered, enjoying my rage. "Tomorrow you *étap* to Mordovia."

Of all the *étap* trains I'd ever seen, I'd never seen one like this. Every cage was a sardine can, smelly and jam-packed. Another *étap* was loading as we pulled out, and at Puotma, another was still

268

unloading as we pulled in. En route I learned that in Moscow, in Kiev, in Minsk, in Leningrad, police were rounding up every troublemaker known to them: drunks, prostitutes, currency traders, youthful rebels, to get them out of Moscow—or to make sure they didn't go to Moscow—during the Olympics. The closest person to me on the train—I mean the guy literally, physically, pressed closest to me—told me that a plainclothes cop had stopped him outside a *valiuta* store and searched him, finding fifty U.S. dollars in his wallet. He was about to enter the store to buy a pair of special shoes for his daughter, some kind not available in regular stores for rubles. The police had snooped on him because he had already done two years for currency dealing. Authorities were determined that Moscow was to be as clean as a whistle when the foreign visitors arrived.

At Puotma I expected to hear my name called, singled out as a foreigner to transfer to the sidetrack for Leplai and Camp 5–1. No one called. Later I heard my name for the stop at the hospital camp, and I realized why. Until a court released me, I was still a patient.

Good. Hospital times were always among the better times.

No, wait. To be a psychiatric patient at the camp hospital means Corpus 12, the psycho-isolator, the only psychiatric "ward" they have.

Getting off the train, I spotted a *zavkhoz* I had known, obviously one of the receiving crew. I told him in my best man-on-a-mission voice, "I'm supposed to report immediately to Viktor Viktorovich."

Not waiting for his assent, I bounded for the administration building, less than a hundred yards away. Luck came my way. My old friend Viktor Viktorovich, the psychiatrist-prisoner in charge of Corpus 12, was there.

"I'm here from Serbsky," I said, racing to give him my story. "I got a three-sixty-two, just have to wait for court and I'm out."

He looked delighted. "A court comes here in two weeks."

"Two *weeks?*" That seemed like another two years. "Look, Viktor, you've got to fix it so I don't stay in the psycho-isolator. I thought it was a couple of days, and that was bad enough. Two weeks will kill me. Please don't make me go through that."

269

Viktor looked at the floor, calculating, considering.

"You must promise me. Maybe I fix you go to medical corpus. But must mean you make no trouble. Somebody make fight with you, no fight. You not visit other buildings, do nothing to make questions. If something happen and you not in psycho-isolator"— he drew his fingers across his throat—"I lose nice job."

I took my promise so seriously I virtually never got out of bed except for meals. That took care of another problem. At a time like this, I didn't want to run into Marinka.

After two interminable weeks the court came. Nobody sent for me. There wouldn't be another court visit for two, maybe three more weeks. What was going on?

Another court came. Still another.

I had heard talk at Serbsky that didn't seem important to me at the time. Later, the madness of that crowded train, the chaos in Puotma of one jam-packed train after another, seemed to have nothing to do with me. Now I heard the same talk I'd heard at Serbsky, from people in the ward, in the mess hall, people I knew to be knowledgeable. Following the Soviet invasion of Afghanistan, President Carter threatened to boycott the Moscow Olympics. I remembered a medical technician at Serbsky who took my blood pressure daily and had kept running it up as he ranted nonstop about the maniac Carter. Since then, daily, people had asked me—guards, prisoners, whoever I met—whether my country's President had gone crazy.

Now all of that had everything to do with me. What all these experienced, knowledgeable guys were saying to me was that there was no way the court, the KGB, the Kremlin, were going to let an American out *now*. Not until the Olympics were past and gone.

I didn't want to believe it, couldn't bring myself to believe it, yet time forced me to. The weeks came and went, the courts came and went, and my precious 362 seemed as worthless as my MasterCard at the *magazin*.

During those weeks I learned that my "deal" with the KGB was not as clean and simple as they'd made it seem. They had demanded silence about the escape and I was absolutely prepared to give them that. But now they wanted more, demanding it relentlessly, yet so subtly I couldn't raise a fuss and charge they were backing down.

At the hospital camp, just about every week at unexpected moments, a KGB interrogator named Sasha, who couldn't be more than twenty-five years old, came calling on me. I assumed his assignment was a form of on-the-job training for a rookie, until his smooth, sharp manipulations of me made me think he could give lessons to his elders.

We'd meet in a small room of the administration building, so that others, I suppose, wouldn't know about our rendezvous. But, of course, secrets like that don't last in a prison hospital, and I became a marked man. In the corridor, in the mess hall, guys would call out:

"Ahmstairr, stomach full, *da?* Eat good when comes KGB man, *da?*"

I hated the searing spotlight of those loud taunts. What the hell did those bastards know of what happened at the meetings?

I especially hated it because those bastards were right. Sasha started every meeting with me, at least in the beginning, by opening his briefcase and passing me a pack of cigarettes and something irresistible to eat: at the least, a couple of tins of tasty conserves from a civilian store; on the best days, a small, sensuously seasoned Finnish salami that some prisoners would kill for.

An old hand had once told me that every KGB prisoner's file had information on what that prisoner couldn't resist. When the KGB wants information out of him, that's what they drive him crazy with. The bait is not necessarily stuff to eat. Recidivists, for example, often have trained themselves out of caring about food. They may be more interested in good tobacco or tea (the KGB man doesn't have to know his client is brewing it down to illegal *chaffir*, does he?). I heard stories about some guys getting nips of vodka. A surprising number of bored Russians talked about starving, really starving, for books. Surely, the surest way to melt some guys would be women, but I doubt that the straitlaced KGB would go that far, at

271

least not for common prisoners, who might boast of it to others. Anyhow, the official file on me was absolutely accurate. The way to get me was with food, at least as prelude to other powerful persuaders that Sasha worked on me.

In our first meetings he pressed me in predictable ways: What was I telling others about my disappearance from camp? What would I say about it after my release? If I saw Darrell, what would I say to him? He never once, in weeks of meetings, used the word "escape." Without exception, he used the word *paiekhel*, the past tense of "leaving": "When you left—" "Then, after you left—"

Then his questions moved up a level. "If you were released soon to go back to America"—the son of a bitch knew what a tease that was—"you know you would be interrogated by the CIA, the FBI. What would you say? Suppose they harassed you for details. They could make trouble for you. How would you handle that?"

"I'll tell them the truth," I kept saying. "I'll tell them I was always treated fairly. I'll tell them the impression we get on American television is wrong, that nobody starves, nobody is beaten or tortured, that we don't do slave labor, that we're paid for our work. The work isn't always too pleasant, but, what the hell, we're prisoners. Work isn't so hot in a civilian factory either."

He'd look at me, partly satisfied, partly skeptical.

"How we know we can trust you?"

"Look, you've been fair to me. We made an agreement. You're keeping your side. Why shouldn't I keep mine?"

"But after you're released—"

"If I'm released, all the more reason I'd want to be fair."

"Suppose someone contacted you after your release."

"Like who?"

"One of my, mmm, colleagues."

I waited for elaboration, but he offered none.

"Contacted me for what?"

"Just to check up on our understanding."

Did I hear him right?

"Sure, he can check up, why not. I'm sure he'd do it in a way

272

that wouldn't make trouble for me with the American government."

"Of course."

"He'd be able to find me easily enough."

"Of course. I'm sure he could always locate you through—" He glanced down at his folder, casually like a TV performer peeking at a cue card, and recited my brother's name and his exact street address in Philadephia, and my aunt's name and her exact street address in New York. Son of a bitch! Was he threatening me? Was he threatening *them?* What did he mean?

I never did find out. He never mentioned the subject again.

But he left me with an idea. Another time when he pressed me about whether I could be trusted, I said, "Look, my good friend Darrell Lean, you know that I've known him practically all my life. I've traveled with him, lived with him. We've had our differences, but I've been like a big brother to him. You'll have him here three more years, with no possibility of early release. Right? If I had some reason to go back on my word, which I don't, how could I do it while you still have him here?"

Sasha's eyes X-rayed me, but I couldn't tell if my point impressed him or not.

Routinely at meeting after meeting, he'd asked me to tell him about Chinese prisoners I knew, in camp or at the hospital. What questions did they ask? Which of them had cash? Did any get favors from guards? "We know which are spies," he said, but what could I tell about these "known" spies to "prove" my trustworthiness while my release was under consideration?

"I don't know them. I don't speak Chinese," I protested. It seemed to work.

Well, it partly worked. My excuse had the weakness of not being an outright refusal. He asked about other prisoners in 5–1. Who had asked me to contact people or mail letters for them in the West? I'd received so many requests of that kind I wouldn't have known where to begin. If I refused outright on some kind of principle, it would be at the cost of the principle that had governed my life for the past risk-filled year—my release. Without overtly threatening or promising anything, Sasha tightened an excruciating, deadly squeeze on me. To show my good will I passed him a few morsels of prisoner gossip I knew the KGB already knew; Svelkov, the interrogator who used to visit me at 5–1, had volunteered them to me, hoping to draw me into telling more. Sasha seemed especially interested in prisoners from other Soviet Bloc countries. To avoid an outright refusal to cooperate, I told him that Poles and Bulgarians, mentioning two or three by name, seemed more interested than others in how the system works in America.

What questions did they ask?

Mostly about the state of Nevada, which permits legal whorehouses.

When it was clear that either my memory or my social connections in Camp 5–1 were deficient, Sasha began testing me with prisoners I was currently meeting in the hospital. The pressure made my neck sweat and my arms itch. Almost every day somebody proposed some hotshot deal for enlisting me in smuggling out his grandmother's icons to make us both rich. Who asked them to? Usually, they were the hospital's most annoying, sneaky jerks, who would sell anybody out for an insulting price. Was I now supposed to endanger my release to protect *their* asses? After the way I'd risked my own to get out of here?

Before I could focus a clear answer for myself about that, strange things began to happen. Business began to boom in requests for my help, but of a special kind: not involving icons and sending photographs to relatives, but the very kinds of requests the KGB seemed most interested in. Just as someone had in Rybinsk, one guy pleaded with me to promise to send an American woman as a tourist about the time of his release to look him up, marry him, and thus give him legal ground for emigration. A Bulgarian wanted me to teach him English so he could befriend American tourists and engage them to do "important tasks in America against the Soviet regime." He oversold his case. If he'd said he wanted to learn English to trade in currency I might have believed him. Another guy, who did look

274

intelligent and well-read, wanted to foist on me "the Moscow telephone number of Andrei Sakharov" (this was before Sakharov was banished to internal exile in Gorki) so I could pass it to someone in the Western press (as though that would be so hard for Sakharov's friends to do right in Moscow).

The suddenness and heavy-footedness of this outburst of proposed little conspiracies reeked of the KGB. Only an idiot wouldn't recognize they were setups. If I didn't report to Sasha something clearly contrived by him, I was as good as condemned to serving three more years—more than the whole sentences of some of these jerks endangering me with their stupid, petty schemes. After all, the Russians hadn't promised my early release. They'd just promised that if I surrendered, my having "left" would not prejudice their *consideration* of release.

At least, that was the reasoning I kept replaying to myself as I proceeded to do what I did. I now admit freely that what I decided was that I couldn't tell the setups from the genuine jerks, so from that point on I had to report all of them to Sasha.

But to this day I like to think every single one of those crackpot proposals—I'd say about six or eight in all—was a test concocted by Sasha. I kept telling myself that every night as I lay awake. By day, every day, all day, I kept thinking of little else but wishing the Olympics were finally over and some judge would stamp a validation of my 362.

In the last week of November, as I half-dozed in my bed, a call from the door awoke me: "Ahmstairr!"

The next day, November 27, court!

Three judges, two women and a man, looked down at me with kindly faces, playing with my life.

"Ever you violated camp rules?" the woman in the middle, the chief judge, asked.

"No." They couldn't know about the escape.

"You learned lesson from camp experience?"

"Yes."

"If released, will you commit crime again in Soviet Union?"

"No. Not in the Soviet Union or anywhere else."

Then the man took his turn.

"If you released and go home, what will you tell American people about Soviet Union?"

We're getting close. Oh God, make this okay.

"I will tell them that the Soviet people are very generous. They have open hearts. In America I heard many stories about terrible Soviet labor camps. I admit I did not do too well with the food, because I wasn't used to it. But at all times I was treated very humanely."

Don't make it sound too good, watch it.

"I don't feel it's my job to go around telling about the camp. Frankly, I want to forget it. But there's something I do want the American people to know. My country does not understand what it means that the Soviet people lost twenty million young men in the Great Patriotic War. My people must know what that means, if there is ever to be world peace."

I was singing their song. I could feel it hit home.

Then the chief judge said the magic word:

"Citizen Ahmstairr—" True, I was not technically a citizen, but that word made me a person again. I hadn't been addressed as a person in more than four years. "Citizen Ahmstairr, you now released from further serving punishment."

Before the thrill ran through me, a doctor from the hospital administration who stood beside the judges' bench, a fellow to whom I'd been supplying United States postage stamps from my letters, stabbed me with a postscript.

"Of course, that means after approval of KGB."

Court or no court, I blurted, "What do you mean, approval?"

He gazed at me, benignly tipping his head. "If KGB not approve, you not come to court today. Must approve final details of departure."

That evening, preparing for the next morning's *étap* back to 5–1, my official address from which I had to be released, for the first

276

time since returning here I let myself think about Marinka. I ached to look into her face. To tell her the story of these past weeks and months. To tell her that the risk of her life had saved mine.

But there was no way I dared send a message to her. I couldn't slip a note under the door of her *protsedurnaia*. I couldn't even be sure she was still there. I lay awake concentrating on a message to her—that I was all right, that I was going home to America—almost believing that my concentration would transmit it telepathically.

Someday I'd find a way to let her know for certain.

Or she would find me in America.

On the train to Camp 5–1, surprised to be going there at all, I wondered how to handle the circle of prisoners who would crowd around me, pressing for details of my disappearance, my adventures.

I had wondered needlessly. A barren private room awaited me at the *sanchast'*, the dispensary, where someone had set up a cot. There I stayed, no one telling me for how long. An elderly Mongolian civilian, who worked as a half-*fel'dsher*, half-orderly, brought my meals.

On Monday, December 1, as he set down my breakfast, the Mongolian looked at me in a curious way and ran his finger down the side of my face.

"You must shave today."

Nobody ever tells a prisoner to shave unless he looks atrocious. I'd shaved Saturday.

"Today? I'm going?"

"You shave."

"Please tell my why. I'm going?"

His face turned official, like an actor playing a generalissimo. "An order. You must shave. I know nothing more."

"I can't stand it. Tell me."

He turned away, flopping his hand, as though he didn't want to say. "*Da, da, da, da*, just shave, just shave." Grudgingly he added, "You must be ready eleven o'clock."

277

Eleven came and went. So did twelve and one. At one-thirty the Mongolian left for home in Leplai.

An officer came by and told me I would leave at four. Four came, four-thirty, five. The day had turned to wintry night. The officer returned and told me I must absolutely be ready at six.

At five minutes after six, still waiting and wondering at the window of the *sanchast'*, I saw the officer in charge of prisoner dossiers enter the camp gate and head for the *sanchast'*. He never appeared except to bring an amnesty or clemency or official word that someone's sentence had reached its completion.

He flung open the door.

"Ahmstairr, get belongings."

That was the official word. Even more official than the court order.

I went to the *sklad* for the duffel bag of stuff from my former existence. Of all the ironies, the camp lights had gone out again. In the pitch darkness of that musty room I felt around for my bag, but couldn't tell mine from anyone else's. I didn't want to leave anything behind, but didn't want to miss that train. The dossier officer entered, carrying a lighted candle, hounding me to hurry.

In the candlelight I found my bag, opened it, pulled out my civilian clothes. I should say my one civilian suit, custom-made, just like for a Malaysian cabinet minister. It was creased and it stank. I ripped off my prisoner's fatigues and pulled it on.

Throwing my duffel bag over my shoulder, I imagined myself entering the lowliest bar in the most forsaken Soviet town looking like this, and getting thrown out as some kind of bum.

The officer took me back to the *shtab*, where two others waited, a young MVD captain named Voloshin, and a guard, a quiet older man. Out of an envelope the dossier officer took twenty-five rubles in cash, instructing me to sign the envelope as a receipt. Voloshin took the money before I touched it, saying he'd hold it.

Voloshin, the older guard, and I half-trotted the length of the village to the Leplai station shack. The moment we climbed aboard,

278

the one-car train that waited started for Puotma. The last time, I had fled this distance through moonlit fog; this time, I rode in a private railroad car.

At Puotma we dashed to the ticket seller's window of the decrepit station.

"No seats, all sold," the seller announced crabbily.

My escorts accepted the verdict with a kind of disciplined resignation, no overt complaint, that I realized I'd seen so often in the Soviet Union. So it was not just a prisoner's attitude, but everyone's.

"Next train, six o'clock morning," Voloshin said. He instructed the older man to go home and we'd meet before six in the station. Voloshin told me he was taking me home.

I had thought during the last few days that I'd like to spend a day or two floating around Leplai and Puotma, gazing leisurely at life in closed Soviet communities, saying good-bye to some of the guards. What was my hurry? I had no wife or kids to rush to. I'd as soon pause here as anywhere else, as long as I was free.

Home, for Voloshin, meant his grandmother's house. When Voloshin announced to her, "Amerikanets, he sleep here tonight," she glowed, expanding like a rising muffin.

Bubbling, the old woman went on the attack in her kitchen, clanking pots and pans, heaping food into them. What came out was a puree of mashed potatoes enriched by cream, then side dishes of noodles and pickles and pickled green tomatoes, followed by slugs of vodka and *samovanka*, a home-brew whiskey. Meanwhile relatives, a half-dozen at least, collected in the living room. After our meal we joined them, taking our shoes off—I had thought only the Japanese did that—before stepping on their Oriental carpet. Then the visitors drifted away.

For a couple of hours I sat on a sofa watching Soviet TV. On the wall behind me hung a crucifix—in this home of a uniformed MVD captain. Would his superiors bust him if they knew? Was official atheism a big flop? These were questions to which I knew I would not have time to get answers. When Voloshin left the room,

279

his grandmother sank herself in the sofa next to me, twinkling and eager, as though grasping a clandestine moment. I knew what was coming. She whispered, "Tell me, how is it in America?"

At five in the morning Voloshin shook me awake, handing me something. It was an egg with a fork, and a small glass of water. I started to crack the eggshell for peeling.

"*Nyet, nyet,*" he commanded. He picked up a second egg, his own, and punctured the shell with a fork, then sucked out its contents. It was not hard-boiled, but raw. Then he slugged down the liquid, which was not water, but vodka. The egg for protein and coating the stomach, the vodka for challenging a cold new day.

Grandma, already long awake, handed us a bag stuffed with food. The hell with those twenty-five rubles Voloshin had pocketed. I was getting my money's worth. We tramped through icy darkness for the train.

In late afternoon, I could scarcely believe that Kazanskii Vokzal, the Moscow station that received trains from the direction of the Republic of Kazan, was the same place that had greeted me on my gloomy, tense morning arrival more than a year earlier with Dmitri. This time it bustled, aglow with dusty sunbeams of freedom—my freedom, at least. Voloshin led us to a kiosk and bought three ice cream cones. I have never particularly liked vanilla. This time I adored vanilla.

He made a phone call and reported that I would fly out next morning, and that we'd spend the night in a police residence, a kind of prefecture.

"You not prisoner, you free man," Voloshin made sure I understood. "But—not total free because no internal visa. *Da?*"

"But I can go out with you, can't I?"

"*Nyet.* If police do control check in streets, how we explain you?"

At the prefecture, where the three of us shared a small room, Voloshin sent the elderly guard out for treats, asking me first if I wanted anything special. I couldn't think of anything beyond kolbasa and chocolate. I ate both, washing them down with vodka till my stomach rebelled. Then they had to inquire around the prefecture for bicarbonate of soda. None. There's never any in this country wherever, whenever you need it. My guards were drunk and so was I, as I drifted off in a fantasy of America's President-elect, Ronald Reagan, declaring our country's indisputable superiority in the baking-soda gap.

Next morning at Sheremet'evo, Dennis Reece showed up with two others from the embassy almost an hour after we expected him, minutes before the Aeroflot departure. Those hand tremors had seized me again as I waited for him—and for my ticket—with visions of missing the plane. One of the other two people was a State Department nurse who would fly with me to the States, the price of her ticket paid by my aunt, as was mine.

Our flight, with few aboard, took off for Frankfurt, where we would change to an American carrier. No wonder flights of Western carriers leave Moscow jam-packed, while Aeroflot flies out almost empty. Like the jet that flew me to Moscow in July 1976—my God, four and a half years ago!—this one was comfortable enough, but colorless, bereft of style.

And that dairy-maid stewardess! In the couple of hours at the airport, even through my slight hangover and early-morning blearies, my eyes attuned themselves to the smart looks of Western women, departing amid the herded groups of tourists. Unless my memory was misleading me, they looked different from the Western women I'd last seen. Even girls of student age looked different: combed and eye-shadowed and tailored, just like middle-aged suburbanites. Had they all washed Woodstock out of their hair?

The buxom stewardess, wearing a smock, brought breakfast. An egg. To suck out of the shell raw, or to bite into? It was hard boiled. Black bread, a glass of tea with sugar cubes—and kasha.

I'd had no kasha for thirty-six hours, ever since my guard's grandmother's feast. A comforting feeling of something from home rose in me. Kasha—I'd missed it.

That surprising, confusing nostalgia mixed with an eagerness to get the hell away. I knew I shouldn't ask her, but I did.

281

"How long until we leave the Soviet Union?"

"Leave? Already we leave. We flying now."

"I mean until we leave Soviet airspace." I thought she'd hate me for the insult.

She didn't. Casting her eyes blankly out the window, then shrugging in puzzlement over why it should matter, she said, "Soon. Few minutes."

She gazed down at me with sympathetic eyes that gave her face a simple loveliness. She looked . . . motherly. No, too young. Sisterly. No, not that. It was a look I'd seen even on the faces of the hardened men at camp: a guileless, peasantlike knowing of the way things are, as simple and direct as potato soup. The look was Russian, that's what it was. I'd grown accustomed to something in her face.

"Do you ever fly to America?"

Her eyes turned off at the touching of a sensitive subject. "No, never. We not go there. Jimmy Carter stop. He stop before I start fly."

She scurried away to her duties.

After a while, my nurse-companion went to the washroom. The stewardess returned with a pleated paper cup of fruit-flavored candies.

"Pilot tell me you American."

"Yes."

With an air of passing me a secret message, she leaned across the empty seat to lower my table and said, "Now we out from Soviet air."

I nodded my thanks.

I drew a breath and momentarily closed my eyes, trying to absorb the meaning of it. I didn't want her to see my relief.

She didn't. She had sat down beside me.

Her glistening peasant eyes were searching for words. She found them.

I knew what they would be.

She said, "Tell me, how is it in America?"

282

AFTERWORD

"What are you working on?" friends ask a writer.

For the past year, I've replied by telling about the man who lived this adventure.

Inevitably, the story would seize their interest and they'd ask, "How did the two of you ever find each other?"

The fact is, we almost didn't.

In the early summer of 1982, Gerald Amster, not knowing where else to begin, fingered the Manhattan Yellow Pages in search of someone he had to find. He located a listing for Dial-a-Writer, an awkwardly named but valuable service of the American Society of Journalists and Authors, which matches available free-lance writers with prospective users of their talents.

A couple of days after he called I happened to be talking on the phone with my friend Dorothy Beach, the elegant and energetic lady who is Dial-a-Writer's chief matchmaker. It was not one of her best days, and she began telling me how bewildered she sometimes feels trying to sort out rock-solid callers, such as a bank wanting an artistic tone to its annual report, from other prospects who may offer livelier material, but who may be screwballs and time-wasters.

"Right here, for example," she said, "is a man's name that's been staring up at me for two days and I don't know what to make of it. This man called out of the blue and says he spent more than four years in a Soviet labor camp."

"I think book editors are tired of Soviet dissidents."

"He's not Soviet."

"What is he?"

"American."

"A spy?"

"No."

She ran down the high points of a story that strained credibility.

"Does he sound like he's telling the truth?"

"He *sounds* like it, yes, but—"

"Well, you know plenty of experienced writers. One of them can test him out pretty quickly."

"You want to talk to him?"

"Me?"

"Sure."

"That's not the kind of book I do. You know that."

"I know. But you've spent time in the Soviet Union."

"But not on this kind of story."

"All right," she said, resigned. "I wish somebody would just talk to him."

"You think he'd talk on the phone?"

"I'm sure he would. I'd like to know how much effort you think this is worth."

The telephone voice of Gerald Amster was deep, resonant, and dignified, alerting me to something hidden beneath his formality. He began his story and answered my questions readily and fully.

I said I'd call him in a couple of days. Like my friend Dorothy, I didn't know what to do about him. I wasn't sure yet that he rang true and was too preoccupied with my own work to get more deeply involved.

On the afternoon of the second day, he called me. The more we talked, the more absorbed I became with his compelling tale.

284

On July 15, 1982, I traveled to New York from my home in Connecticut and visited him in a one-room basement apartment on West Eleventh Street in Greenwich Village, where he then lived. He was tall and muscular, with a full, neat head of hair and a mustache, both starting to gray, and with an upright bearing that exactly suited the deep, controlled voice. But his eyes bespoke an extreme shyness. They focused uneasily, not as though to assess the visitor, but to catch whether the visitor was assessing him.

I ran a tape recorder as we talked, which may have prolonged his formal air. But after the second or third cassette, he gave up reaching for euphemisms and his voice and enunciation relaxed. Recollections poured from him that were concrete, precise, and abundant. During our breaks he showed me papers and souvenirs relating to his adventure: U.S. State Department documents, Soviet documents, newspaper clippings of his Moscow trial, the Malaysian suit he wore when he was arrested.

I left him that day surprised at myself. I had decided that there was no way I was going to miss the chance of writing this man's story.

Our subsequent talks, generally running two to four hours each, spread over a period of eleven months until the writing began, and they continued into the months of writing. We grew easy with each other, each learning the other's soft spots and strengths, quirks, and styles of humor.

As Amster poured out details that were constantly surprising, my thoughts were drawn to one fact of this story that seemed impossible to verify.

"The escape," I challenged him. "Other than your say-so, there's no tangible proof that it actually took place."

He threw up his hands. "What kind of proof can there be? You want to go ask the KGB? They were so scared someone might find out an American got away that they didn't tell my doctors at Serbsky. I don't think they told the court that officially released me. You want to go ask Dmitri, who harbored me? Even if I wanted to, I couldn't tell someone how to begin looking for him. You want to go ask the State Department? The Soviets promised the embassy 'unofficially' that they'd take me back without penalty—on the condition of absolute silence. You think the State Department is going to mess up its future 'unofficial' deals with the Russians?"

I couldn't call on Peter Benack to help. He had been released from the prison camp before the time in question. A few days after Darrell Lean's release and return to the United States, I asked him about the escape. His response, I thought, would be of particular interest. First of all, owing to the strains in their friendship, I didn't think Darrell would go out of his way to lie in Amster's behalf. Second, even if he would, based on everything I'd learned about Darrell, I didn't think he would be a skillful dissembler.

Darrell told me that all he knew was that one morning he woke up and Jerry was gone, and that he'd never seen him again until Jerry met him at Kennedy Airport in July 1983.

"How was his disappearance explained? What did you think happened to him?"

He shrugged. (A convincing shrug, I was glad to see.) "Nobody explains, there's nothing to think. He was gone, that's all. That's how guys disappear there. When they want to send you somewhere and don't want any talk, they come and get you in the middle of the night. Maybe some of those other guys ran away. Who knows? In the morning they're gone. Nobody explains."

The editor in chief of Holt, Rinehart and Winston, Jack Macrae, put some questions to Soviet émigrés in New York, among whom he is well connected. Yes, they said, escapes from relatively low-security gulags, as described by Amster, are not uncommon, and underground groups like Dmitri's exist. They found the details of the escape plausible.

As our interviews progressed, I'd question and requestion Amster— at unexpected moments, from unexpected angles—about his time as a fugitive in Moscow. This would sometimes annoy him, but never catch him off balance. He always answered specifically and convincingly, no detail ever in conflict with anything he had told me weeks, months earlier.

Still, I decided to approach the State Department, particularly since I had thought of a simple, factual question that would nail down a corroboration to satisfy any skeptic. I traced the whereabouts of T. Dennis Reece, the vice consul in Moscow at the time of Amster's departure from camp, locating him at a remote post as consul on the island of Cape Verde, off the western shoulder of Africa. Trying to get a call through to Cape Verde took days. Finally, on the day before New Year's Eve, 1983, I reached him and posed my simple, factual question:

"Did you receive a call at the Moscow embassy early in 1980 from someone who claimed to be Gerald Amster and who stated that he had escaped from his labor camp?"

The question protected him from verifying that Jerry had escaped. Officially, the Soviets had never acknowledged that he had. I wasn't asking him to reveal any "unofficial" deal with the Soviets, or even whether the voice on the phone was Jerry's. I simply asked if such a call was received.

The question did not seem to surprise Reece, who remembered Amster instantly, with no prompting. He sounded vaguely troubled and asked that I send him a Freedom of Information Act form, signed and notarized by Amster, and that a photocopy be addressed to "EurSov," internal jargon for the Soviet affairs office at the State Department. Amster readily signed the request and I followed Reece's instructions. As long as I was taking all this trouble I did ask Reece to add whatever detail he might feel at liberty to provide about the "informal" contact with the Soviets. Maybe I shouldn't have breathed that subject.

More than a month later, I had received no reply. Sensing that the delay might have been caused by my added request, I cabled Reece: "RE MY INQUIRY ON AMSTER, PLEASE RUSH VIA MAILGRAM ANSWER TO FIRST QUESTION ONLY. DID PHONE CALL OCCUR?"

Five days later what came was not a mailgram from Reece but a phone call from a woman in the Soviet affairs office in Washington. Reece had cabled her, she said, that "according to my recollection" he did not have evidence of an escape from confinement by Amster.

287

I pointed out to her that Amster himself quotes Reece as having had no official information from the Soviets about the escape, even up to the time of Amster's release. I stated that, having followed his instructions, I was surprised that Reece did not communicate with me directly. Nevertheless, I asked if she would send me a copy of his message, hedged wording and all.

She said she could not because his cable was classified.

Why?

She said she didn't know.

My first reaction was frustration and irritation. Why their tight-fisted caution and defensiveness? Neither I nor Amster was accusing the government of doing anything wrong. In fact, the embassy had done everything exactly right. So why all this, this . . . and then it came clear.

Of course. If Amster's adventure happened exactly as he's told it, which I am convinced it did, the State Department has no choice but to say exactly what I was told Reece said in his classified cable, then insist on leaving it at that, nothing in writing.

Suppose another Amster comes along, or any American needing "informal" extrication from a foreign government's embarrassment. Would that person want our State Department to have burned its bridges—breaching a promise to the Soviets over, of all things, this?

While the events and characterizations portrayed here carefully reflect the descriptions given me by Amster, I take responsibility for creating much of the dialogue.

The names of his two American accomplices have been changed. They have paid their penalty and I see no reason to expose them to any more public discomfort than they have already endured.

I have changed the names of a number of Soviet citizens whose words or acts, as described here, might bring them trouble. In particular, I have changed not only the name but other identifying facts about the woman doctor named Marinka who appears in the last third of this story.

As our many interviews unfolded, I became increasingly fasci-

288

nated with perceiving the psychological themes that helped explain, at least to me, why the man who was telling me his life had chosen such a high-risk lifestyle. While Amster endorses this story as written, I take responsibility for shaping it according to those perceptions.

I am indebted to my editor, Jennifer Josephy, for her enthusiasm and skilled attention to editing detail, which has become a rarity in publishing houses, and to Regina Ryan, my agent, for accurately spotting Mr. Macrae and Miss Josephy as the right editors for the book. Karen Wynn, globetrotter and devotee of stories of international intrigue, as well as dear friend, read and reread these pages in manuscript, made valuable suggestions, challenged and encouraged me. Laura Hagfeldt transcribed dozens of interview tapes, then saw the manuscript through the pressure of final deadlines.

Bernard Asbell

APPENDIX

On the criminal affair No. 150

APPROVED

THE FIRST DEPUTY-PROSECUTOR-GENERAL
OF THE USSR
The State Adviser of Justice of the 1st Class

A. REKUNKOV

05 08 1976

ACCUSATORY RESOLUTION

On accusation of AMSTER Gerald Robert, BENACK Peter, and LEAN Darrell* in committing a criminal affair, envisaged by paragraph 78 of the Criminal Code of the Russian Federation.

*These names have been changed to conform with the substituted names in the text.

This criminal affair was instituted by the Investigating Department of the KGB at the Council of Ministers of the USSR on June 27th, 1976 based on the materials about the illegal moving-into the Soviet Union of some narcotic substance—heroin. The materials were received from the Sheremet'evo Customs Office of the Chief Customs Department of the Ministry for Foreign Trade of the USSR.

Vol. 1, pages 1–2, 4–25

On the same day AMSTER, BENACK, and LEAN were detained in compliance with paragraph 122 of the Criminal-Processual Code of the Russian Federation. On June 29, 1976 they were put under arrest.

Vol. 1, pages 31–33, 118–119, 196–197

In course of the preliminary investigation the following was established.

Having the intention to take up speculating narcotics, at the end of April, 1976 AMSTER and LEAN arrived in Holland.

On June 14, 1976 in Amsterdam they got acquainted with a person of Chinese nationality, Lee by name, and accepted his offer to transport narcotics from Malaysia to Europe for some payment.

BENACK, who arrived in Amsterdam on June 20 this year, also agreed on AMSTER proposition to take part in smuggling narcotics.

On June 21, 1976 the accused got from Lee tickets as well as 1.000 Dutch guilders for their expenses during the trip and on the same day they left Amsterdam for Kuala-Lumpur—the capital of Malaysia—where they received from three Chinese, accomplices of Lee, the double-bottom suitcases with narcotics as well as with clothing which didn't belong to them. In accordance with the bargain made earlier AMSTER, BENACK, and LEAN expressed their willingness to transport the narcotics to Paris for the reward of 30.000 Dutch guilders and about 1.5 kg of heroin.

292

On June 27, 1976 the accused arrived in Moscow by the Aeroflot plane flying from Kuala-Lumpur via Singapore and Moscow to Paris. On the same day during the customs check-in in the Sheremet'evo international airport the narcotic substance of 28 kg 144 gr of heroin they transported was found and seized from them. In the suitcases of AMSTER, BENACK, and LEAN there were accordingly 7 kg 268 gr, 10 kg 383 gr, and 10 kg 493 gr of that narcotic.

AMSTER, BENACK, and LEAN pleaded completely guilty on the accusation presented and stated that they had known about narcotics in their luggage and had smuggled narcotics for the purpose of gaining money. Hoping to transport narcotics across the State border of the USSR freely they deliberately didn't point out in the Customs Declarations that in their luggage there were narcotics which didn't belong to them.

Vol. 1, pages 63, 89, 92, 147, 169, 244, 245

The guilt of AMSTER, BENACK, and LEAN in the crime committed is also proved by the following testimony:

—Evidence of the witnesses—members of Sheremet'evo Customs personnel and separate checking post "Moscow" Silantiev E.V., Popivoda V.P., Cherny E.P., Bykov G.N., Ivanov G.G., and Beresovsky E.V., who were present during the customs check-in and found heroin in the suitcases of the accused. Vol. 1, pages 261-277

—Statements made on June 27, 1976 about seizing the items of smuggling from AMSTER, BENACK, and LEAN. Vol. 1, pages 7, 14, 21

—Material evidence: narcotic substance heroin and three suitcases with special compartments mounted in them. Vol. 2, page 31

—The Customs Declarations in which the accused didn't point out that there was some heroin in their suitcases that belonged to some other persons. Vol. 1, pages 6, 13, 20, 89-90

—The resolution of the experts-criminalists made on July 16, 1976, saying that the substance seized from the accused is a narcotic. Vol. 2, pages 21-30

293

—Material evidence: tickets for AMSTER, BENACK, and LEAN for the flight from Amsterdam to Kuala-Lumpur and from Kuala-Lumpur via Moscow to Paris, boarding passes and luggage cards testifying to their being in Malaysia and crossing the State border of the USSR during their flight from Malaysia to Moscow. Vol. 2, pages 8–10, 79–82, 89–90

—Foreign currency received by the accused from the Chinese Lee as well as clothing which was found in the suitcases of AMSTER, BENACK, and LEAN but belonged to none of them. Vol. 2, pages 91, 97–99, 137

—The statements of examination of the material evidence mentioned above. Vol. 2, pages 35, 37, 38–39, 94–96, 131, 153

ON THE BASIS OF THE ABOVE-MENTIONED ARE ACCUSED:

AMSTER Gerald Robert, born on February 19, 1943 in the state of New Jersey (USA), American, citizen of the USA, finished two years of studying at Columbia University in New York, divorced, has no children, has no certain occupation, lived in New York (USA).

Of his being initiator of smuggling narcotics and having entered a criminal alliance with BENACK and LEAN on June 27, 1976, when on board the plane going from Kuala-Lumpur to Paris with a stop-over in Moscow; of having transported together with them illegally across the State border of the USSR some narcotic substance—28 kg 144 gr of heroin, 7 kg 269 gr of which he had transported personally, that is of committing the crime envisaged by paragraph 78 of the Criminal Code of the Russian Federation.

BENACK Peter, born on May 23, 1945, in the state of Pennsylvania (USA), American, citizen of the USA, finished three

294

years of studying at the technical college in Scranton, married, has four young children dependent on him, was the chief of the building department of . . . company, lived in Las Vegas (USA).

Of the fact that he had entered the criminal alliance with AMSTER and LEAN and going by plane from Kuala-Lumpur to Paris via Moscow on June 27, 1976, together with them he illegally transported across the State border of the USSR some narcotic substance—28 kg 144 gr of heroin, 10 kg 383 gr of which he had transported personally in his double-bottom suitcase, that is, of committing the crime envisaged by paragraph 78 of the Criminal Code of the Russian Federation:

LEAN Darrell, born on July 5, 1950, in Chicago (USA), American, citizen of the USA, finished the 11th grade, unmarried, has no certain occupation, lived in New York (USA).

Of the fact that he had entered the criminal alliance with AMSTER and BENACK and going by plane from Kuala-Lumpur to Paris via Moscow on June 27, 1976, together with them he illegally transported across the State border of the USSR in the double-bottom suitcases some narcotic substance—28 kg 144 gr of heroin, 10 kg 493 gr of which he had transported personally, that is of committing the crime envisaged by paragraph 78 of the Criminal Code of the Russian Federation.

In accordance with paragraph 207 of the Criminal-Procedural Code of the Russian Federation all the documents of the criminal affair on accusation of AMSTER Gerald Robert, BENACK Peter, and LEAN Darrell are to be sent to the USSR Prosecutors' Office.

The accusatory Resolution was made on July 26, 1976, in Moscow.

SENIOR INVESTIGATOR OF THE INVESTIGATION
DEPARTMENT OF THE STATE SECURITY COMMITTEE
OF THE COUNCIL OF MINISTERS OF THE USSR

Major BELIAEV O.